BOOK FOUR - M. I. A.

D1097656

CALIBER
COMICS

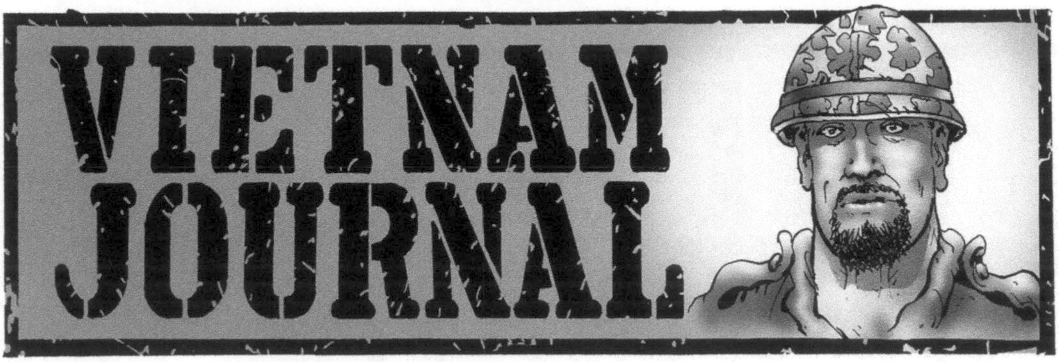
VIETNAM
JOURNAL

BOOK FOUR - M. I. A.

Written and Illustrated
By
DON LOMAX

Lettered
By
CLEM ROBINS

THIS VOLUME COLLECTS:
ISSUE #13 - " The Ballad of Luther Wolfe"
ISSUE #14 - "Cordon and Search"
ISSUE #15 - "Coastal Pink and Almond Eyes"
ISSUE #16 - "M. I. A."

Originally published by Apple Comics

POINT

I kinda like point.

A lotta grunts think you gotta have a death wish to volunteer for point.

But I'd rather be on point than clanging and banging along with the main body in the middle of a bunch of green-assed replacements doing everything they possibly can to get me K.I.A.

I look at it this way. The main thing you gotta look out for are traps and tripwires. When you've been on as many missions as I have you learn what to watch out for. As for ambushes, Chuck-Chuck-the-Mother-Fuck, ain't no fool. He wants the most blood he can get for his rounds expended. Ammunition is hard to come by for Chuck. He will usually let the point man diddy-bop on past 'cause he knows the main body of the patrol is just 50 or so meters behind.

So he waits.

He generally hits hard, with everything he's got, exacting as many casualties as possible in the ▮mad moment▮ of first contact and immediately fades back into the bush before the RTO can call in Arty.

By the time the point man gets back to the shit-storm it's all over but cussing and the bleeding.

Yeah.

Point ain't so bad.

Corporal Lennard Keno

First Cavalry, Vietnam,1967

The Ballad of Luther Wolfe

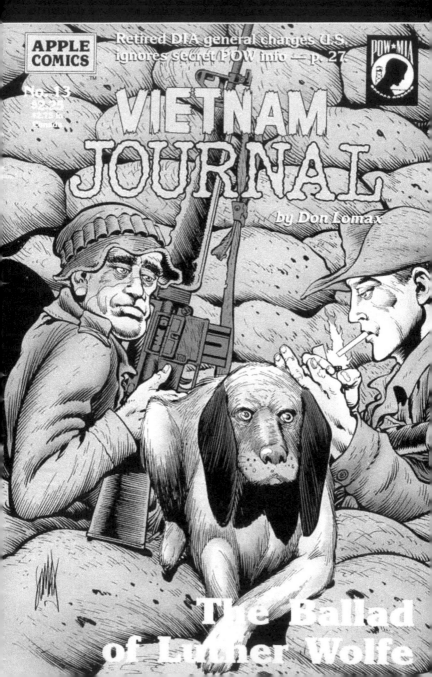

APPLE COMICS ™

No. 13
$2.25
$2.75 in Canada

Retired DIA general charges U.S. ignores secret POW info — p. 27.

POW★MIA

VIETNAM JOURNAL

by Don Lomax

The Ballad of Luther Wolfe

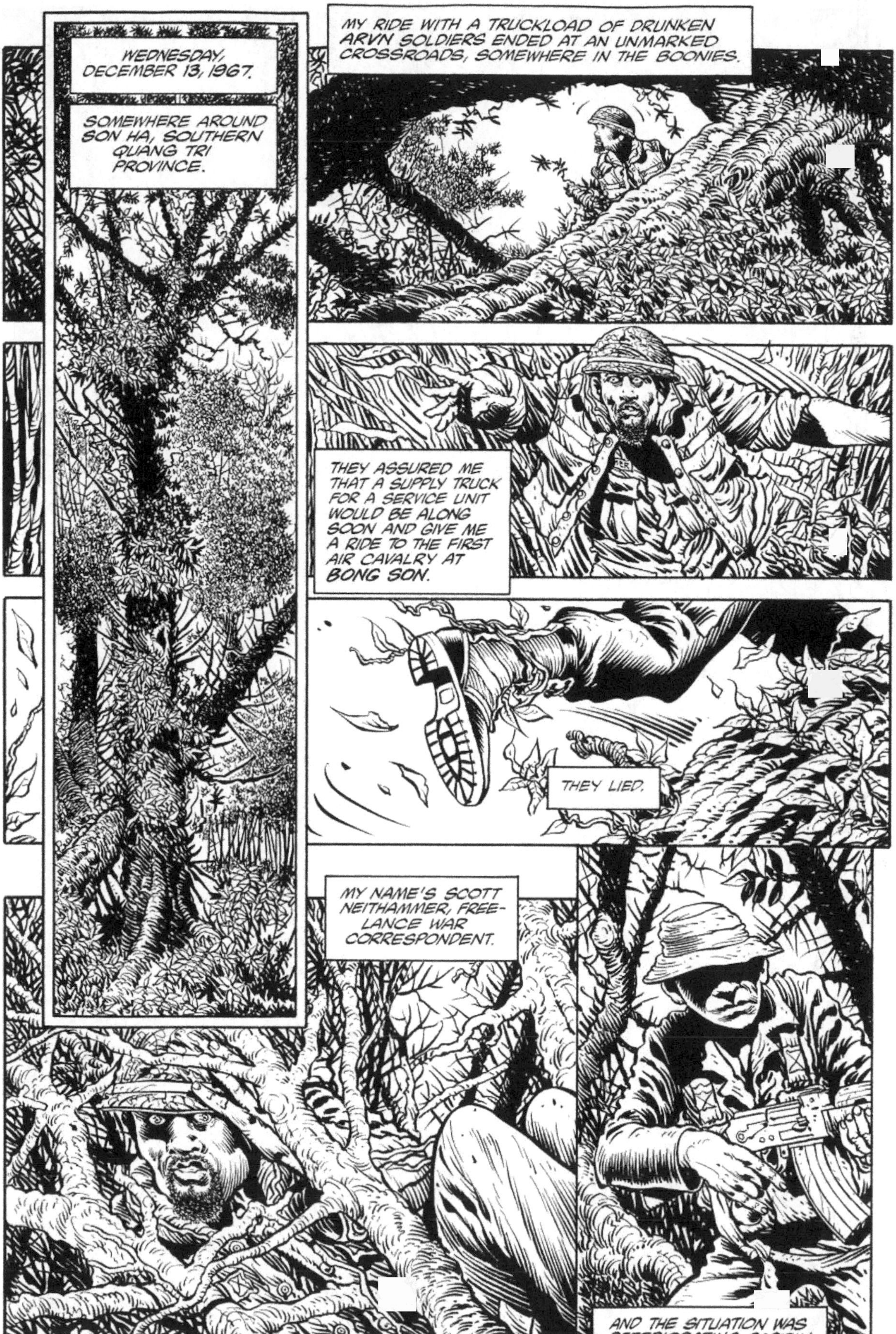
WEDNESDAY, DECEMBER 13, 1967.
SOMEWHERE AROUND SON HA, SOUTHERN QUANG TRI PROVINCE.
MY RIDE WITH A TRUCKLOAD OF DRUNKEN ARVN SOLDIERS ENDED AT AN UNMARKED CROSSROADS, SOMEWHERE IN THE BOONIES.
THEY ASSURED ME THAT A SUPPLY TRUCK FOR A SERVICE UNIT WOULD BE ALONG SOON AND GIVE ME A RIDE TO THE FIRST AIR CAVALRY AT BONG SON.
THEY LIED.
MY NAME'S SCOTT NEITHAMMER, FREE-LANCE WAR CORRESPONDENT.
AND THE SITUATION WAS DETERIORATING RAPIDLY.

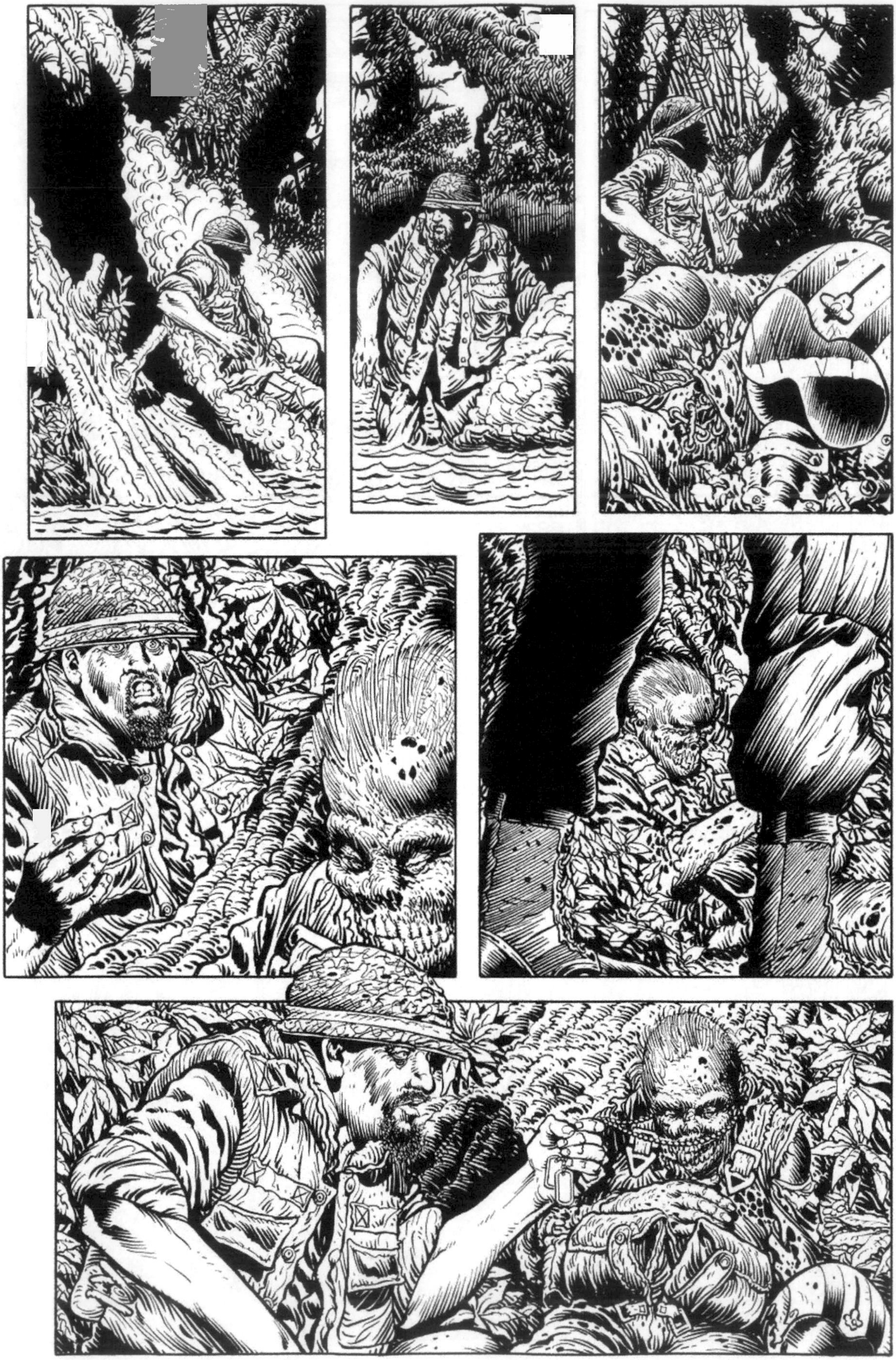

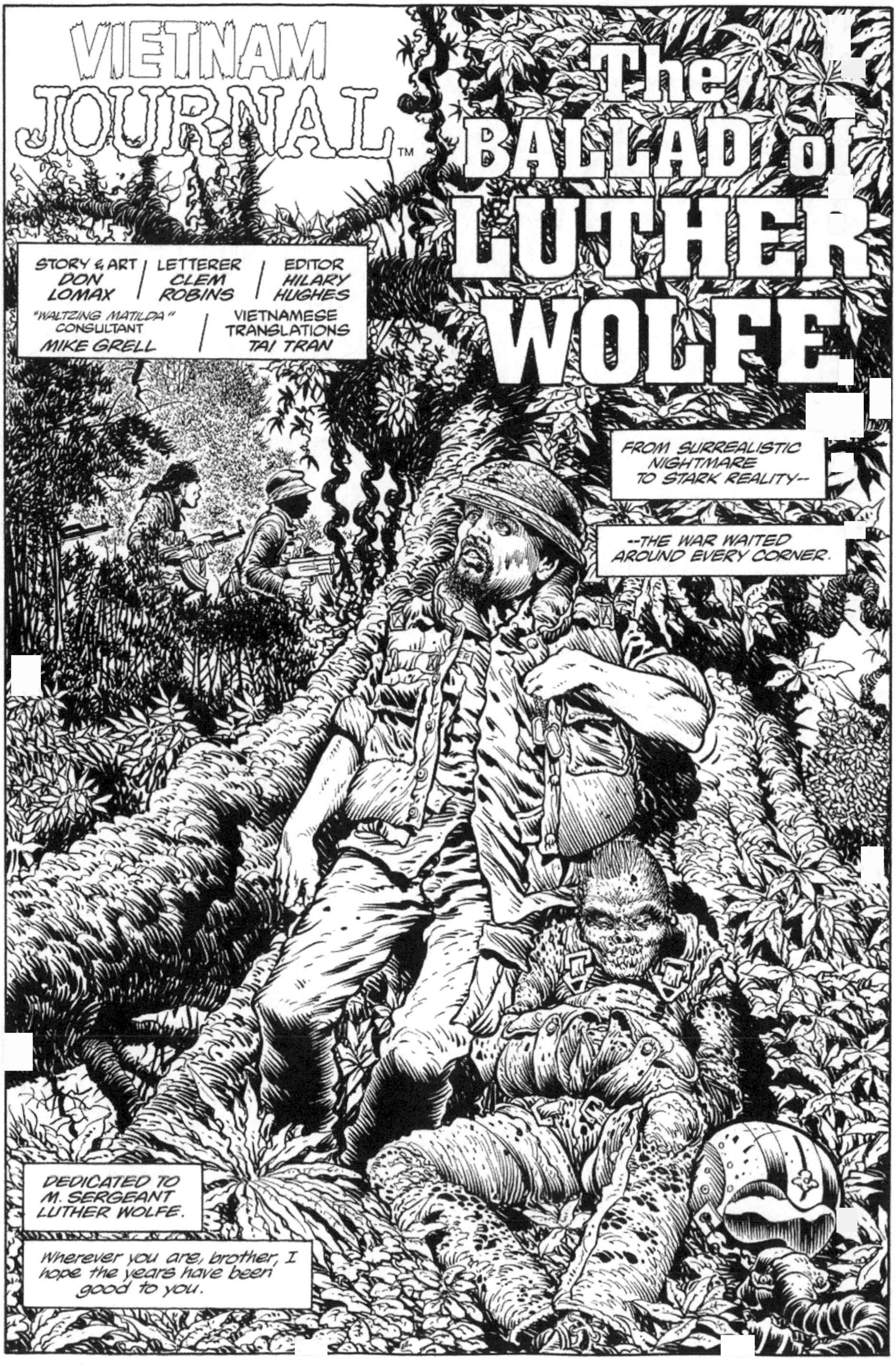
VIETNAM JOURNAL™
The BALLAD of LUTHER WOLFE
STORY & ART DON LOMAX
LETTERER CLEM ROBINS
EDITOR HILARY HUGHES
"WALTZING MATILDA" CONSULTANT MIKE GRELL
VIETNAMESE TRANSLATIONS TAI TRAN
FROM SURREALISTIC NIGHTMARE TO STARK REALITY--
--THE WAR WAITED AROUND EVERY CORNER.
DEDICATED TO M. SERGEANT LUTHER WOLFE.
Wherever you are, brother, I hope the years have been good to you.

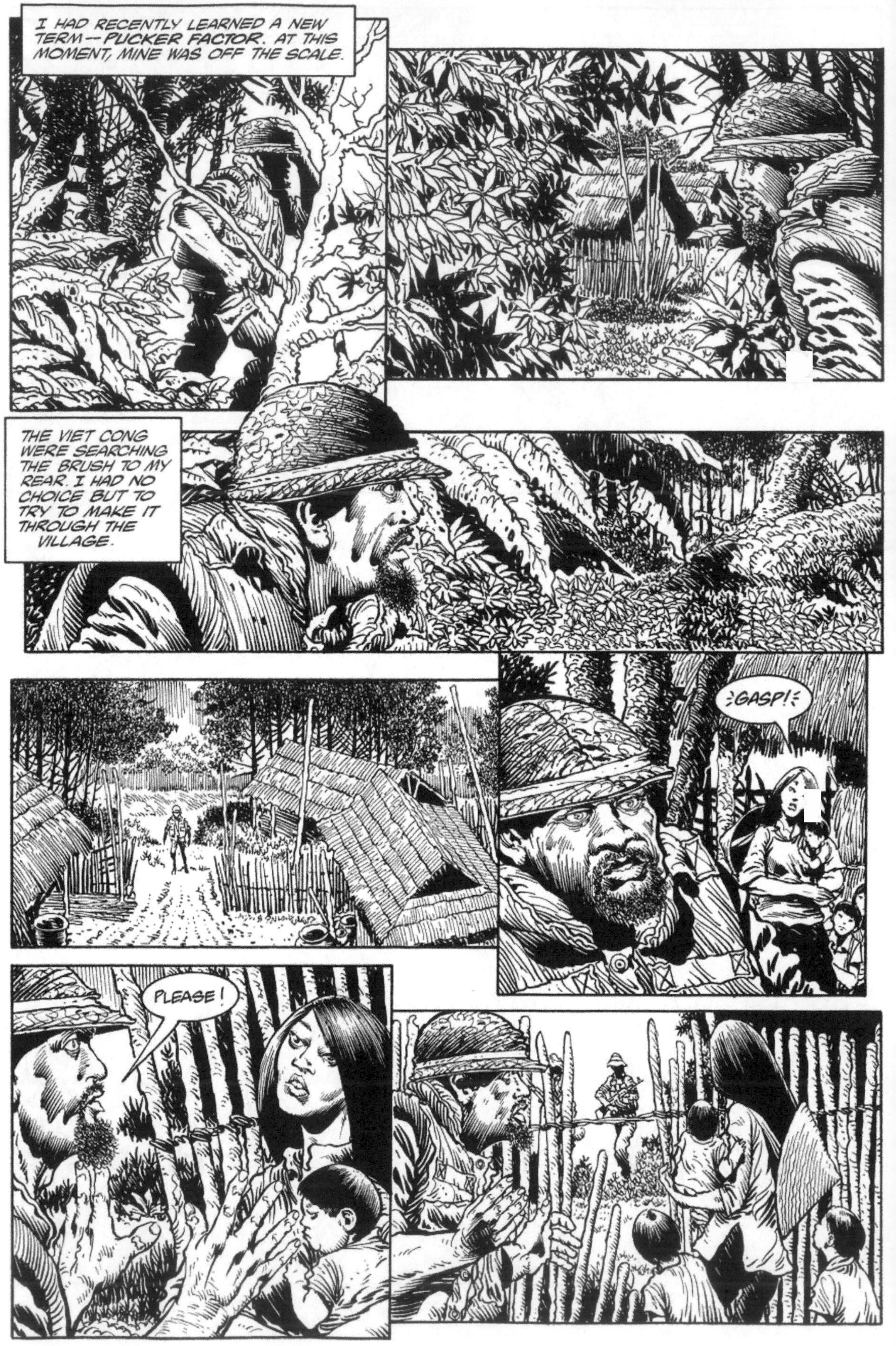
I HAD RECENTLY LEARNED A NEW TERM -- PUCKER FACTOR. AT THIS MOMENT, MINE WAS OFF THE SCALE.
THE VIET CONG WERE SEARCHING THE BRUSH TO MY REAR. I HAD NO CHOICE BUT TO TRY TO MAKE IT THROUGH THE VILLAGE.
GASP!
PLEASE!

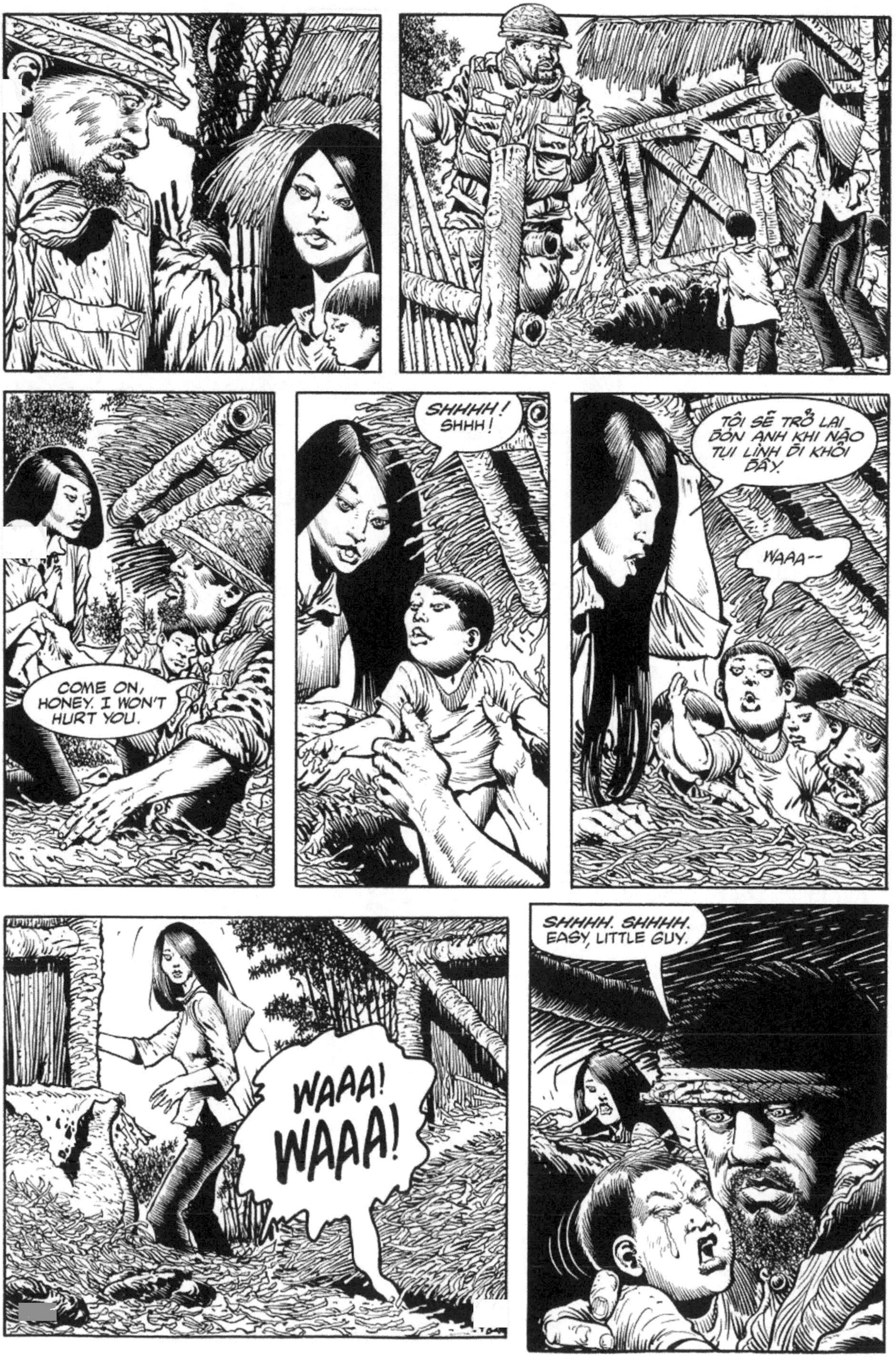
COME ON, HONEY. I WON'T HURT YOU.
SHHHH! SHHH!
TÔI SẼ TRỞ LẠI ĐÓN ANH KHI NÀO TỤI LÍNH ĐI KHỎI ĐÂY.
WAAA--
WAAA! WAAA!
SHHHH. SHHHH. EASY, LITTLE GUY.

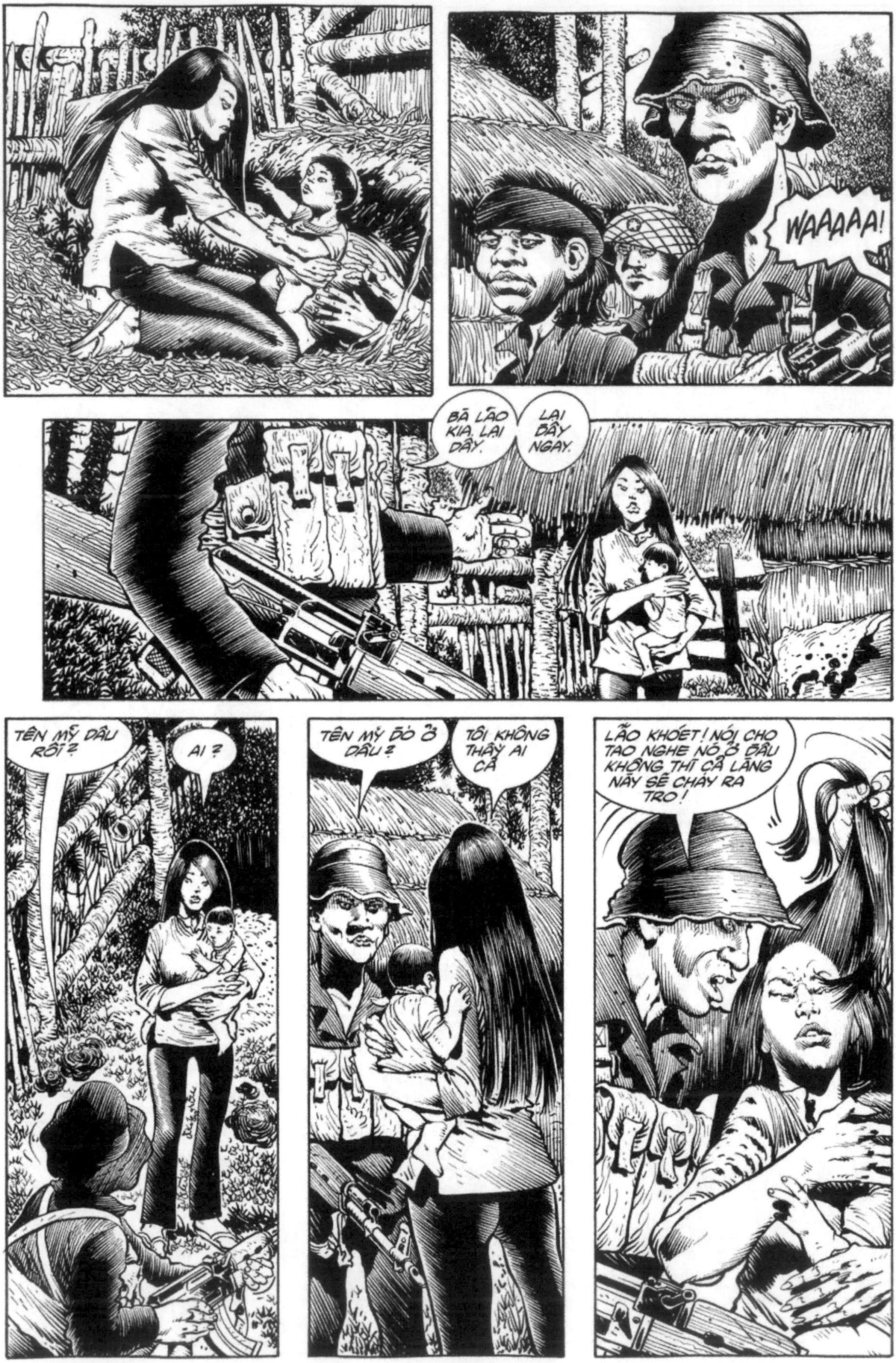
WAAAAA!
BÀ LÃO KIA. LẠI ĐÂY.
LẠI ĐÂY NGAY.
TÊN MỸ DÂU RỒI?
AI?
TÊN MỸ ĐÓ Ở DÂU?
TÔI KHÔNG THẤY AI CẢ
LÃO KHOÉT! NÓI CHO TAO NGHE NÓ Ở ĐÂU KHÔNG THÌ CẢ LÀNG NÀY SẼ CHÁY RA TRO!

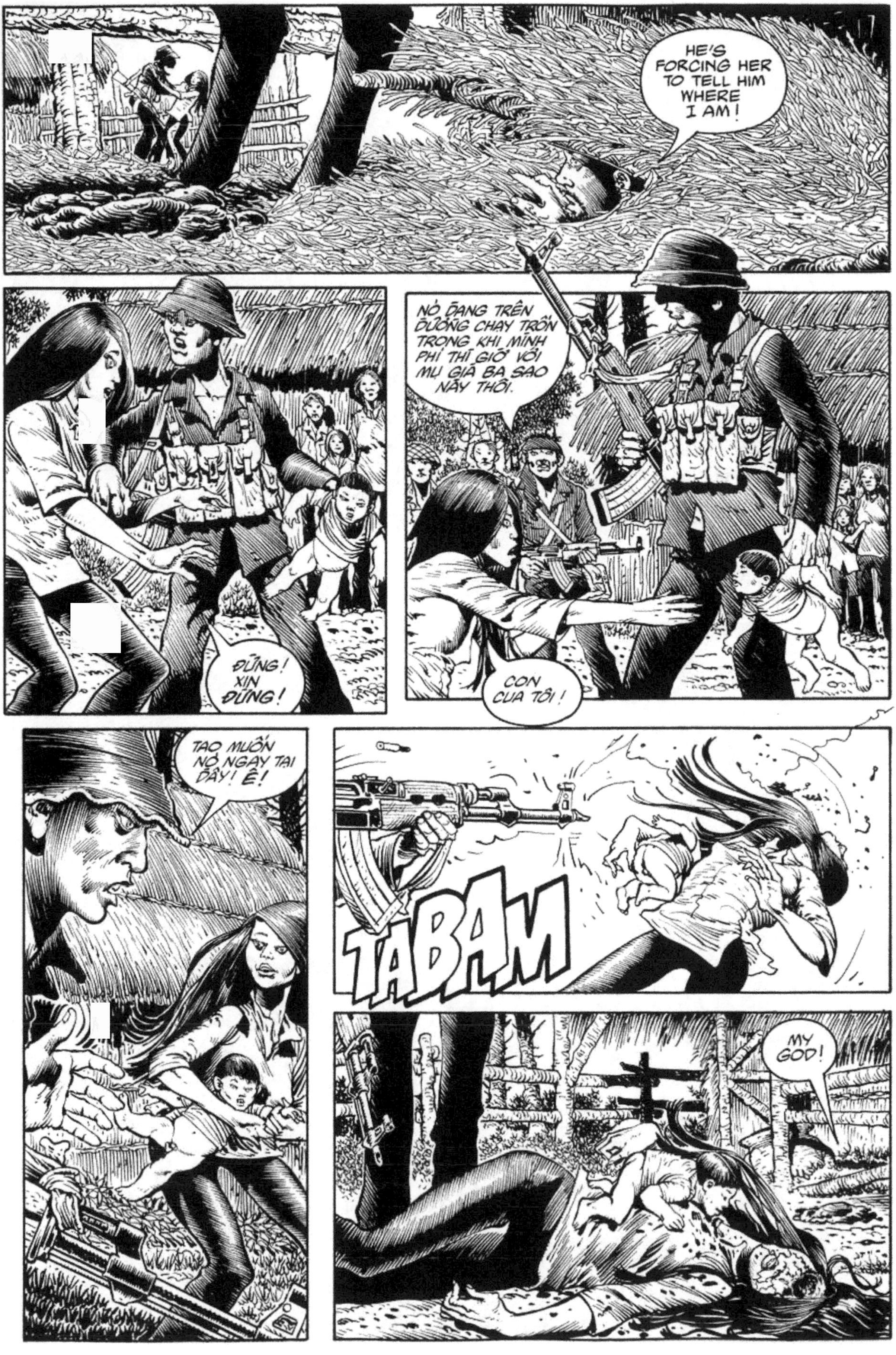
HE'S FORCING HER TO TELL HIM WHERE I AM!
NỎ ĐANG TRÊN ĐƯỜNG CHẠY TRỐN TRONG KHI MÌNH PHÍ THÌ GIỜ VỚI MỤ GIÀ BA SAO NẪY THÔI.
ĐỪNG! XIN ĐỪNG!
CON CỦA TÔI!
TAO MUỐN NỞ NGAY TẠI ĐÂY! Ê!
TABAM
MY GOD!

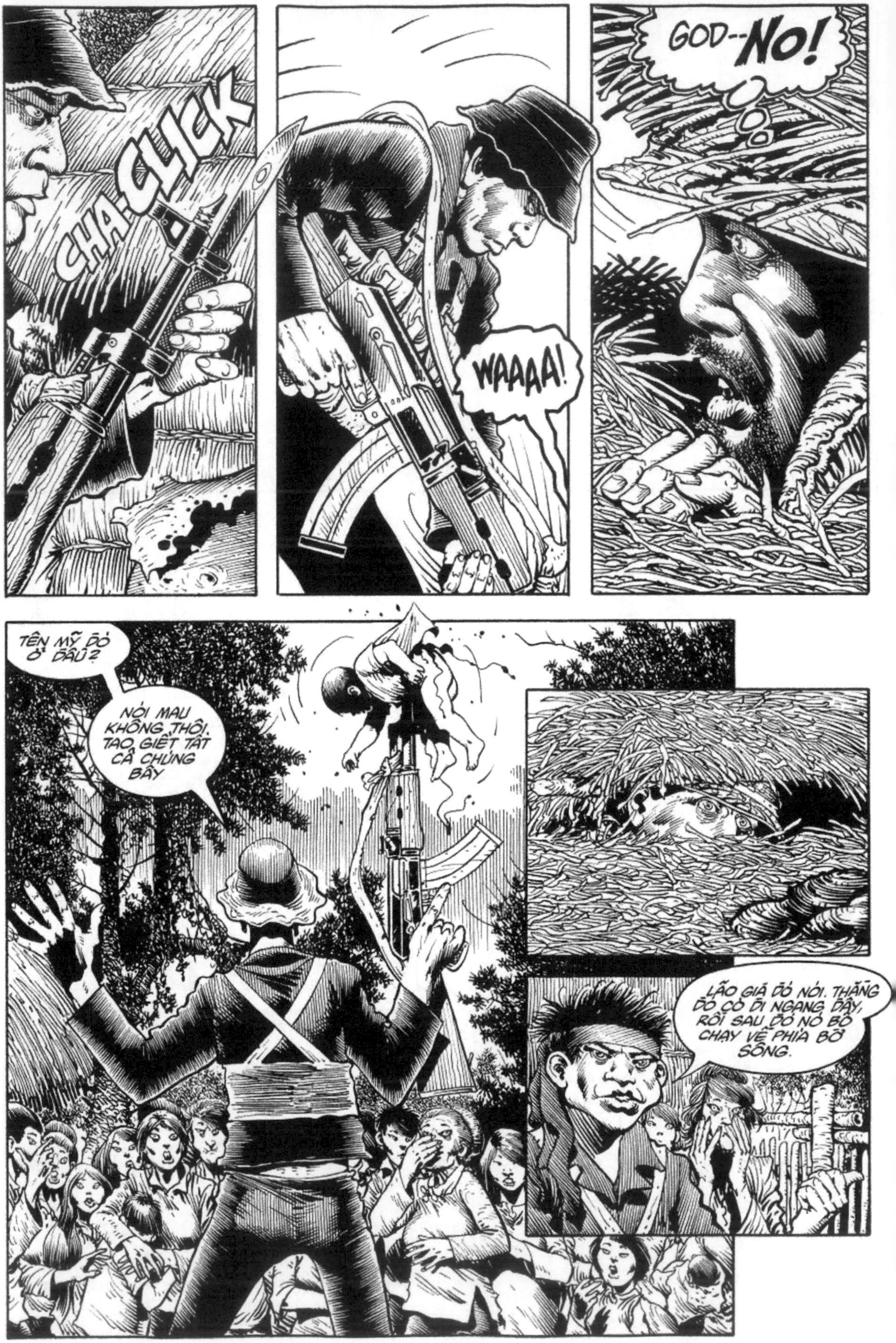
CHA-CLICK
WAAAA!
GOD--NO!
TÊN MỸ ĐÓ Ở ĐÂU?
NÓI MAU KHÔNG THÔI, TAO GIẾT TẤT CẢ CHÚNG BÂY
LÃO GIÀ ĐÓ NÓI. THẰNG ĐÓ CÓ ĐI NGANG ĐÂY, RỒI SAU ĐÓ NÓ BỎ CHẠY VỀ PHÍA BỜ SÔNG.

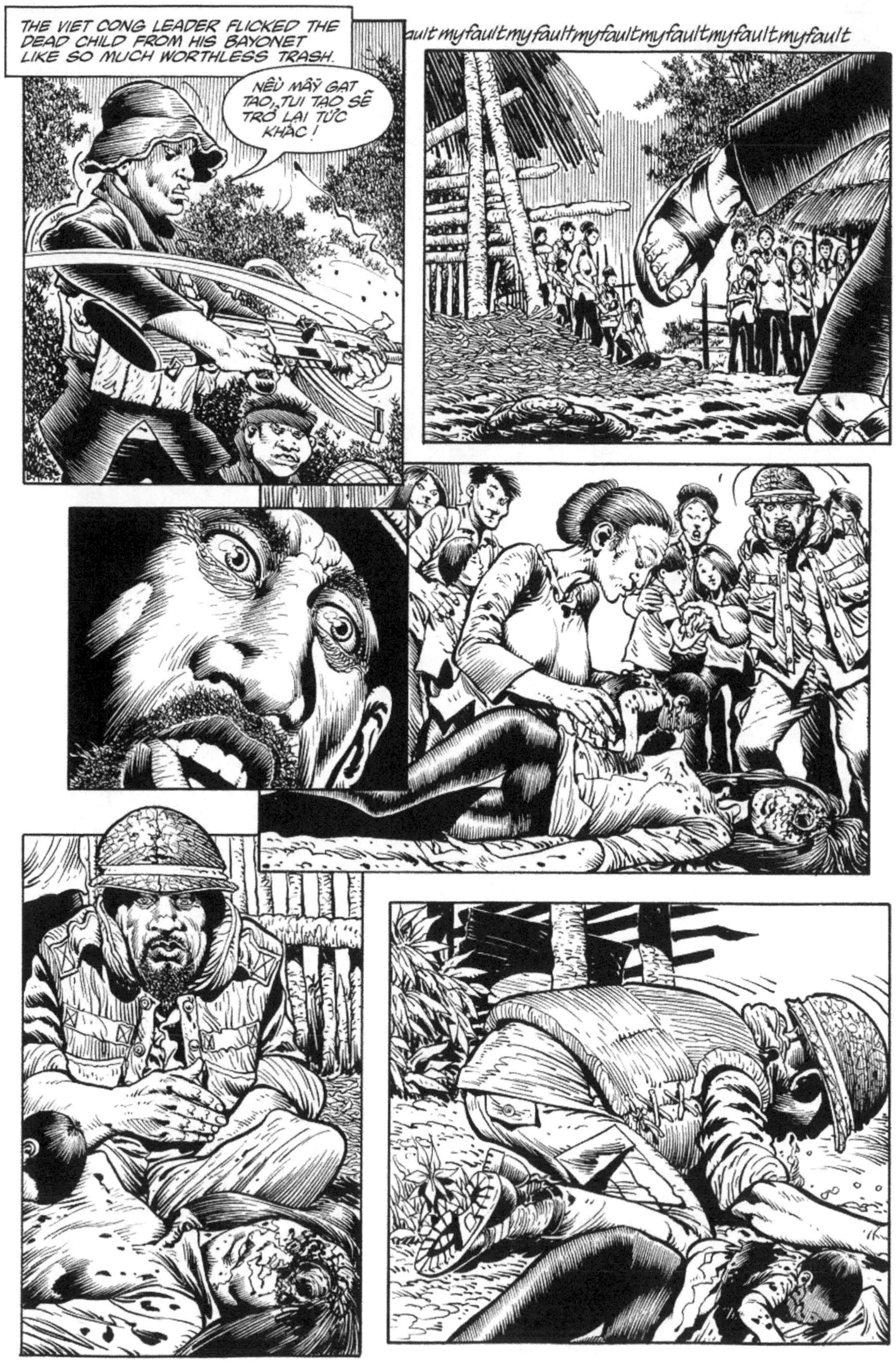
THE VIET CONG LEADER FLICKED THE DEAD CHILD FROM HIS BAYONET LIKE SO MUCH WORTHLESS TRASH.
NẾU MÀY GẠT TAO,, TỤI TAO SẼ TRỞ LẠI TỨC KHẮC!
ault myfault myfault myfault myfault myfault myfault

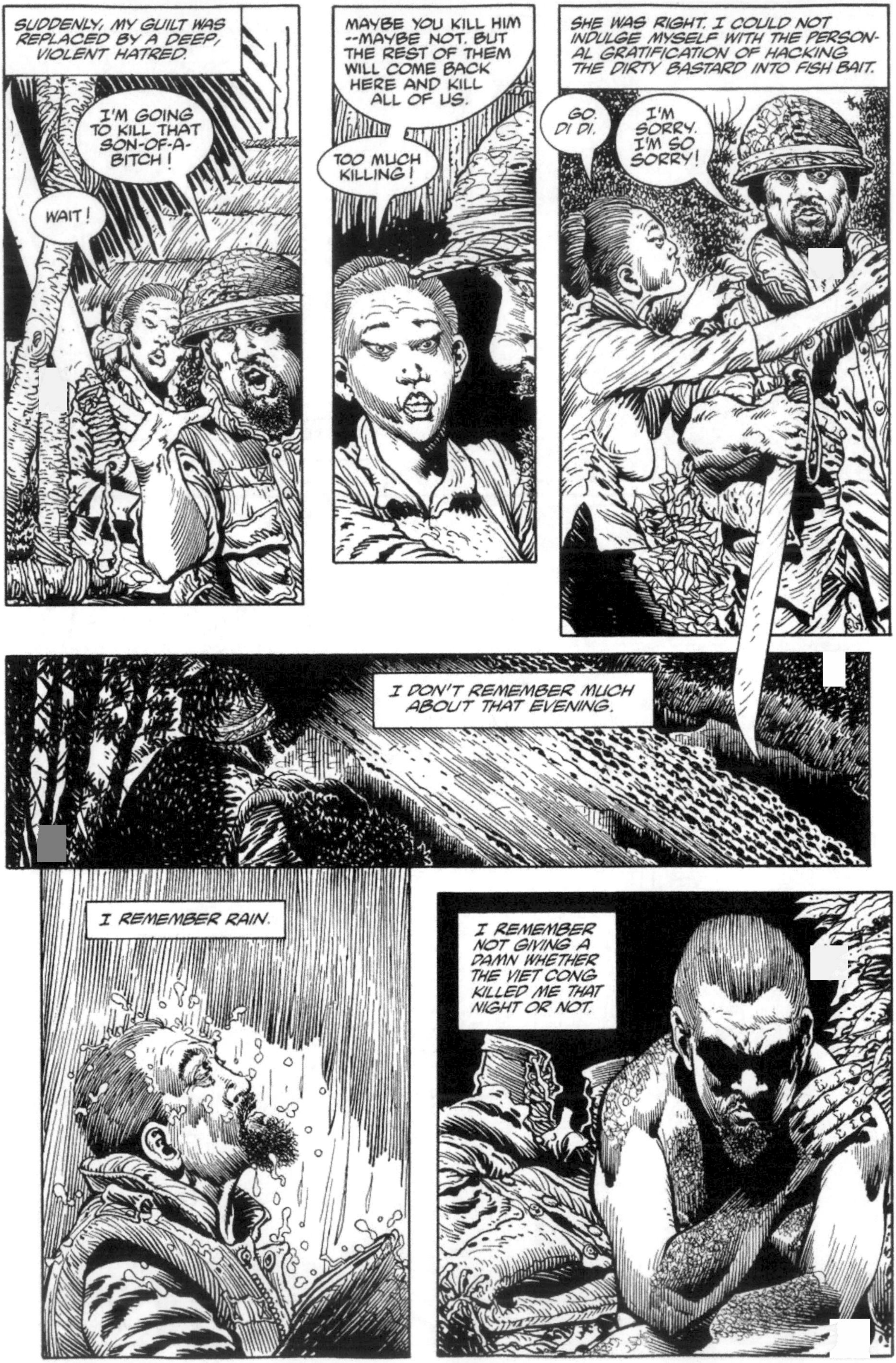
SUDDENLY, MY GUILT WAS REPLACED BY A DEEP, VIOLENT HATRED.
I'M GOING TO KILL THAT SON-OF-A-BITCH!
WAIT!
MAYBE YOU KILL HIM --MAYBE NOT. BUT THE REST OF THEM WILL COME BACK HERE AND KILL ALL OF US.
TOO MUCH KILLING!
SHE WAS RIGHT. I COULD NOT INDULGE MYSELF WITH THE PERSONAL GRATIFICATION OF HACKING THE DIRTY BASTARD INTO FISH BAIT.
GO. DI DI.
I'M SORRY. I'M SO SORRY!
I DON'T REMEMBER MUCH ABOUT THAT EVENING.
I REMEMBER RAIN.
I REMEMBER NOT GIVING A DAMN WHETHER THE VIET CONG KILLED ME THAT NIGHT OR NOT.

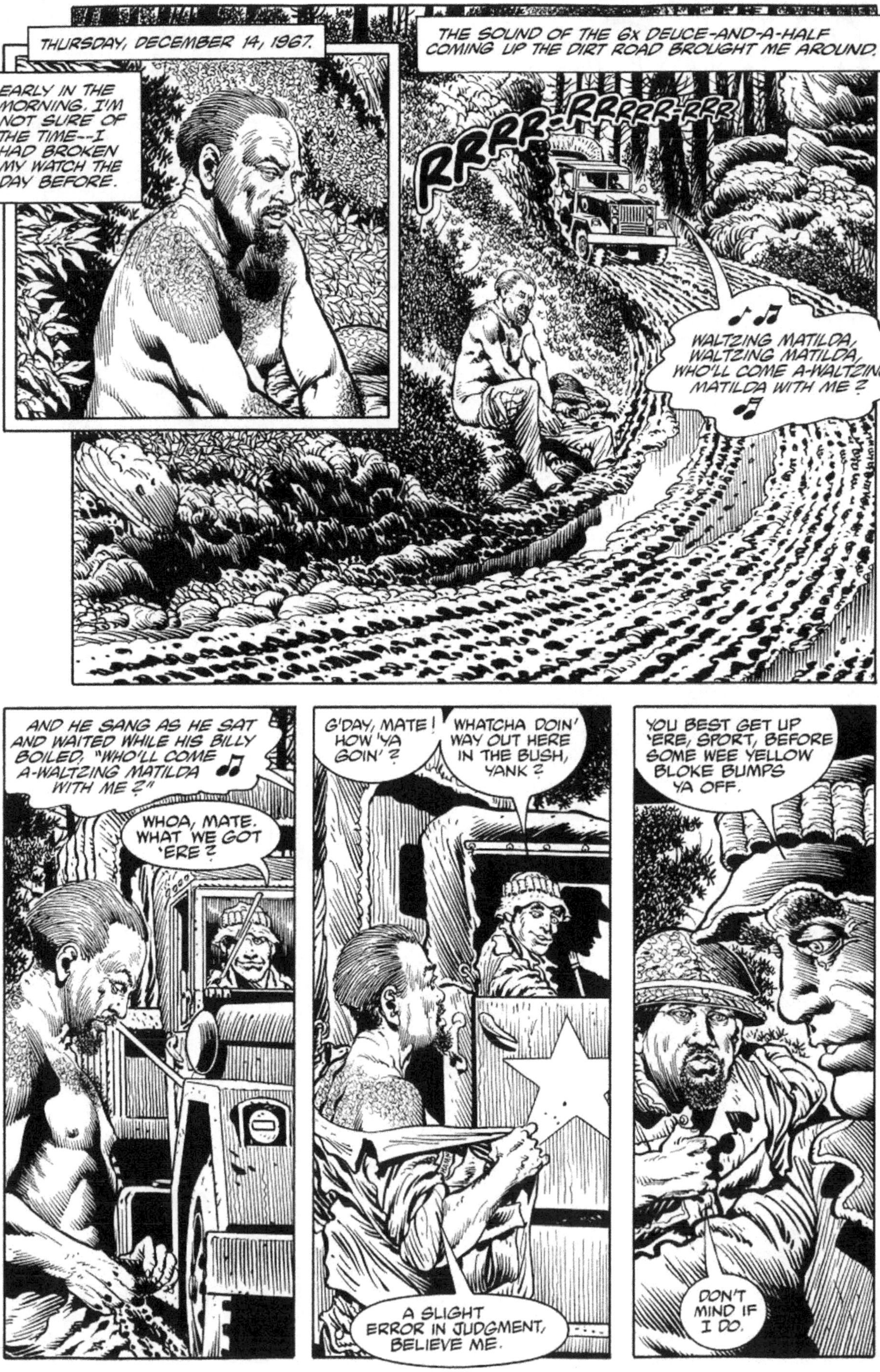
THURSDAY, DECEMBER 14, 1967.
EARLY IN THE MORNING, I'M NOT SURE OF THE TIME--I HAD BROKEN MY WATCH THE DAY BEFORE.
THE SOUND OF THE 6x DEUCE-AND-A-HALF COMING UP THE DIRT ROAD BROUGHT ME AROUND.
RRRR-RRRRR-RRR
WALTZING MATILDA, WALTZING MATILDA, WHO'LL COME A-WALTZING MATILDA WITH ME ?
AND HE SANG AS HE SAT AND WAITED WHILE HIS BILLY BOILED, "WHO'LL COME A-WALTZING MATILDA WITH ME ?"
WHOA, MATE. WHAT WE GOT 'ERE ?
G'DAY, MATE ! HOW 'YA GOIN' ?
WHATCHA DOIN' WAY OUT HERE IN THE BUSH, YANK ?
A SLIGHT ERROR IN JUDGMENT, BELIEVE ME.
YOU BEST GET UP 'ERE, SPORT, BEFORE SOME WEE YELLOW BLOKE BUMPS YA OFF.
DON'T MIND IF I DO.

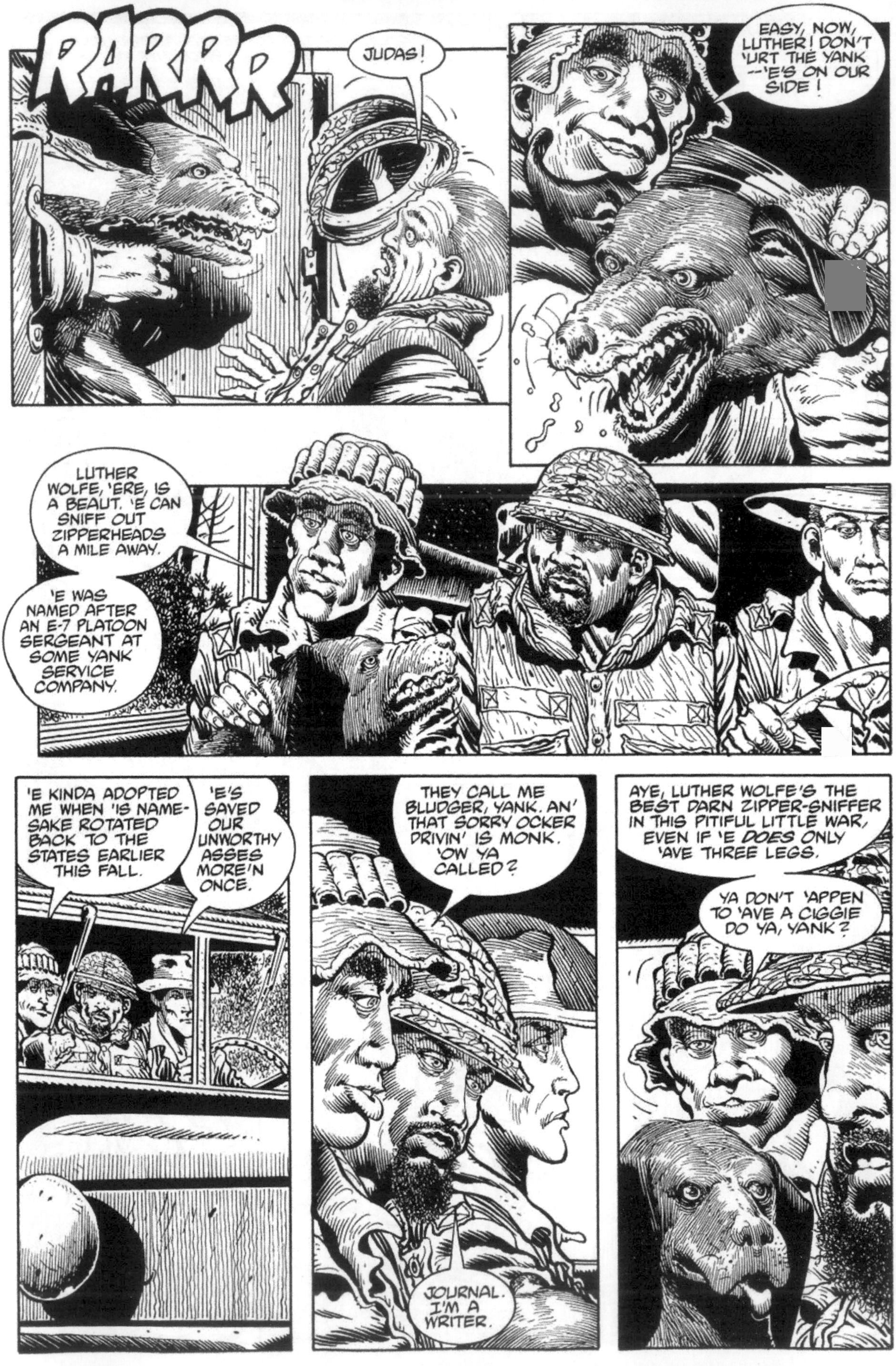
RARRR
JUDAS!
EASY, NOW, LUTHER! DON'T 'URT THE YANK --'E'S ON OUR SIDE!
LUTHER WOLFE, 'ERE, IS A BEAUT. 'E CAN SNIFF OUT ZIPPERHEADS A MILE AWAY.
'E WAS NAMED AFTER AN E-7 PLATOON SERGEANT AT SOME YANK SERVICE COMPANY.
'E KINDA ADOPTED ME WHEN 'IS NAME-SAKE ROTATED BACK TO THE STATES EARLIER THIS FALL.
'E'S SAVED OUR UNWORTHY ASSES MORE'N ONCE.
THEY CALL ME BLUDGER, YANK. AN' THAT SORRY OCKER DRIVIN' IS MONK. 'OW YA CALLED?
JOURNAL. I'M A WRITER.
AYE, LUTHER WOLFE'S THE BEST DARN ZIPPER-SNIFFER IN THIS PITIFUL LITTLE WAR, EVEN IF 'E *DOES* ONLY 'AVE THREE LEGS.
YA DON'T 'APPEN TO 'AVE A CIGGIE DO YA, YANK?

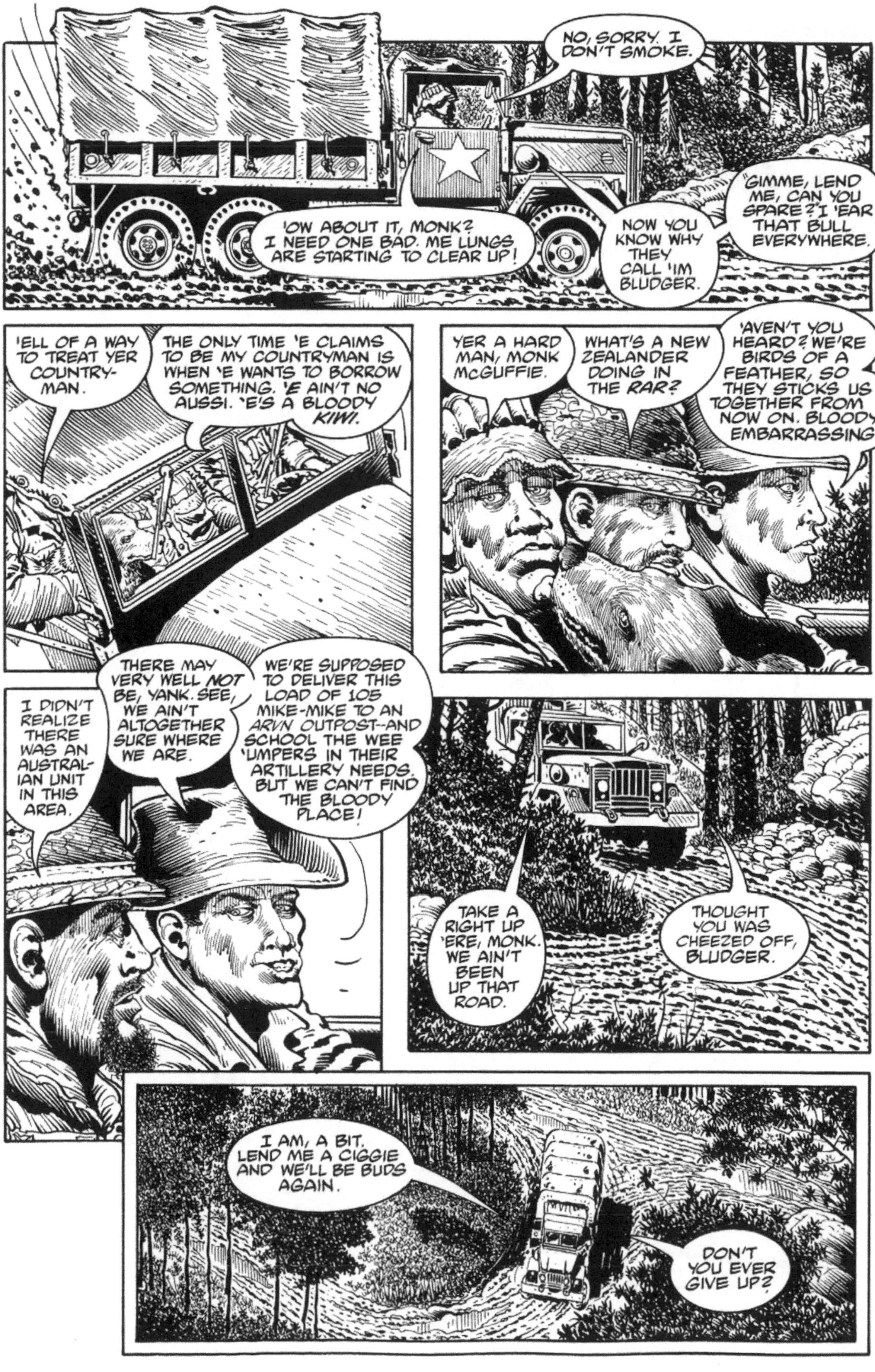
NO, SORRY. I DON'T SMOKE.
'OW ABOUT IT, MONK? I NEED ONE BAD. ME LUNGS ARE STARTING TO CLEAR UP!
NOW YOU KNOW WHY THEY CALL 'IM BLUDGER.
"GIMME, LEND ME, CAN YOU SPARE?" I 'EAR THAT BULL EVERYWHERE.
'ELL OF A WAY TO TREAT YER COUNTRYMAN.
THE ONLY TIME 'E CLAIMS TO BE MY COUNTRYMAN IS WHEN 'E WANTS TO BORROW SOMETHING. 'E AIN'T NO AUSSI. 'E'S A BLOODY KIWI.
YER A HARD MAN, MONK McGUFFIE.
WHAT'S A NEW ZEALANDER DOING IN THE RAR?
'AVEN'T YOU HEARD? WE'RE BIRDS OF A FEATHER, SO THEY STICKS US TOGETHER FROM NOW ON. BLOODY EMBARRASSING.
I DIDN'T REALIZE THERE WAS AN AUSTRALIAN UNIT IN THIS AREA.
THERE MAY VERY WELL NOT BE, YANK. SEE, WE AIN'T ALTOGETHER SURE WHERE WE ARE.
WE'RE SUPPOSED TO DELIVER THIS LOAD OF 105 MIKE-MIKE TO AN ARVN OUTPOST--AND SCHOOL THE WEE 'UMPERS IN THEIR ARTILLERY NEEDS. BUT WE CAN'T FIND THE BLOODY PLACE!
TAKE A RIGHT UP 'ERE, MONK. WE AIN'T BEEN UP THAT ROAD.
THOUGHT YOU WAS CHEEZED OFF, BLUDGER.
I AM, A BIT. LEND ME A CIGGIE AND WE'LL BE BUDS AGAIN.
DON'T YOU EVER GIVE UP?

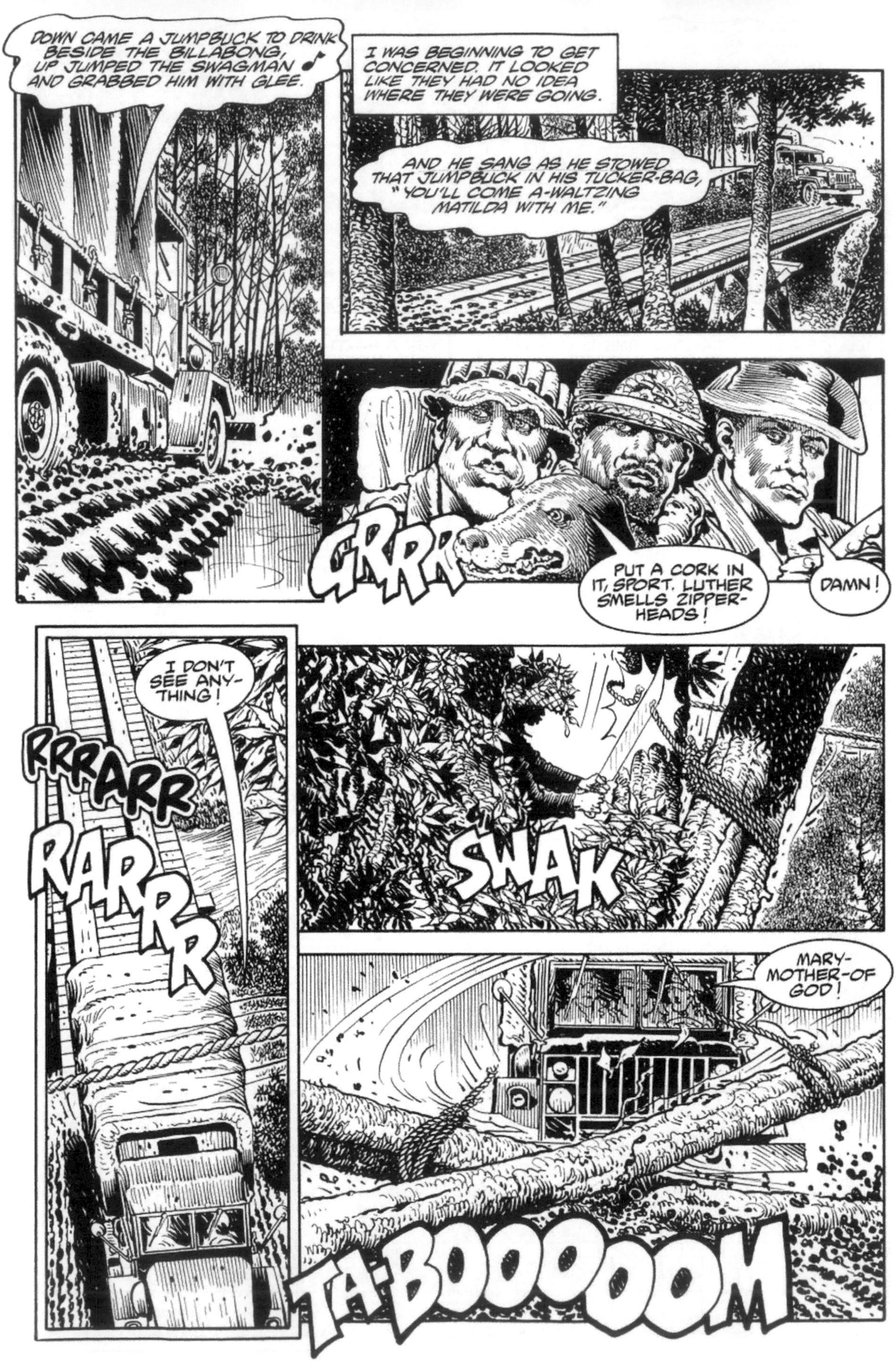
DOWN CAME A JUMPBUCK TO DRINK BESIDE THE BILLABONG, UP JUMPED THE SWAGMAN AND GRABBED HIM WITH GLEE.
I WAS BEGINNING TO GET CONCERNED. IT LOOKED LIKE THEY HAD NO IDEA WHERE THEY WERE GOING.
AND HE SANG AS HE STOWED THAT JUMPBUCK IN HIS TUCKER-BAG, "YOU'LL COME A-WALTZING MATILDA WITH ME."
GRRRR
PUT A CORK IN IT, SPORT. LUTHER SMELLS ZIPPER-HEADS!
DAMN!
I DON'T SEE ANY-THING!
RRRARR
RARRR
SWAK
MARY-MOTHER-OF GOD!
TA-BOOOOOOM

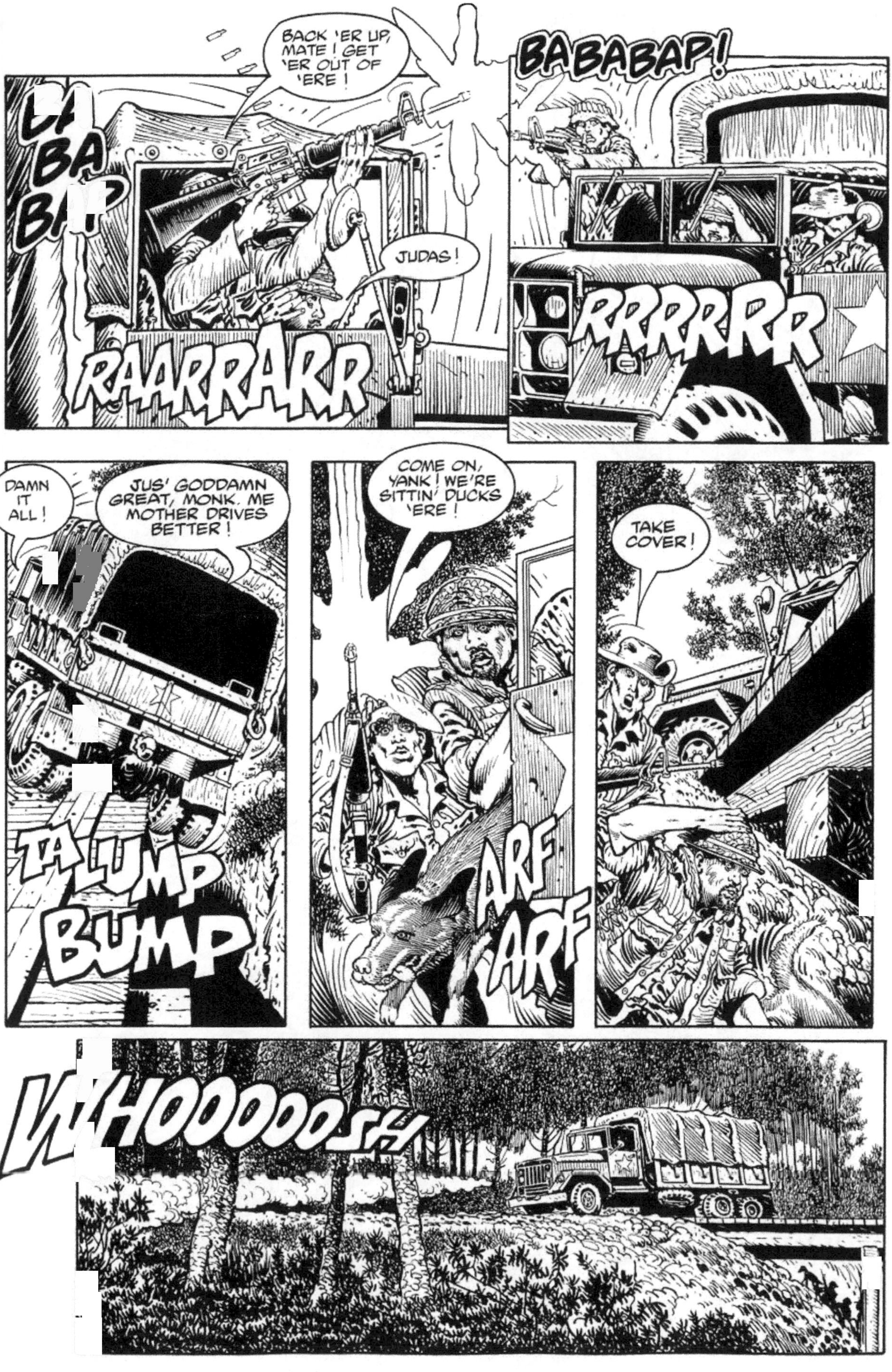

BACK 'ER UP, MATE! GET 'ER OUT OF 'ERE!
BA BA BAP
JUDAS!
RAARRARR
BABABAP!
RRRRRRR
DAMN IT ALL!
JUS' GODDAMN GREAT, MONK. ME MOTHER DRIVES BETTER!
TALUMP BUMP
COME ON, YANK! WE'RE SITTIN' DUCKS 'ERE!
ARF ARF
TAKE COVER!
WHOOOOOSH

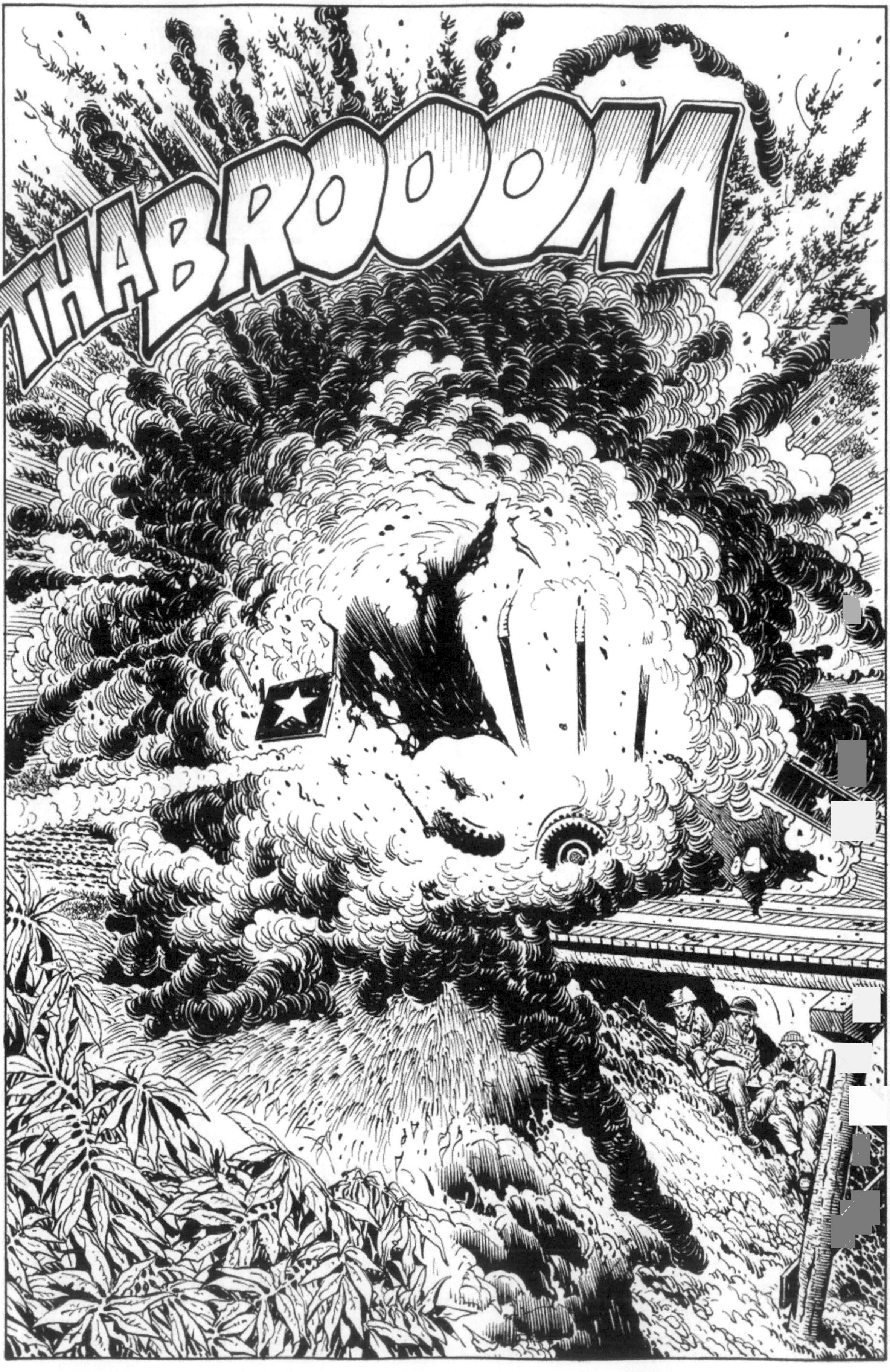
THABROOOM

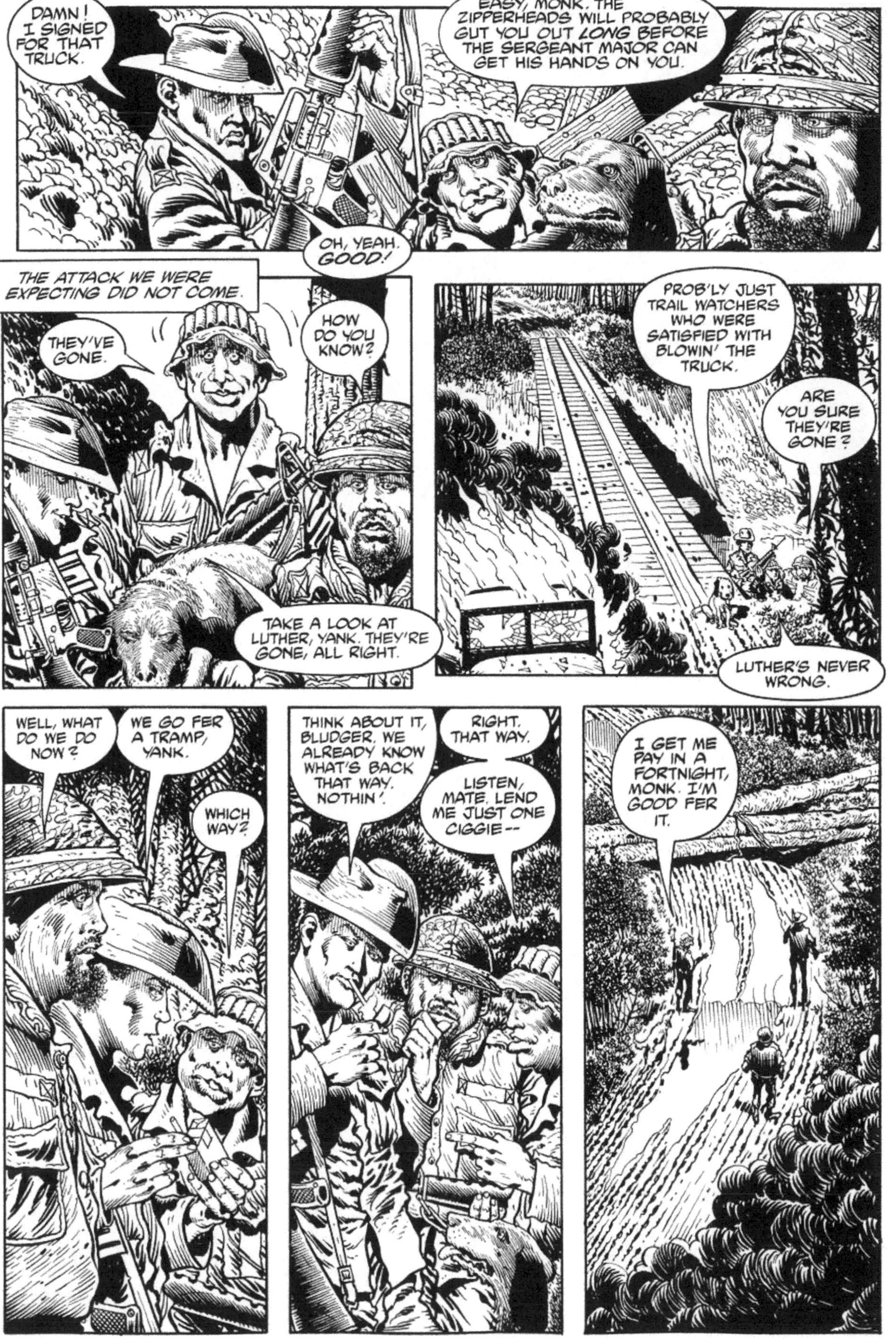

DAMN! I SIGNED FOR THAT TRUCK.
EASY, MONK. THE ZIPPERHEADS WILL PROBABLY GUT YOU OUT LONG BEFORE THE SERGEANT MAJOR CAN GET HIS HANDS ON YOU.
OH, YEAH. GOOD!
THE ATTACK WE WERE EXPECTING DID NOT COME.
THEY'VE GONE.
HOW DO YOU KNOW?
TAKE A LOOK AT LUTHER, YANK. THEY'RE GONE, ALL RIGHT.
PROB'LY JUST TRAIL WATCHERS WHO WERE SATISFIED WITH BLOWIN' THE TRUCK.
ARE YOU SURE THEY'RE GONE?
LUTHER'S NEVER WRONG.
WELL, WHAT DO WE DO NOW?
WE GO FER A TRAMP, YANK.
WHICH WAY?
THINK ABOUT IT, BLUDGER. WE ALREADY KNOW WHAT'S BACK THAT WAY. NOTHIN'.
RIGHT. THAT WAY.
LISTEN, MATE. LEND ME JUST ONE CIGGIE--
I GET ME PAY IN A FORTNIGHT, MONK. I'M GOOD FER IT.

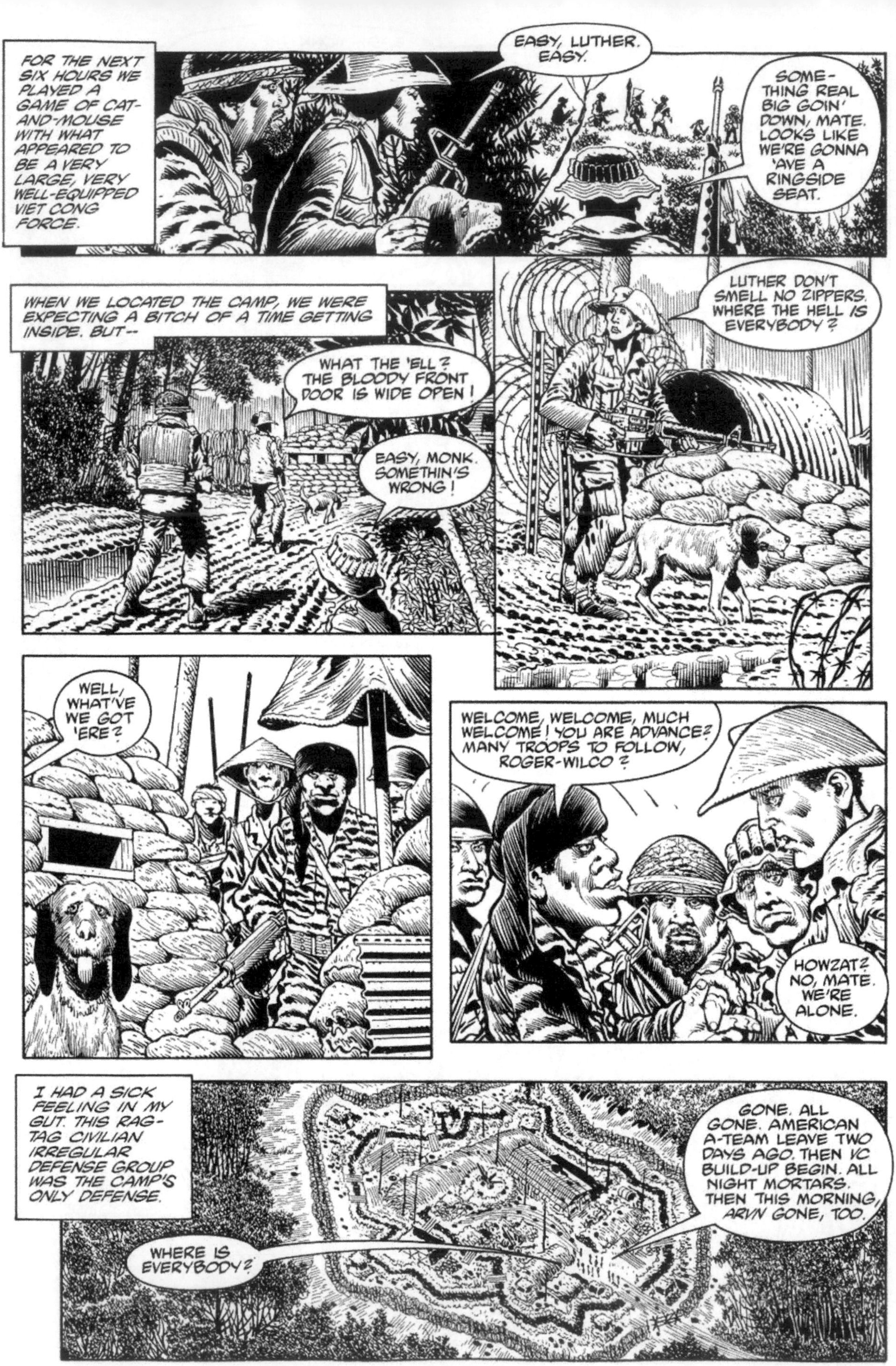
FOR THE NEXT SIX HOURS WE PLAYED A GAME OF CAT-AND-MOUSE WITH WHAT APPEARED TO BE A VERY LARGE, VERY WELL-EQUIPPED VIET CONG FORCE.
EASY, LUTHER. EASY.
SOME-THING REAL BIG GOIN' DOWN, MATE. LOOKS LIKE WE'RE GONNA 'AVE A RINGSIDE SEAT.
WHEN WE LOCATED THE CAMP, WE WERE EXPECTING A BITCH OF A TIME GETTING INSIDE. BUT--
WHAT THE 'ELL? THE BLOODY FRONT DOOR IS WIDE OPEN!
EASY, MONK. SOMETHIN'S WRONG!
LUTHER DON'T SMELL NO ZIPPERS. WHERE THE HELL IS EVERYBODY?
WELL, WHAT'VE WE GOT 'ERE?
WELCOME, WELCOME, MUCH WELCOME! YOU ARE ADVANCE? MANY TROOPS TO FOLLOW, ROGER-WILCO?
HOWZAT? NO, MATE. WE'RE ALONE.
I HAD A SICK FEELING IN MY GUT. THIS RAG-TAG CIVILIAN IRREGULAR DEFENSE GROUP WAS THE CAMP'S ONLY DEFENSE.
WHERE IS EVERYBODY?
GONE. ALL GONE. AMERICAN A-TEAM LEAVE TWO DAYS AGO. THEN VC BUILD-UP BEGIN. ALL NIGHT MORTARS. THEN THIS MORNING, ARVN GONE, TOO.

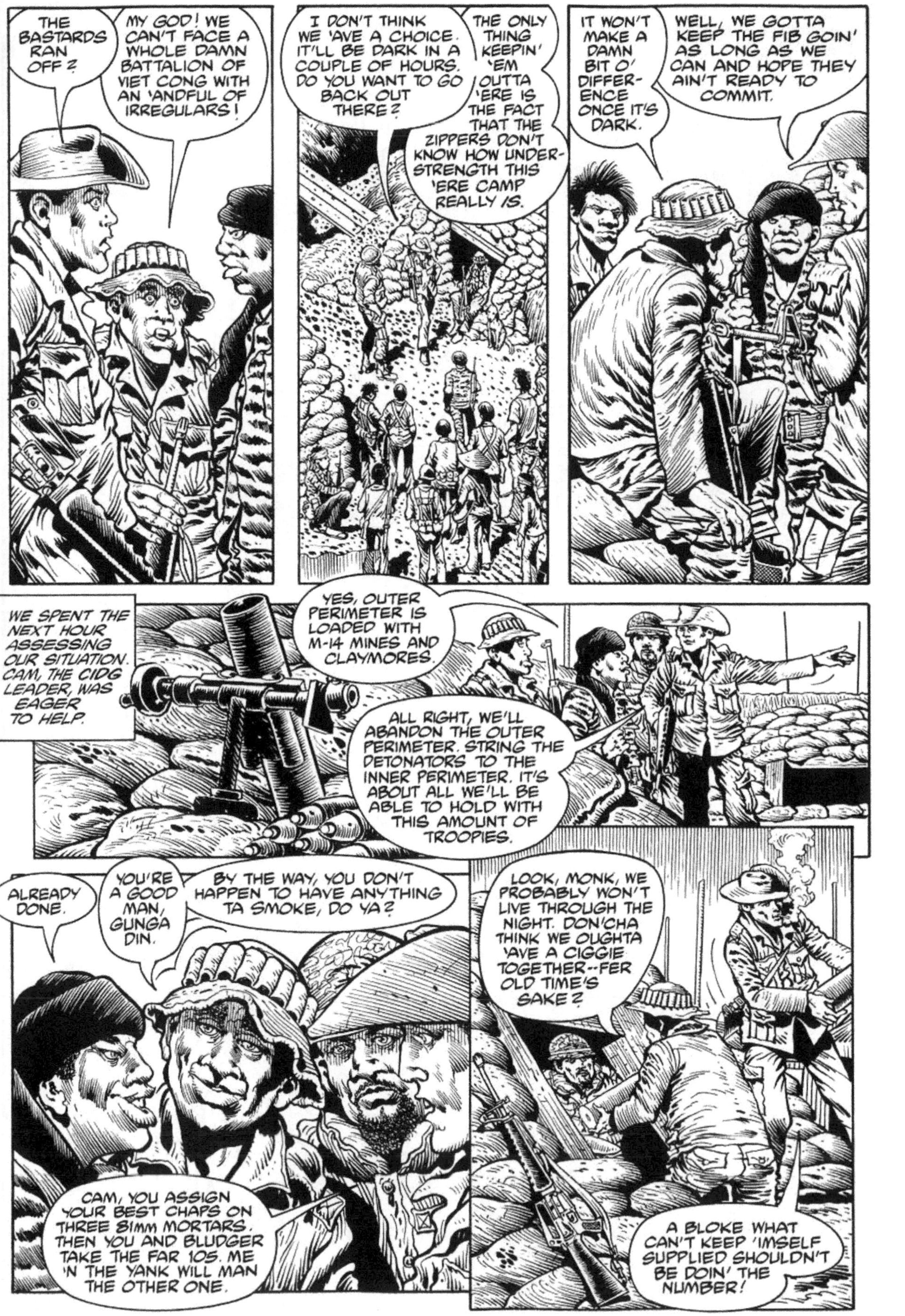

THE BASTARDS RAN OFF?
MY GOD! WE CAN'T FACE A WHOLE DAMN BATTALION OF VIET CONG WITH AN 'ANDFUL OF IRREGULARS!
I DON'T THINK WE 'AVE A CHOICE. IT'LL BE DARK IN A COUPLE OF HOURS. DO YOU WANT TO GO BACK OUT THERE?
THE ONLY THING KEEPIN' 'EM OUTTA 'ERE IS THE FACT THAT THE ZIPPERS DON'T KNOW HOW UNDER-STRENGTH THIS 'ERE CAMP REALLY IS.
IT WON'T MAKE A DAMN BIT O' DIFFER-ENCE ONCE IT'S DARK.
WELL, WE GOTTA KEEP THE FIB GOIN' AS LONG AS WE CAN AND HOPE THEY AIN'T READY TO COMMIT.
WE SPENT THE NEXT HOUR ASSESSING OUR SITUATION. CAM, THE CIDG LEADER, WAS EAGER TO HELP.
YES, OUTER PERIMETER IS LOADED WITH M-14 MINES AND CLAYMORES.
ALL RIGHT, WE'LL ABANDON THE OUTER PERIMETER. STRING THE DETONATORS TO THE INNER PERIMETER. IT'S ABOUT ALL WE'LL BE ABLE TO HOLD WITH THIS AMOUNT OF TROOPIES.
CAM, YOU ASSIGN YOUR BEST CHAPS ON THREE 81MM MORTARS. THEN YOU AND BLUDGER TAKE THE FAR 105. ME 'N THE YANK WILL MAN THE OTHER ONE.
ALREADY DONE.
YOU'RE A GOOD MAN, GUNGA DIN.
BY THE WAY, YOU DON'T HAPPEN TO HAVE ANYTHING TA SMOKE, DO YA?
LOOK, MONK, WE PROBABLY WON'T LIVE THROUGH THE NIGHT. DON'CHA THINK WE OUGHTA 'AVE A CIGGIE TOGETHER--FER OLD TIME'S SAKE?
A BLOKE WHAT CAN'T KEEP 'IMSELF SUPPLIED SHOULDN'T BE DOIN' THE NUMBER!

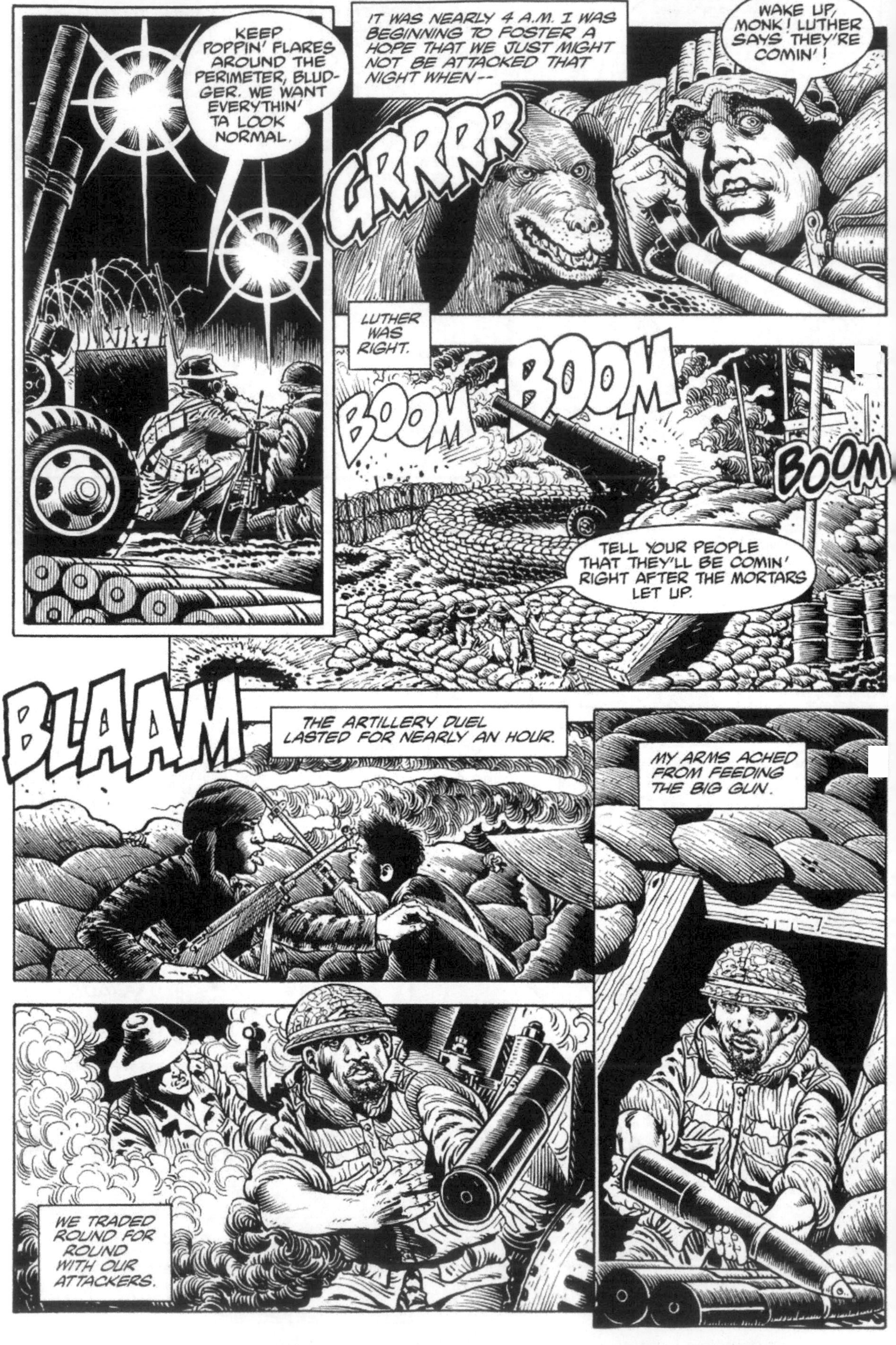
KEEP POPPIN' FLARES AROUND THE PERIMETER, BLUDGER. WE WANT EVERYTHIN' TA LOOK NORMAL.
IT WAS NEARLY 4 A.M. I WAS BEGINNING TO FOSTER A HOPE THAT WE JUST MIGHT NOT BE ATTACKED THAT NIGHT WHEN--
WAKE UP, MONK! LUTHER SAYS THEY'RE COMIN'!
GRRRR
LUTHER WAS RIGHT.
BOOM
BOOM
BOOM
TELL YOUR PEOPLE THAT THEY'LL BE COMIN' RIGHT AFTER THE MORTARS LET UP.
BLAAM
THE ARTILLERY DUEL LASTED FOR NEARLY AN HOUR.
MY ARMS ACHED FROM FEEDING THE BIG GUN.
WE TRADED ROUND FOR ROUND WITH OUR ATTACKERS.

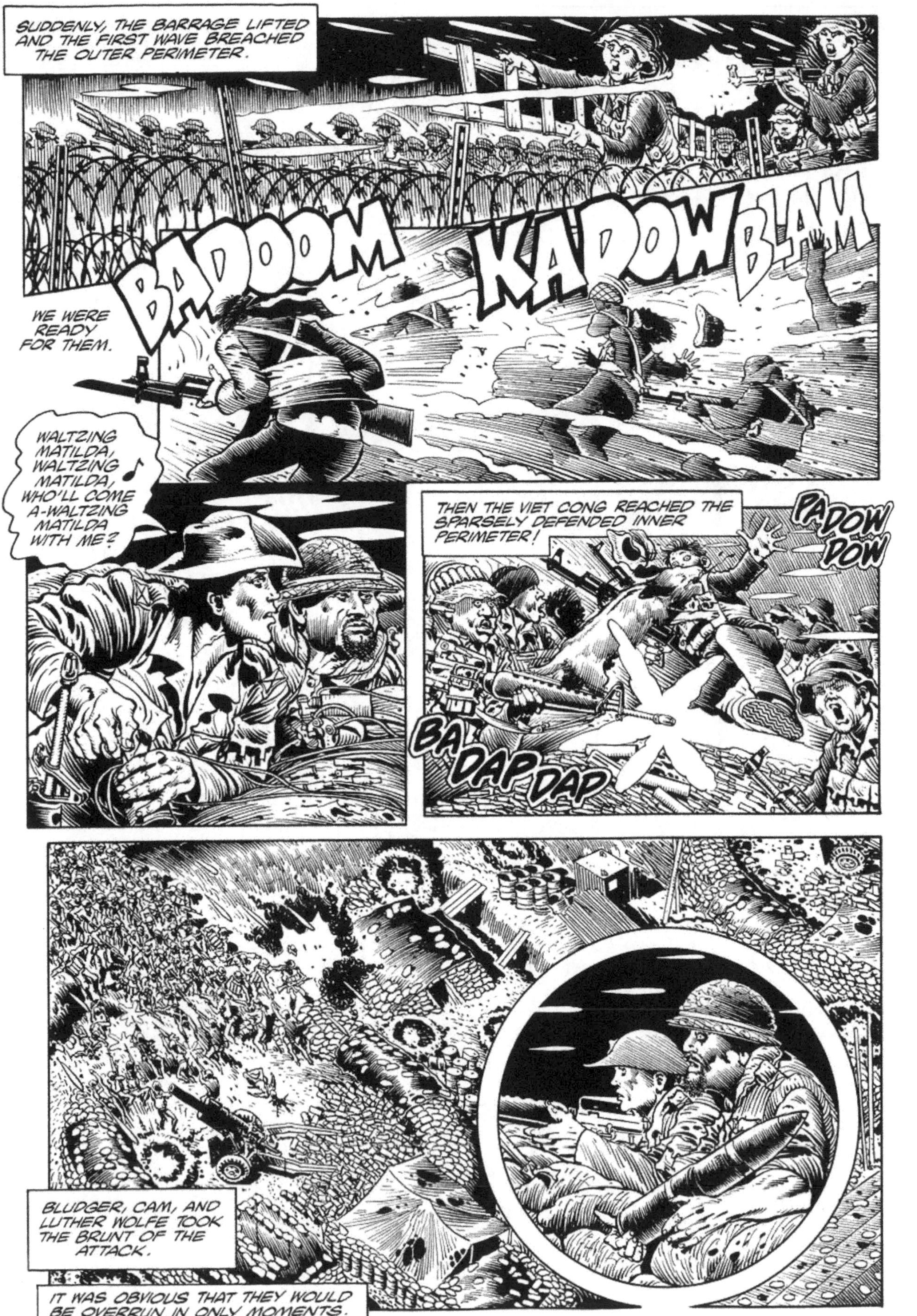
SUDDENLY, THE BARRAGE LIFTED AND THE FIRST WAVE BREACHED THE OUTER PERIMETER.
BADOOM
KADOW
BLAM
WE WERE READY FOR THEM.
WALTZING MATILDA, WALTZING MATILDA, WHO'LL COME A-WALTZING MATILDA WITH ME?
THEN THE VIET CONG REACHED THE SPARSELY DEFENDED INNER PERIMETER!
PADOW DOW
BA DAP DAP
BLUDGER, CAM, AND LUTHER WOLFE TOOK THE BRUNT OF THE ATTACK.
IT WAS OBVIOUS THAT THEY WOULD BE OVERRUN IN ONLY MOMENTS.

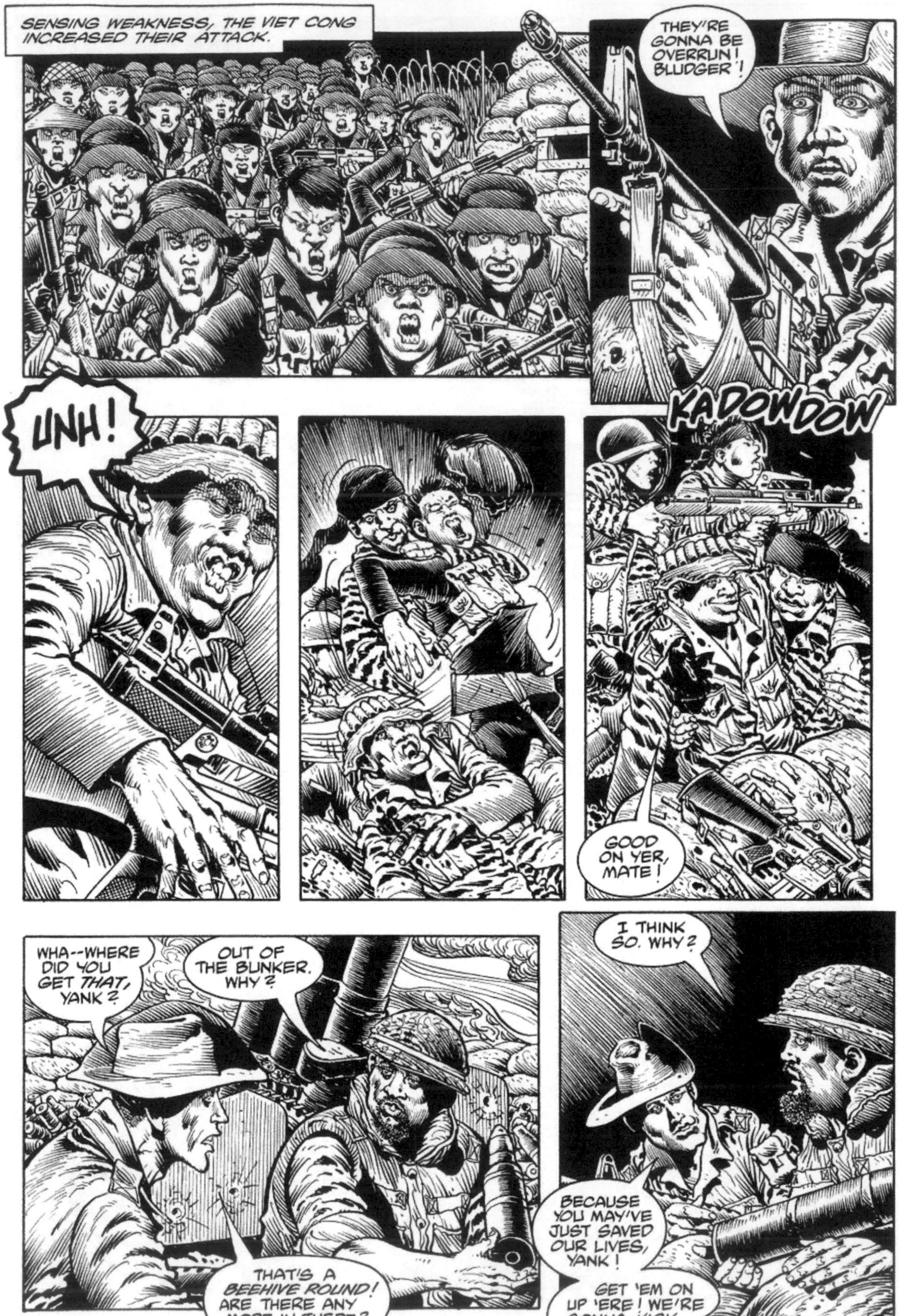
SENSING WEAKNESS, THE VIET CONG INCREASED THEIR ATTACK.
THEY'RE GONNA BE OVERRUN! BLUDGER'!
KADOWDOW
UNH!
GOOD ON YER, MATE!
WHA--WHERE DID YOU GET THAT, YANK?
OUT OF THE BUNKER. WHY?
THAT'S A BEEHIVE ROUND! ARE THERE ANY MORE IN THERE?
I THINK SO. WHY?
BECAUSE YOU MAY'VE JUST SAVED OUR LIVES, YANK!
GET 'EM ON UP 'ERE! WE'RE GONNA KICK SOME ASS!

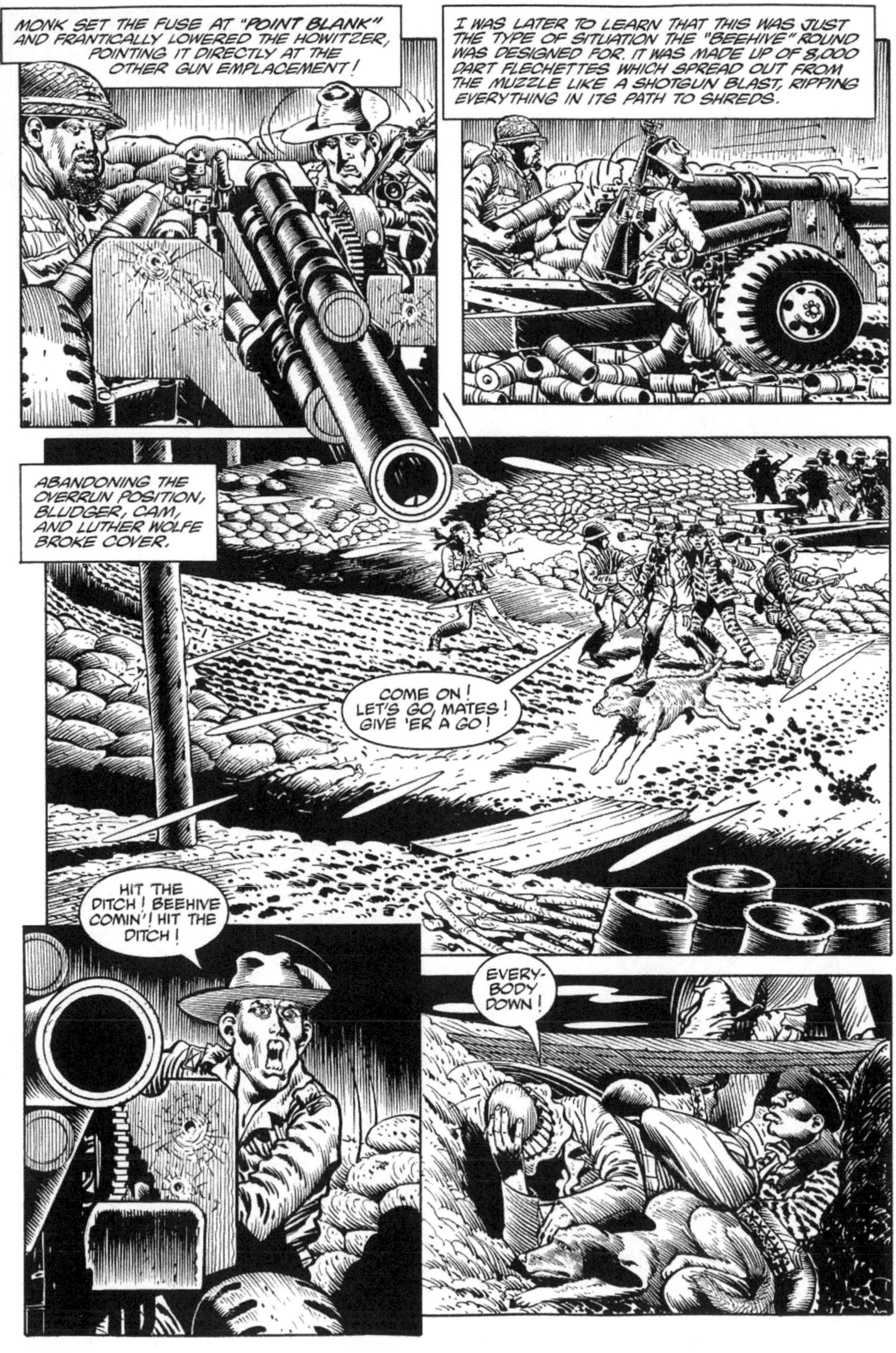
MONK SET THE FUSE AT "POINT BLANK" AND FRANTICALLY LOWERED THE HOWITZER, POINTING IT DIRECTLY AT THE OTHER GUN EMPLACEMENT!
I WAS LATER TO LEARN THAT THIS WAS JUST THE TYPE OF SITUATION THE "BEEHIVE" ROUND WAS DESIGNED FOR. IT WAS MADE UP OF 8,000 DART FLECHETTES WHICH SPREAD OUT FROM THE MUZZLE LIKE A SHOTGUN BLAST, RIPPING EVERYTHING IN ITS PATH TO SHREDS.
ABANDONING THE OVERRUN POSITION, BLUDGER, CAM, AND LUTHER WOLFE BROKE COVER.
COME ON! LET'S GO, MATES! GIVE 'ER A GO!
HIT THE DITCH! BEEHIVE COMIN'! HIT THE DITCH!
EVERY-BODY DOWN!

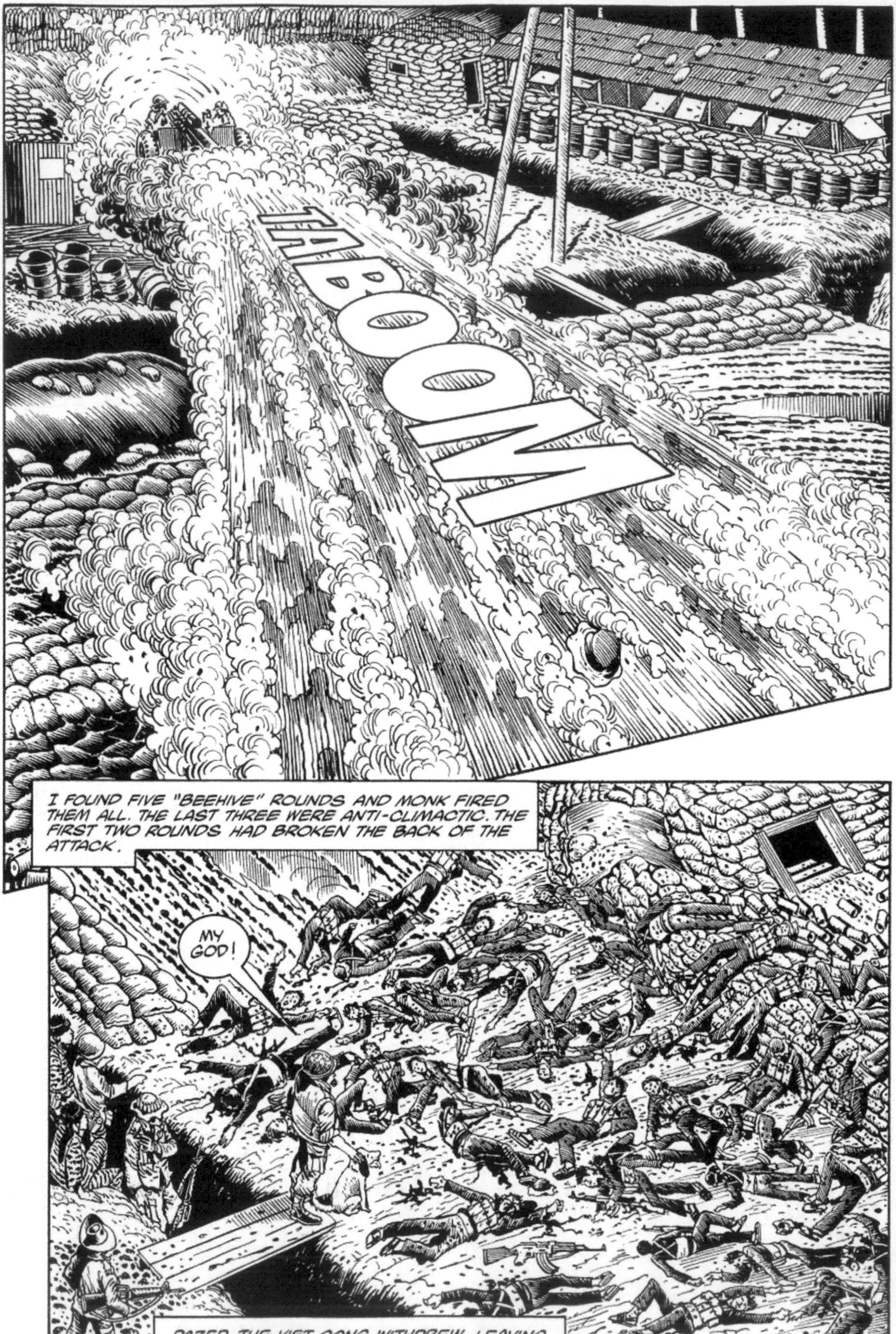
TABOOM
I FOUND FIVE "BEEHIVE" ROUNDS AND MONK FIRED THEM ALL. THE LAST THREE WERE ANTI-CLIMACTIC. THE FIRST TWO ROUNDS HAD BROKEN THE BACK OF THE ATTACK.
MY GOD!
DAZED, THE VIET CONG WITHDREW, LEAVING 51 DEAD OR WOUNDED IN THEIR WAKE.

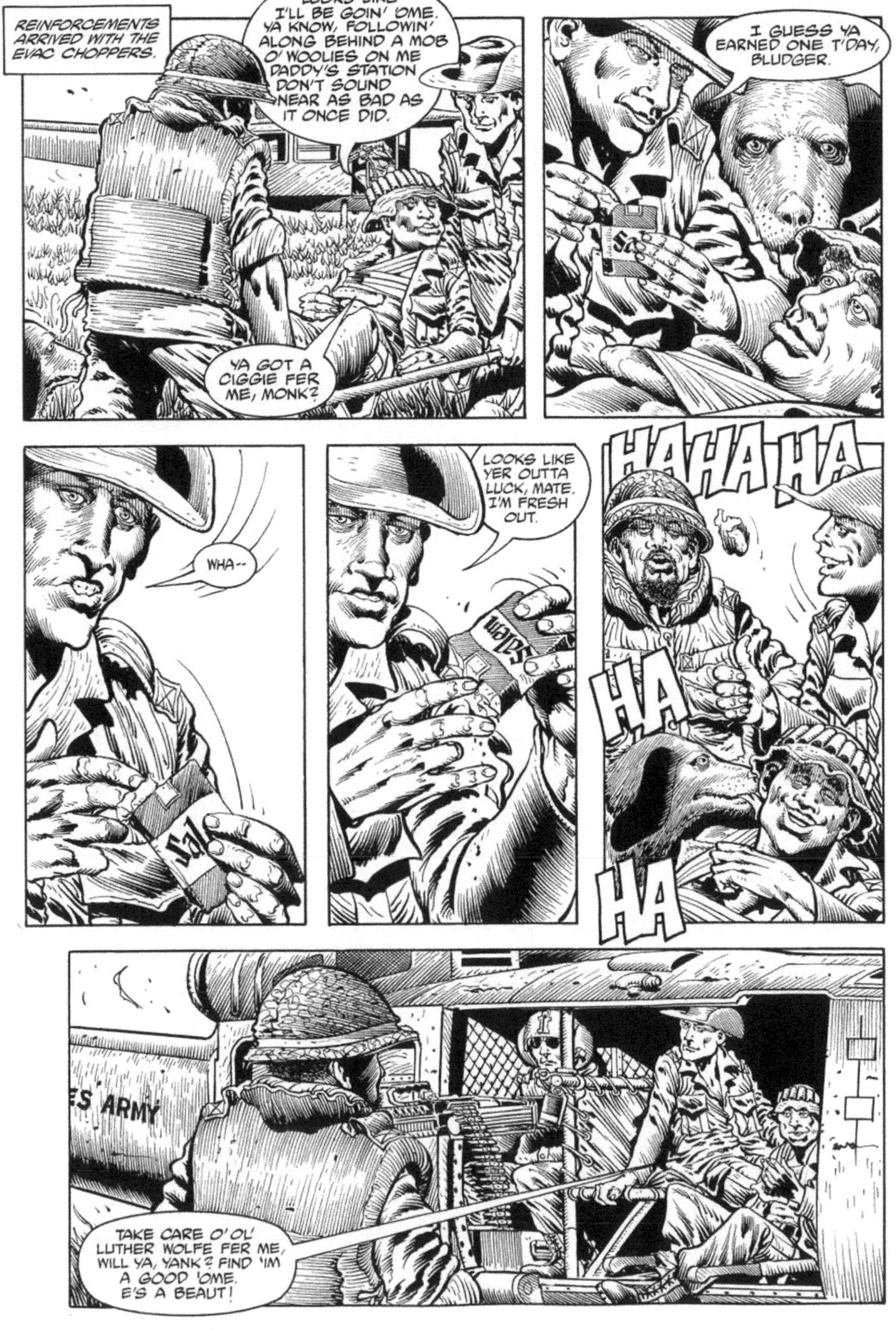

REINFORCEMENTS ARRIVED WITH THE EVAC CHOPPERS.
LOOKS LIKE I'LL BE GOIN' 'OME. YA KNOW, FOLLOWIN' ALONG BEHIND A MOB O' WOOLIES ON ME DADDY'S STATION DON'T SOUND NEAR AS BAD AS IT ONCE DID.
YA GOT A CIGGIE FER ME, MONK?
I GUESS YA EARNED ONE T'DAY, BLUDGER.
WHA--
LOOKS LIKE YER OUTTA LUCK, MATE. I'M FRESH OUT.
HAHAHA
HA
HA
HA
ES ARMY
TAKE CARE O' OL' LUTHER WOLFE FER ME, WILL YA, YANK? FIND 'IM A GOOD 'OME. E'S A BEAUT!

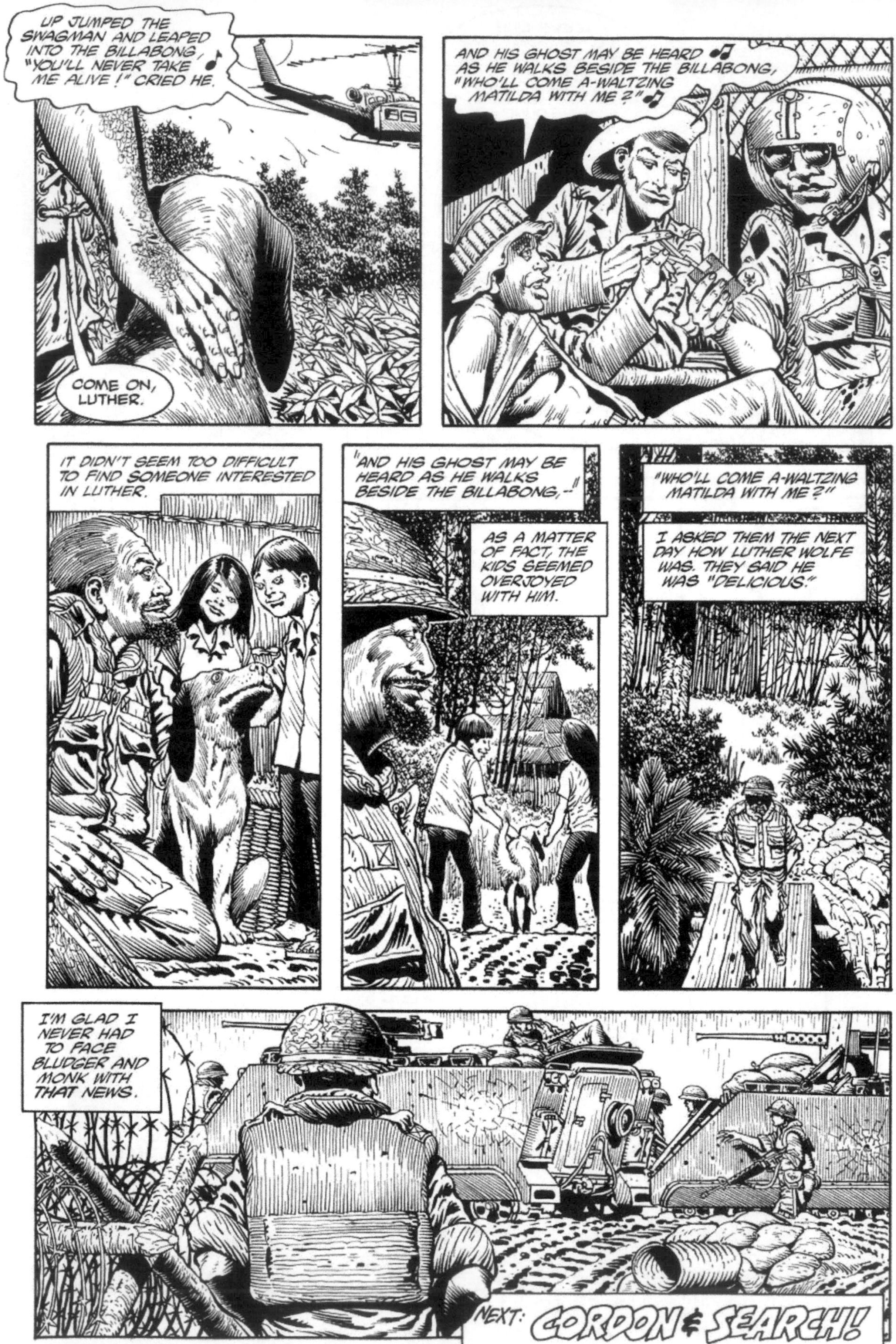

UP JUMPED THE SWAGMAN AND LEAPED INTO THE BILLABONG, "YOU'LL NEVER TAKE ME ALIVE!" CRIED HE.
COME ON, LUTHER.
AND HIS GHOST MAY BE HEARD AS HE WALKS BESIDE THE BILLABONG, "WHO'LL COME A-WALTZING MATILDA WITH ME?"
IT DIDN'T SEEM TOO DIFFICULT TO FIND SOMEONE INTERESTED IN LUTHER.
"AND HIS GHOST MAY BE HEARD AS HE WALKS BESIDE THE BILLABONG,--"
AS A MATTER OF FACT, THE KIDS SEEMED OVERJOYED WITH HIM.
"WHO'LL COME A-WALTZING MATILDA WITH ME?"
I ASKED THEM THE NEXT DAY HOW LUTHER WOLFE WAS. THEY SAID HE WAS "DELICIOUS."
I'M GLAD I NEVER HAD TO FACE BLUDGER AND MONK WITH THAT NEWS.
NEXT: CORDON & SEARCH!

POW Forum: What evidence do we have that POWs are still being held in Southeast Asia?

On February 1, 1988, The Connecticut chapter of the National Forget-Me-Not Association sponsored a Prisoner-of-War Forum at Western Connecticut State University in Danbury, Connecticut.

Participants included Bill Paul, a reporter for The Wall Street Journal, *and U.S. Rep. John Rowland (R-Conn.), a leader in Congress on the issue of POWs abandoned in Vietnam. The Departments of Defense and State were invited to send representatives to participate, but declined, saying no one was available.*

In part 3 of our edited transcript of the proceedings, Mr. Paul continues his historical overview of the issue...

Thirdly, what is the evidence that should lead any of us to believe that they're still alive in Vietnam? — or that they were there in the first place? Okay, you've got the historical background, but do you really think they're there? Or is it just my propaganda?

Let's begin by referring to a gentleman by the name of Eugene Tighe, General, Retired, Defense Intelligence Agency — which is the Pentagon's equivalent of the CIA.

He was running the Defense Intelligence Agency back in the 70's, and he remembers that when the first group — mind you he said "first group" — when the first group of men came out of North Vietnam in early 1973, he expected another shipment. At least that many, and more. He said, "Oh, well, surely there's going to be another group." There was never another group.

After he retired, he was asked to look at some of the intelligence that boat people have told our officials in Washington upon their getting out of Vietnam and Laos. General Tighe said, "It's overwhelming. On any other intelligence issue I have ever been involved with, this would be enough to move, to act, to get it done."

But he even went further in his denunciation of his own military establishment. He said "They don't do it. There's a mindset to debunk here. It's not that they're stupid, it's not that they're ignorant. There is a mindset to debunk the good information." And that's from a member of the establishment.

Let's move on. There's a gentleman living in the wilds of Montana today by the name of Jerry Mooney. Back in the early 70's, he had a job to intercept and decode Vietnamese radio messages. Jerry Mooney used to keep track of the planes that were shot down.

Every time a plane went down and he knew that the men had survived — remember, the Vietnamese's own communications on this — he would write down the names of the two men in that plane. Or the one man, if only one was known to have survived according to the Vietnamese. By the time the U.S. involvement ended and the men came home, Jerry Mooney had a list of 700 names, of whom at least 300 had to be alive, based upon the Vietnamese's own information.

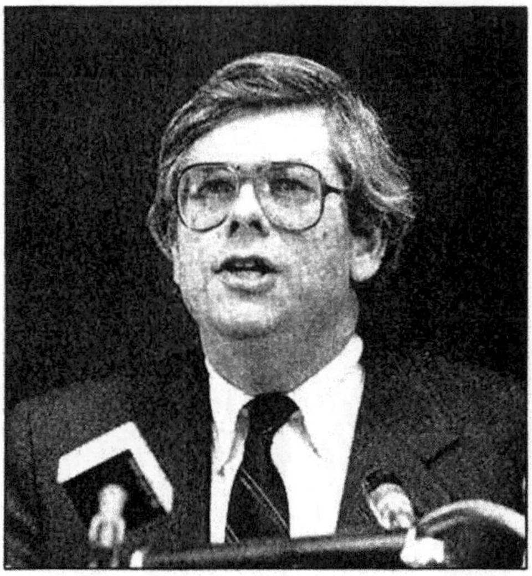

"The men who had the special training didn't come back." — Bill Paul
Photo by Carol Kaliff. Copyright ©1990 The Danbury (Ct.) News-Times

In other words, if there was a plane that went down and only one of the two men was known to have survived, he had to put both names. But he had a minimum of 300. He sat there, as many of us did, the day that the men came off the plane and started marking them down. He expected to hit 300 very quickly.

He got 5% of them. He got 15 or 20 of them, out of his 700-man list. And he started scratching his head and he said, "Now what the devil's going on here?"

Then he looked and he noticed something peculiar. The *pilots* were coming back — the men in the front seats who piloted the planes. The men in the *back seats,* who had all the special training — the electronic warfare training, the coding information, the nuclear missile information — they didn't come back.

Funny thing about that — the men who had the information highly valued by the Vietnamese didn't come back.

Search

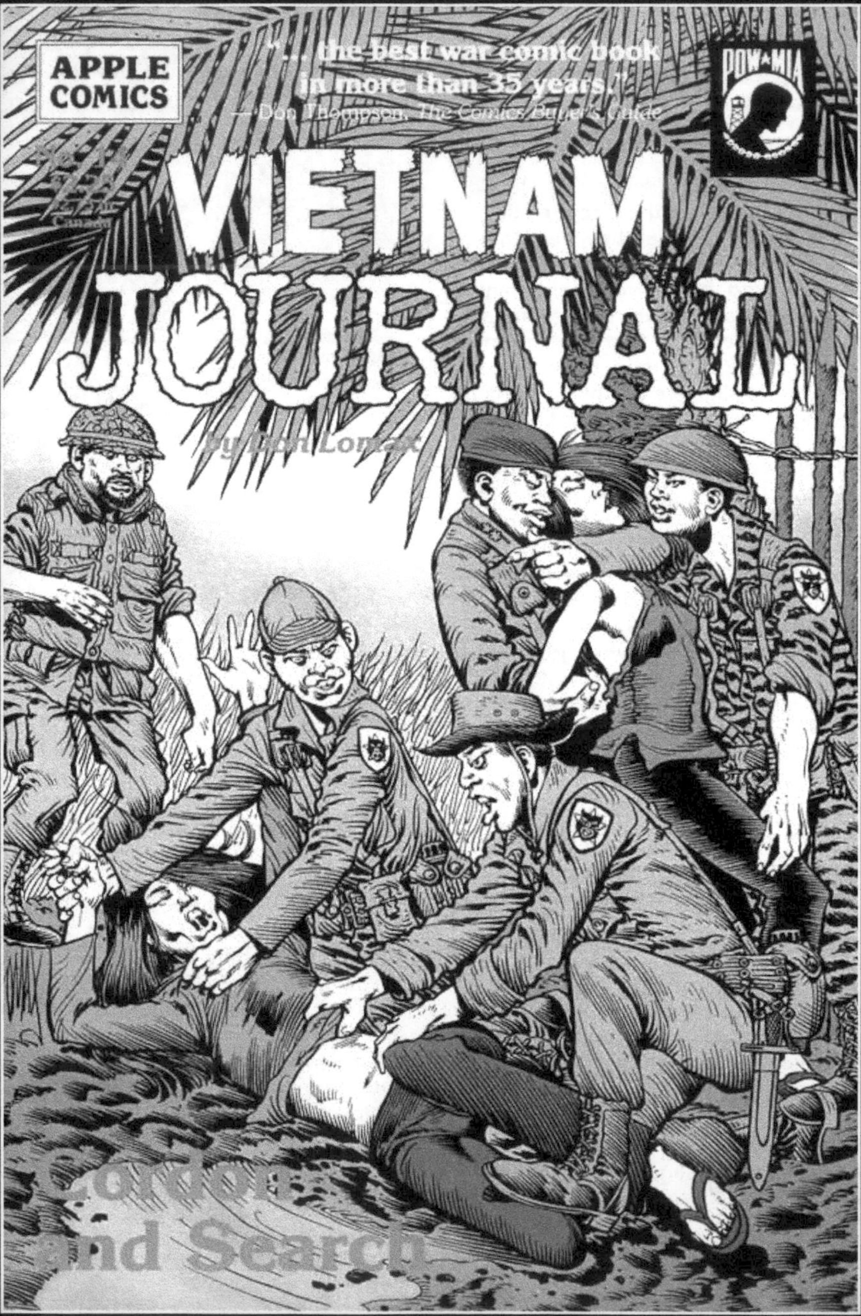
APPLE COMICS
"... the best war comic book in more than 35 years."
—Don Thompson, The Comics Buyer's Guide
POW★MIA
VIETNAM JOURNAL
Cordon and Search

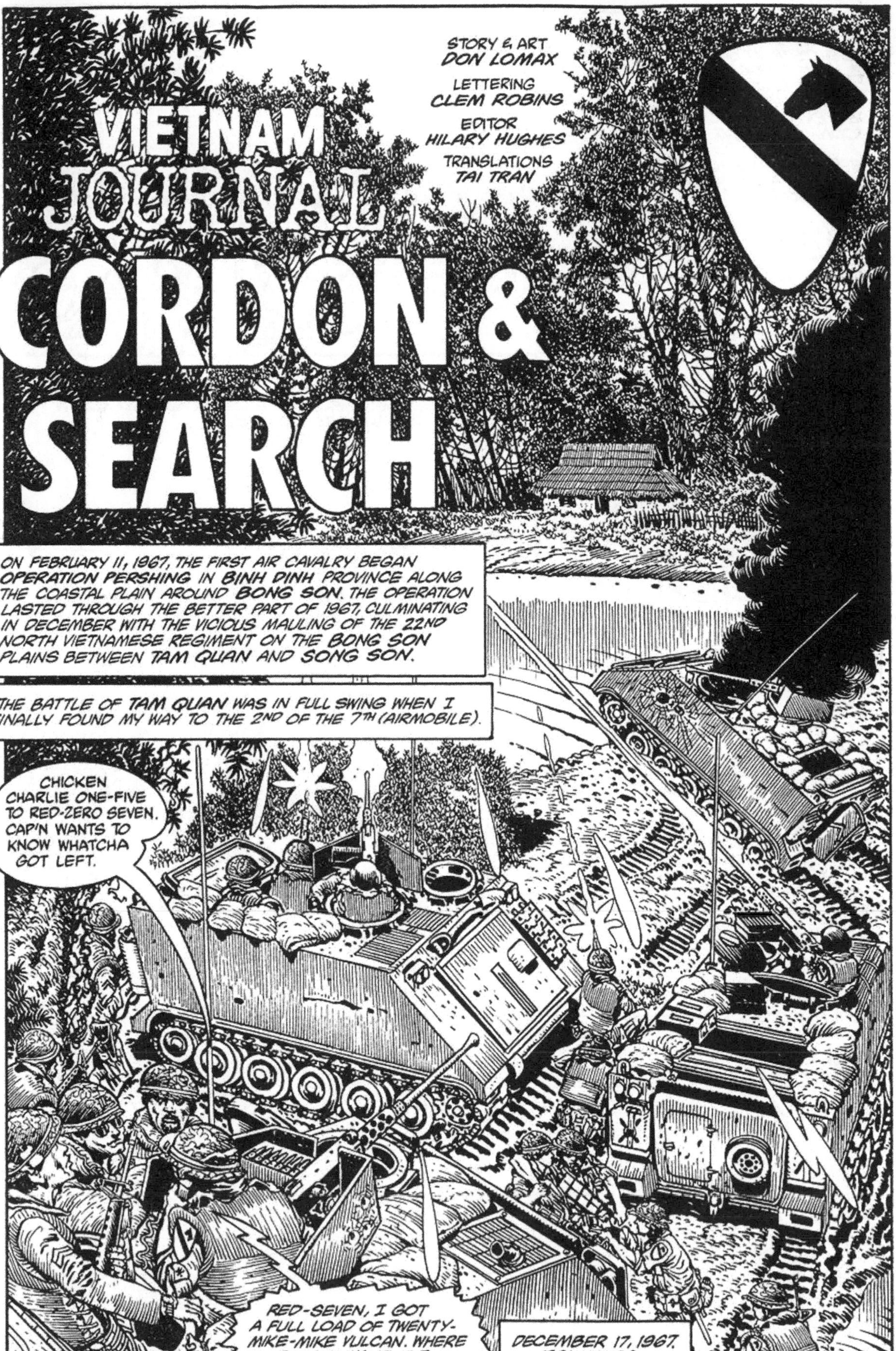
VIETNAM JOURNAL
CORDON & SEARCH
STORY & ART DON LOMAX
LETTERING CLEM ROBINS
EDITOR HILARY HUGHES
TRANSLATIONS TAI TRAN
ON FEBRUARY 11, 1967, THE FIRST AIR CAVALRY BEGAN OPERATION PERSHING IN BINH DINH PROVINCE ALONG THE COASTAL PLAIN AROUND BONG SON. THE OPERATION LASTED THROUGH THE BETTER PART OF 1967, CULMINATING IN DECEMBER WITH THE VICIOUS MAULING OF THE 22ND NORTH VIETNAMESE REGIMENT ON THE BONG SON PLAINS BETWEEN TAM QUAN AND SONG SON.
THE BATTLE OF TAM QUAN WAS IN FULL SWING WHEN I FINALLY FOUND MY WAY TO THE 2ND OF THE 7TH (AIRMOBILE).
CHICKEN CHARLIE ONE-FIVE TO RED-ZERO SEVEN. CAP'N WANTS TO KNOW WHATCHA GOT LEFT.
RED-SEVEN, I GOT A FULL LOAD OF TWENTY-MIKE-MIKE VULCAN. WHERE DO YOU WANT IT?
DECEMBER 17, 1967. 1321 HOURS.

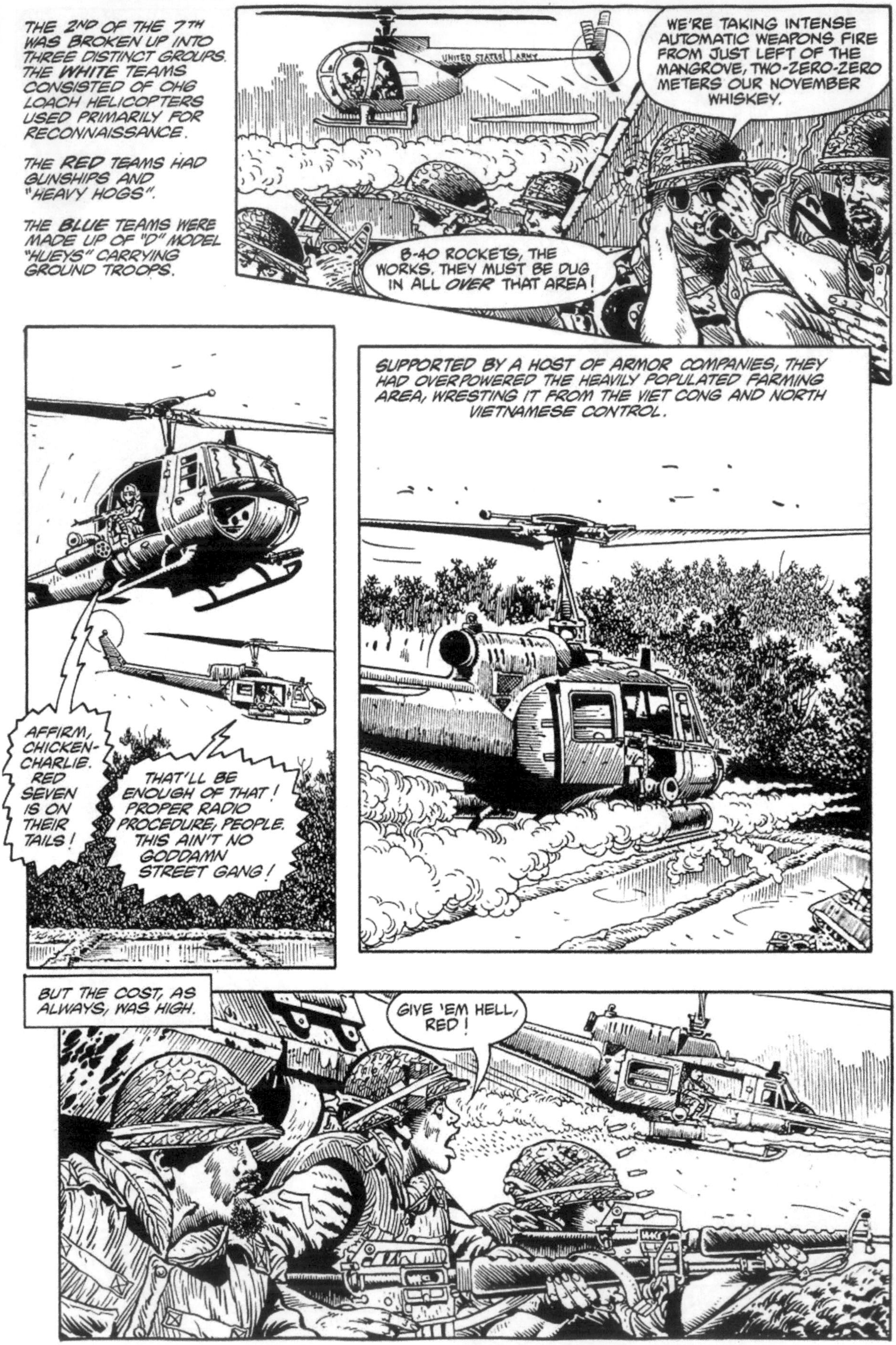
THE 2ND OF THE 7TH WAS BROKEN UP INTO THREE DISTINCT GROUPS. THE WHITE TEAMS CONSISTED OF OH6 LOACH HELICOPTERS USED PRIMARILY FOR RECONNAISSANCE.
THE RED TEAMS HAD GUNSHIPS AND "HEAVY HOGS".
THE BLUE TEAMS WERE MADE UP OF "D" MODEL "HUEYS" CARRYING GROUND TROOPS.
WE'RE TAKING INTENSE AUTOMATIC WEAPONS FIRE FROM JUST LEFT OF THE MANGROVE, TWO-ZERO-ZERO METERS OUR NOVEMBER WHISKEY.
B-40 ROCKETS, THE WORKS. THEY MUST BE DUG IN ALL OVER THAT AREA!
UNITED STATES ARMY
AFFIRM, CHICKEN-CHARLIE. RED SEVEN IS ON THEIR TAILS!
THAT'LL BE ENOUGH OF THAT! PROPER RADIO PROCEDURE, PEOPLE. THIS AIN'T NO GODDAMN STREET GANG!
SUPPORTED BY A HOST OF ARMOR COMPANIES, THEY HAD OVERPOWERED THE HEAVILY POPULATED FARMING AREA, WRESTING IT FROM THE VIET CONG AND NORTH VIETNAMESE CONTROL.
BUT THE COST, AS ALWAYS, WAS HIGH.
GIVE 'EM HELL, RED!

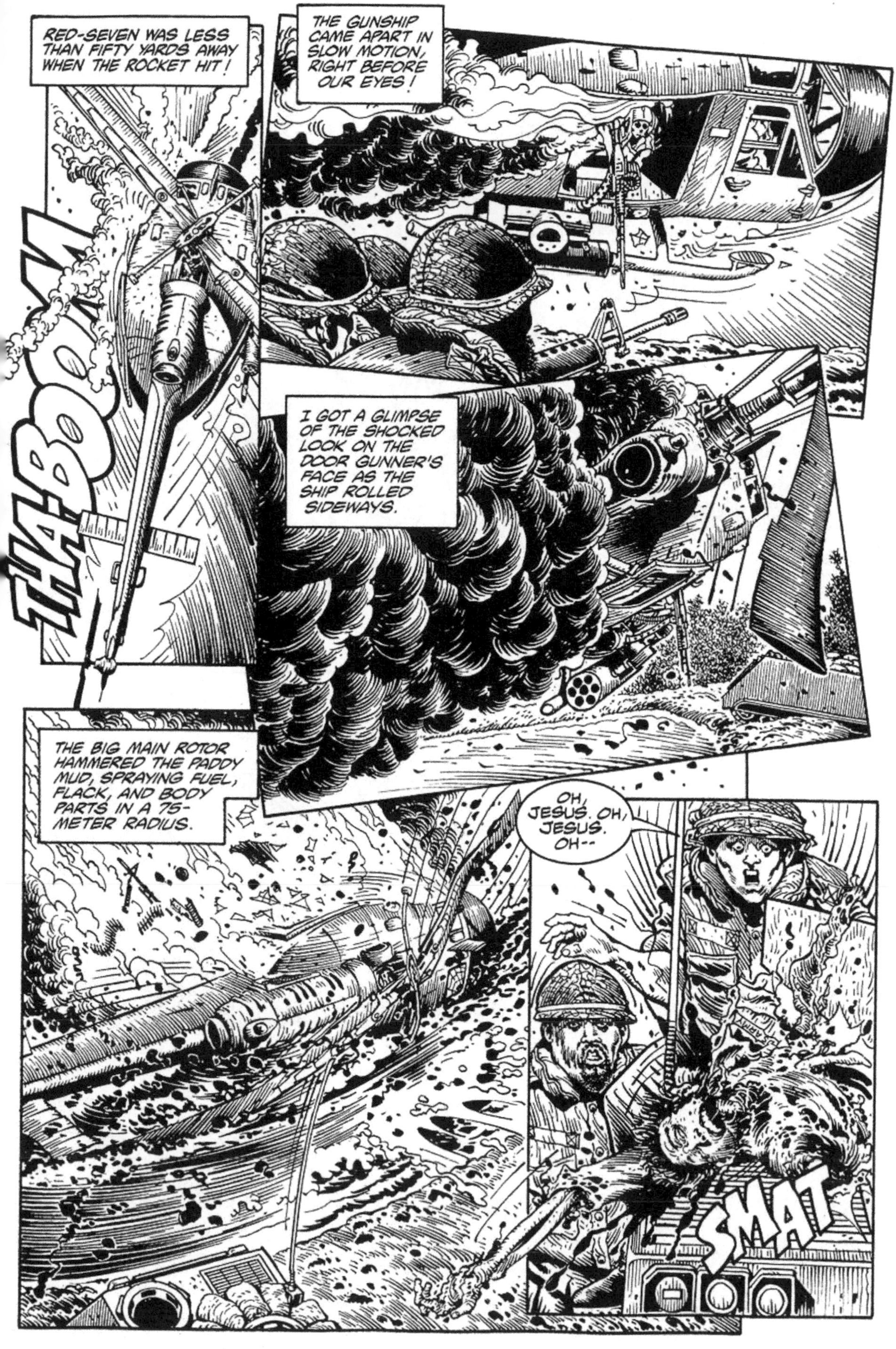
RED-SEVEN WAS LESS THAN FIFTY YARDS AWAY WHEN THE ROCKET HIT!
THABOOM
THE GUNSHIP CAME APART IN SLOW MOTION, RIGHT BEFORE OUR EYES!
I GOT A GLIMPSE OF THE SHOCKED LOOK ON THE DOOR GUNNER'S FACE AS THE SHIP ROLLED SIDEWAYS.
THE BIG MAIN ROTOR HAMMERED THE PADDY MUD, SPRAYING FUEL, FLACK, AND BODY PARTS IN A 75-METER RADIUS.
OH, JESUS. OH, JESUS. OH--
SMAT

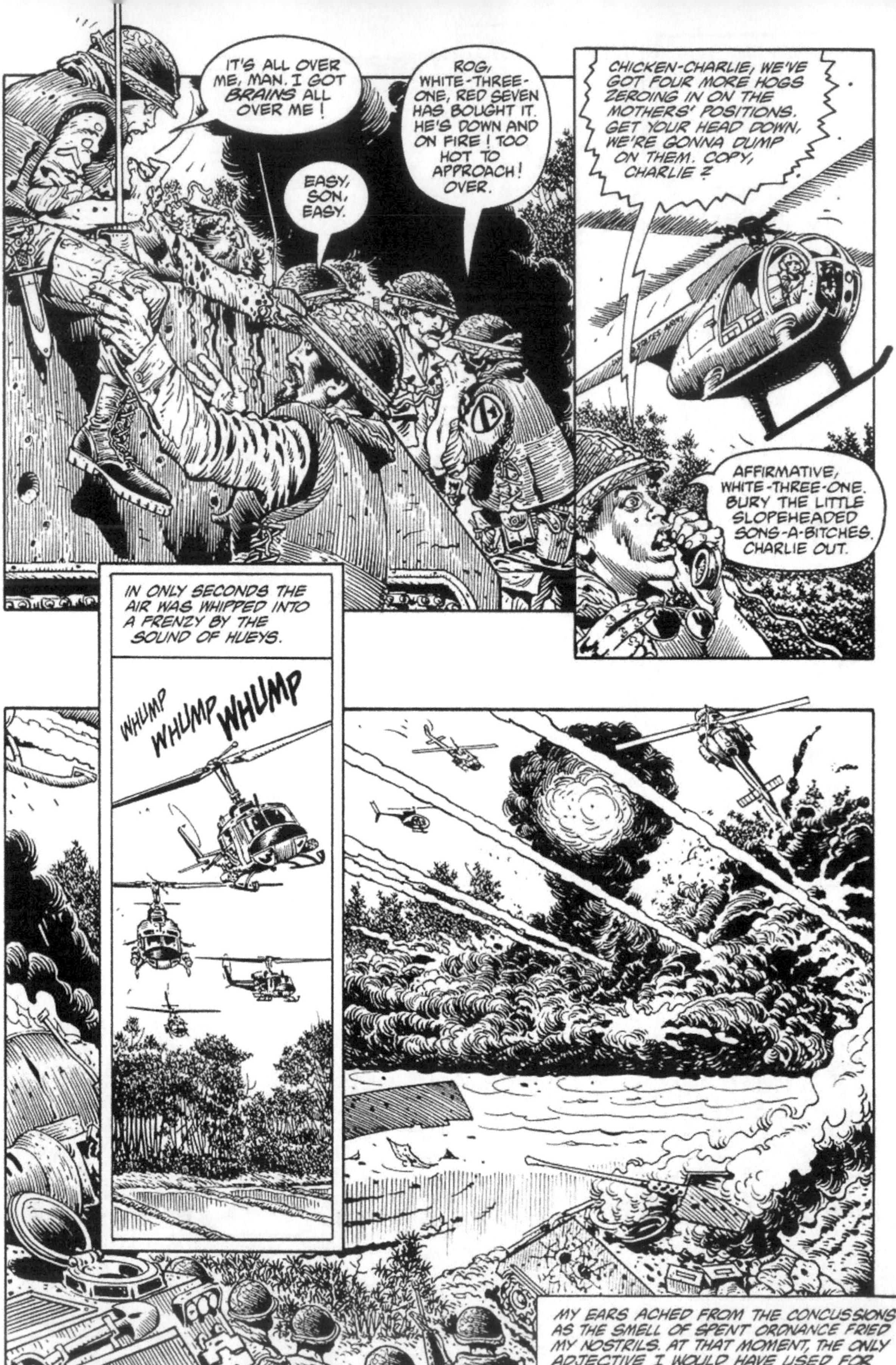

IT'S ALL OVER ME, MAN. I GOT BRAINS ALL OVER ME!
EASY, SON, EASY.
ROG, WHITE-THREE-ONE, RED SEVEN HAS BOUGHT IT. HE'S DOWN AND ON FIRE! TOO HOT TO APPROACH! OVER.
CHICKEN-CHARLIE, WE'VE GOT FOUR MORE HOGS ZEROING IN ON THE MOTHERS' POSITIONS. GET YOUR HEAD DOWN, WE'RE GONNA DUMP ON THEM. COPY, CHARLIE?
AFFIRMATIVE, WHITE-THREE-ONE. BURY THE LITTLE SLOPEHEADED SONS-A-BITCHES. CHARLIE OUT.
IN ONLY SECONDS THE AIR WAS WHIPPED INTO A FRENZY BY THE SOUND OF HUEYS.
WHUMP WHUMP WHUMP
MY EARS ACHED FROM THE CONCUSSIONS AS THE SMELL OF SPENT ORDNANCE FRIED MY NOSTRILS. AT THAT MOMENT, THE ONLY ADJECTIVE I WOULD HAVE USED FOR WAR WOULD HAVE BEEN 'NOISY'.

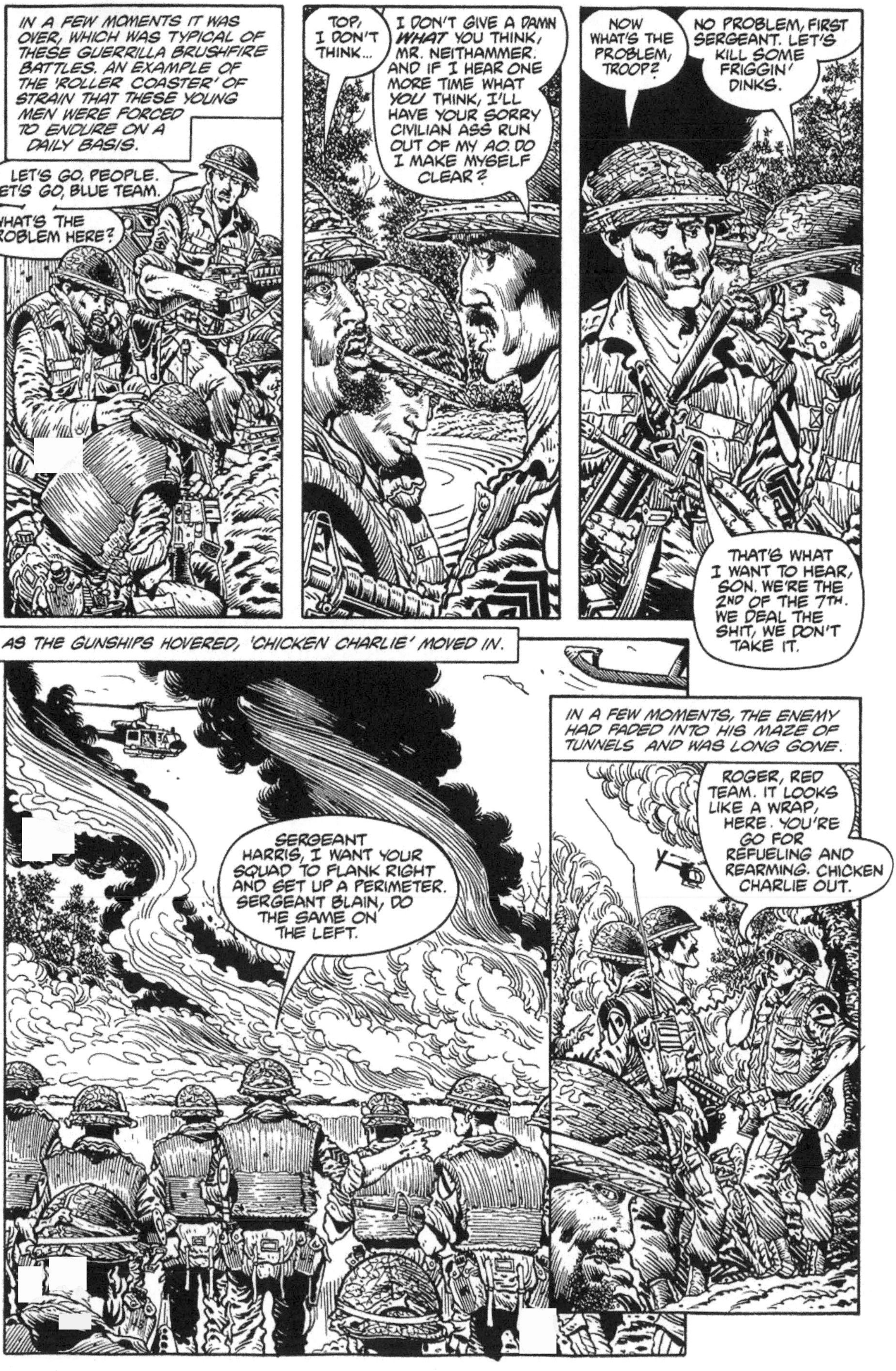
IN A FEW MOMENTS IT WAS OVER, WHICH WAS TYPICAL OF THESE GUERRILLA BRUSHFIRE BATTLES. AN EXAMPLE OF THE 'ROLLER COASTER' OF STRAIN THAT THESE YOUNG MEN WERE FORCED TO ENDURE ON A DAILY BASIS.
LET'S GO, PEOPLE. LET'S GO, BLUE TEAM.
WHAT'S THE PROBLEM HERE?
TOP, I DON'T THINK...
I DON'T GIVE A DAMN WHAT YOU THINK, MR. NEITHAMMER. AND IF I HEAR ONE MORE TIME WHAT YOU THINK, I'LL HAVE YOUR SORRY CIVILIAN ASS RUN OUT OF MY AO. DO I MAKE MYSELF CLEAR?
NOW WHAT'S THE PROBLEM, TROOP?
NO PROBLEM, FIRST SERGEANT. LET'S KILL SOME FRIGGIN' DINKS.
THAT'S WHAT I WANT TO HEAR, SON. WE'RE THE 2ND OF THE 7TH. WE DEAL THE SHIT, WE DON'T TAKE IT.
AS THE GUNSHIPS HOVERED, 'CHICKEN CHARLIE' MOVED IN.
SERGEANT HARRIS, I WANT YOUR SQUAD TO FLANK RIGHT AND SET UP A PERIMETER. SERGEANT BLAIN, DO THE SAME ON THE LEFT.
IN A FEW MOMENTS, THE ENEMY HAD FADED INTO HIS MAZE OF TUNNELS AND WAS LONG GONE.
ROGER, RED TEAM. IT LOOKS LIKE A WRAP, HERE. YOU'RE GO FOR REFUELING AND REARMING. CHICKEN CHARLIE OUT.

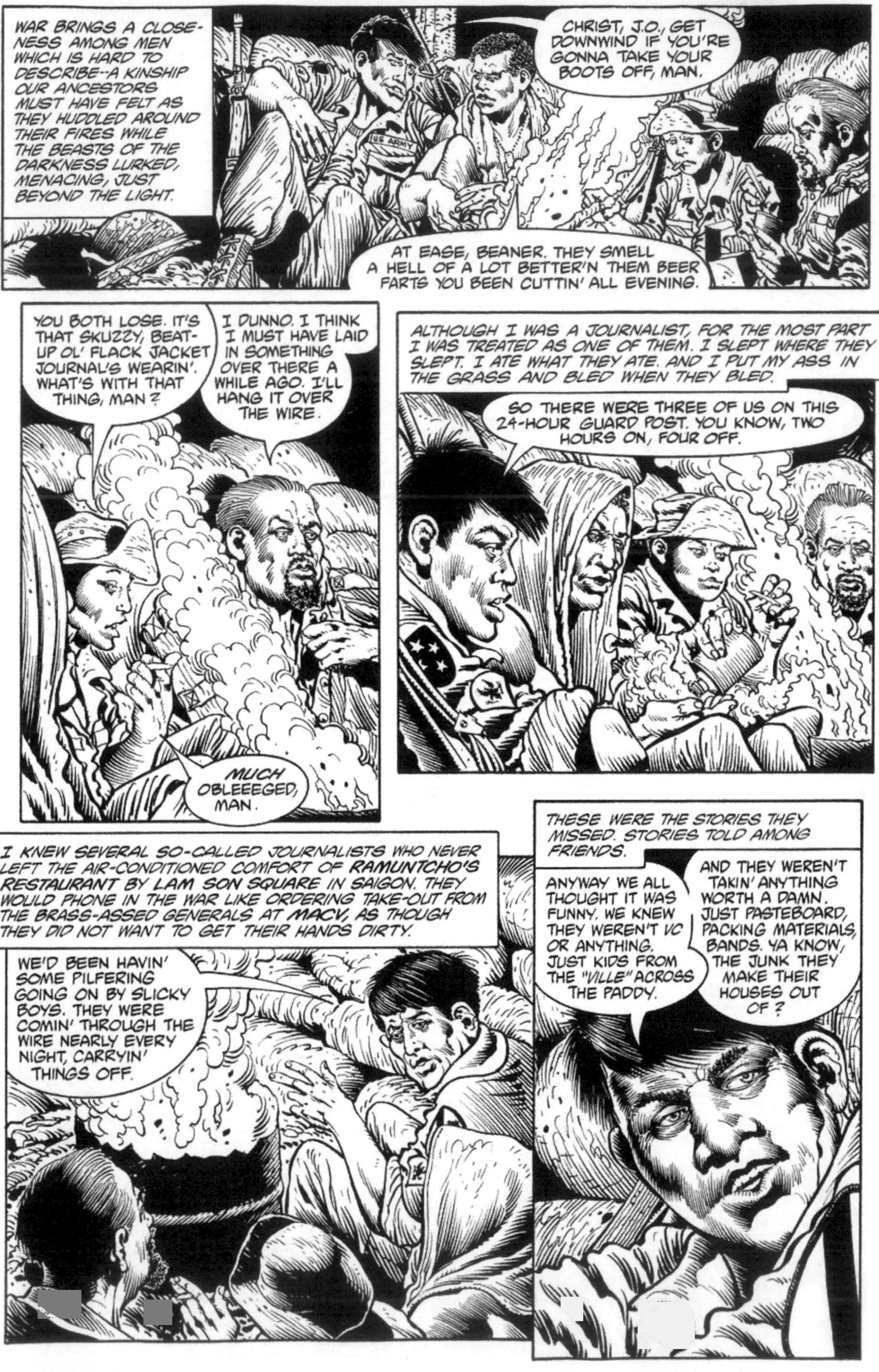
WAR BRINGS A CLOSENESS AMONG MEN WHICH IS HARD TO DESCRIBE--A KINSHIP OUR ANCESTORS MUST HAVE FELT AS THEY HUDDLED AROUND THEIR FIRES WHILE THE BEASTS OF THE DARKNESS LURKED, MENACING, JUST BEYOND THE LIGHT.
CHRIST, J.O., GET DOWNWIND IF YOU'RE GONNA TAKE YOUR BOOTS OFF, MAN.
US ARMY
AT EASE, BEANER. THEY SMELL A HELL OF A LOT BETTER'N THEM BEER FARTS YOU BEEN CUTTIN' ALL EVENING.
YOU BOTH LOSE. IT'S THAT SKUZZY, BEAT-UP OL' FLACK JACKET JOURNAL'S WEARIN'. WHAT'S WITH THAT THING, MAN?
I DUNNO. I THINK I MUST HAVE LAID IN SOMETHING OVER THERE A WHILE AGO. I'LL HANG IT OVER THE WIRE.
MUCH OBLEEEGED, MAN.
ALTHOUGH I WAS A JOURNALIST, FOR THE MOST PART I WAS TREATED AS ONE OF THEM. I SLEPT WHERE THEY SLEPT. I ATE WHAT THEY ATE. AND I PUT MY ASS IN THE GRASS AND BLED WHEN THEY BLED.
SO THERE WERE THREE OF US ON THIS 24-HOUR GUARD POST. YOU KNOW, TWO HOURS ON, FOUR OFF.
I KNEW SEVERAL SO-CALLED JOURNALISTS WHO NEVER LEFT THE AIR-CONDITIONED COMFORT OF RAMUNTCHO'S RESTAURANT BY LAM SON SQUARE IN SAIGON. THEY WOULD PHONE IN THE WAR LIKE ORDERING TAKE-OUT FROM THE BRASS-ASSED GENERALS AT MACV, AS THOUGH THEY DID NOT WANT TO GET THEIR HANDS DIRTY.
WE'D BEEN HAVIN' SOME PILFERING GOING ON BY SLICKY BOYS. THEY WERE COMIN' THROUGH THE WIRE NEARLY EVERY NIGHT, CARRYIN' THINGS OFF.
THESE WERE THE STORIES THEY MISSED. STORIES TOLD AMONG FRIENDS.
ANYWAY WE ALL THOUGHT IT WAS FUNNY. WE KNEW THEY WEREN'T VC OR ANYTHING. JUST KIDS FROM THE "VILLE" ACROSS THE PADDY.
AND THEY WEREN'T TAKIN' ANYTHING WORTH A DAMN. JUST PASTEBOARD, PACKING MATERIALS, BANDS. YA KNOW, THE JUNK THEY MAKE THEIR HOUSES OUT OF?

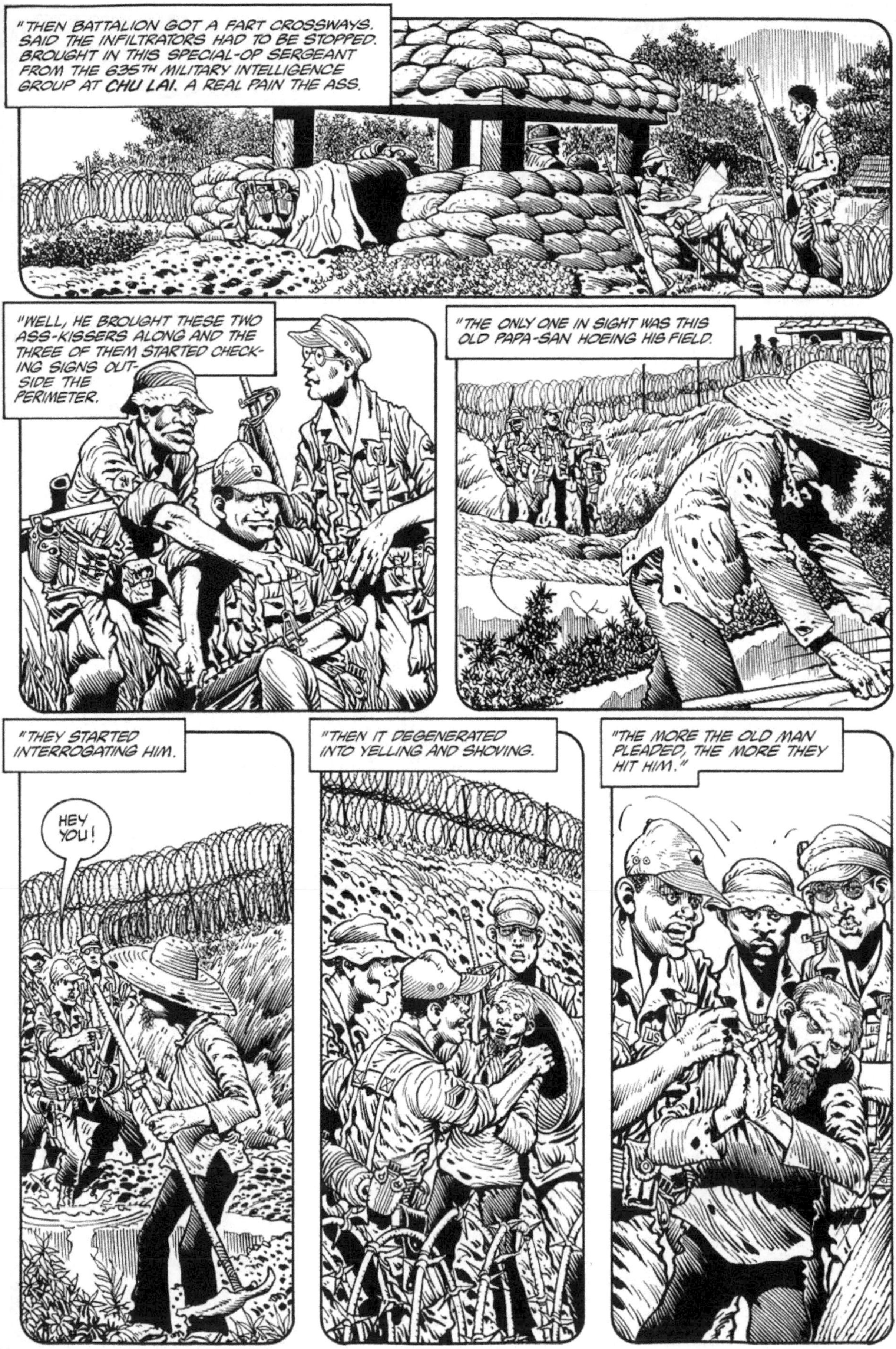
"THEN BATTALION GOT A FART CROSSWAYS. SAID THE INFILTRATORS HAD TO BE STOPPED. BROUGHT IN THIS SPECIAL-OP SERGEANT FROM THE 635TH MILITARY INTELLIGENCE GROUP AT CHU LAI. A REAL PAIN THE ASS.
"WELL, HE BROUGHT THESE TWO ASS-KISSERS ALONG AND THE THREE OF THEM STARTED CHECKING SIGNS OUTSIDE THE PERIMETER.
"THE ONLY ONE IN SIGHT WAS THIS OLD PAPA-SAN HOEING HIS FIELD.
"THEY STARTED INTERROGATING HIM.
HEY YOU!
"THEN IT DEGENERATED INTO YELLING AND SHOVING.
"THE MORE THE OLD MAN PLEADED, THE MORE THEY HIT HIM."

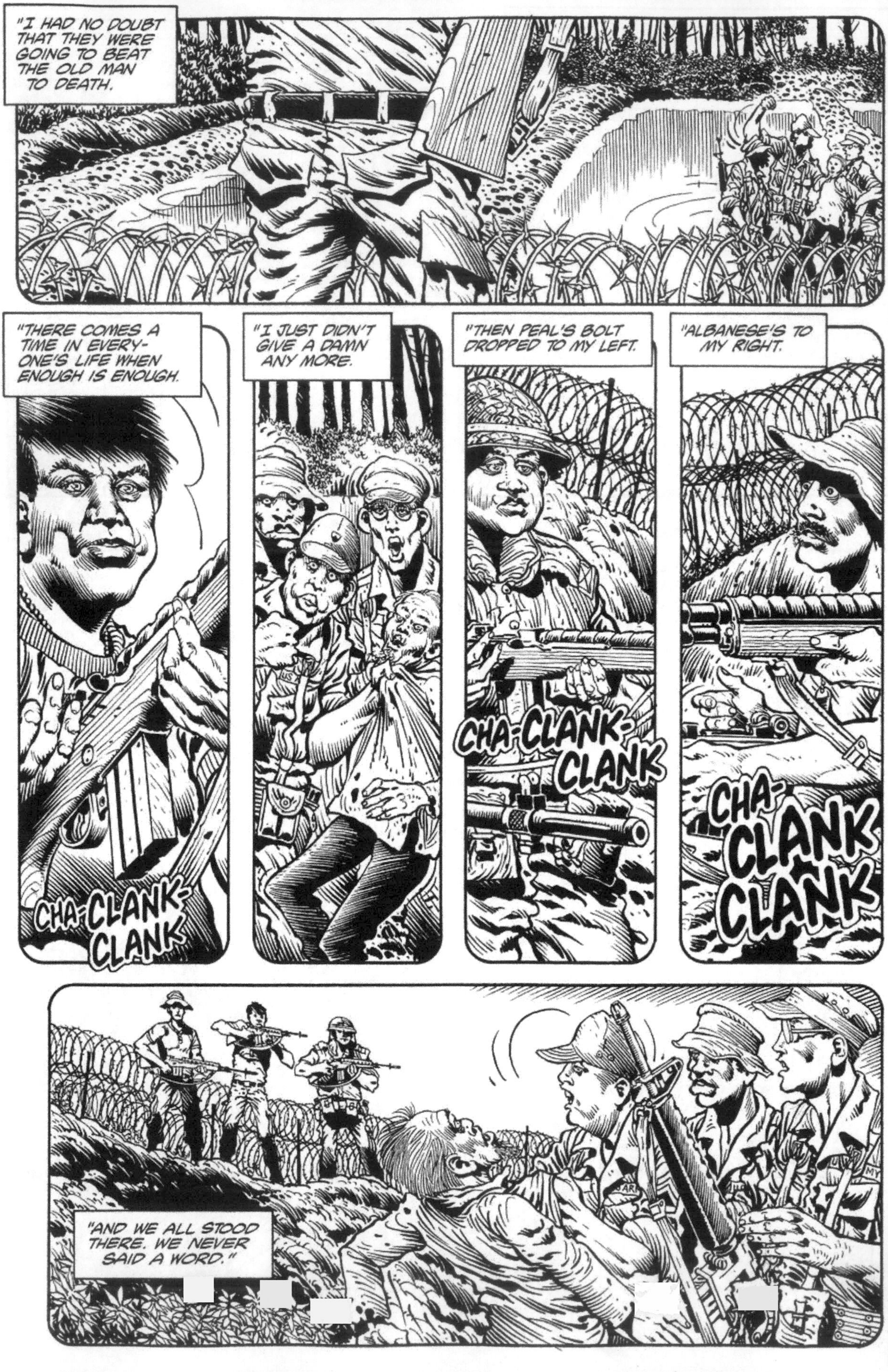
"I HAD NO DOUBT THAT THEY WERE GOING TO BEAT THE OLD MAN TO DEATH.
"THERE COMES A TIME IN EVERY-ONE'S LIFE WHEN ENOUGH IS ENOUGH.
CHA-CLANK-CLANK
"I JUST DIDN'T GIVE A DAMN ANY MORE.
"THEN PEAL'S BOLT DROPPED TO MY LEFT.
CHA-CLANK-CLANK
"ALBANESE'S TO MY RIGHT.
CHA-CLANK CLANK
"AND WE ALL STOOD THERE. WE NEVER SAID A WORD."

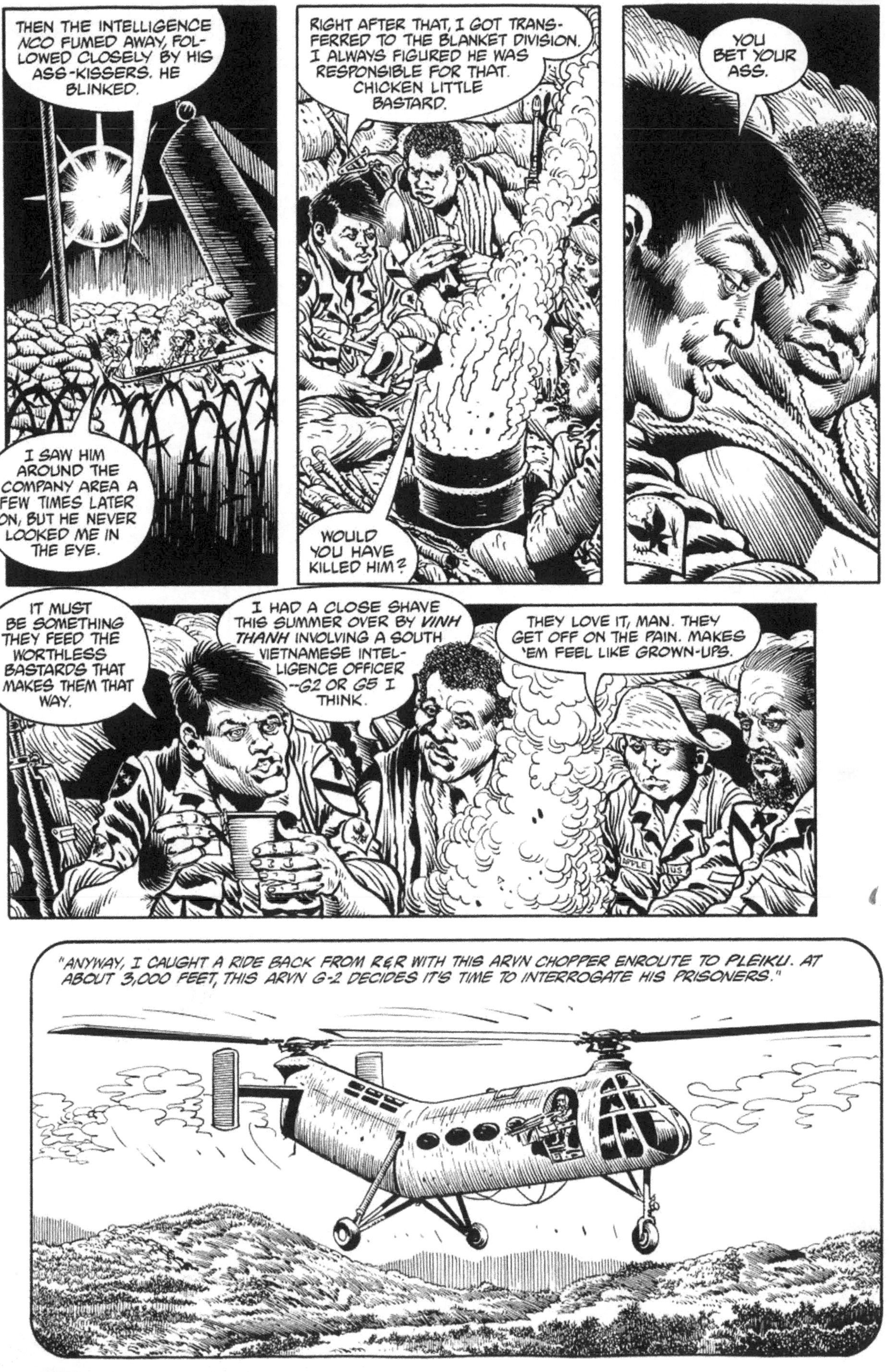
THEN THE INTELLIGENCE NCO FUMED AWAY, FOL-LOWED CLOSELY BY HIS ASS-KISSERS. HE BLINKED.
I SAW HIM AROUND THE COMPANY AREA A FEW TIMES LATER ON, BUT HE NEVER LOOKED ME IN THE EYE.
RIGHT AFTER THAT, I GOT TRANS-FERRED TO THE BLANKET DIVISION. I ALWAYS FIGURED HE WAS RESPONSIBLE FOR THAT. CHICKEN LITTLE BASTARD.
WOULD YOU HAVE KILLED HIM?
YOU BET YOUR ASS.
IT MUST BE SOMETHING THEY FEED THE WORTHLESS BASTARDS THAT MAKES THEM THAT WAY.
I HAD A CLOSE SHAVE THIS SUMMER OVER BY VINH THANH INVOLVING A SOUTH VIETNAMESE INTEL-LIGENCE OFFICER --G2 OR G5 I THINK.
THEY LOVE IT, MAN. THEY GET OFF ON THE PAIN. MAKES 'EM FEEL LIKE GROWN-UPS.
APPLE
U.S.
"ANYWAY, I CAUGHT A RIDE BACK FROM R&R WITH THIS ARVN CHOPPER ENROUTE TO PLEIKU. AT ABOUT 3,000 FEET, THIS ARVN G-2 DECIDES IT'S TIME TO INTERROGATE HIS PRISONERS."

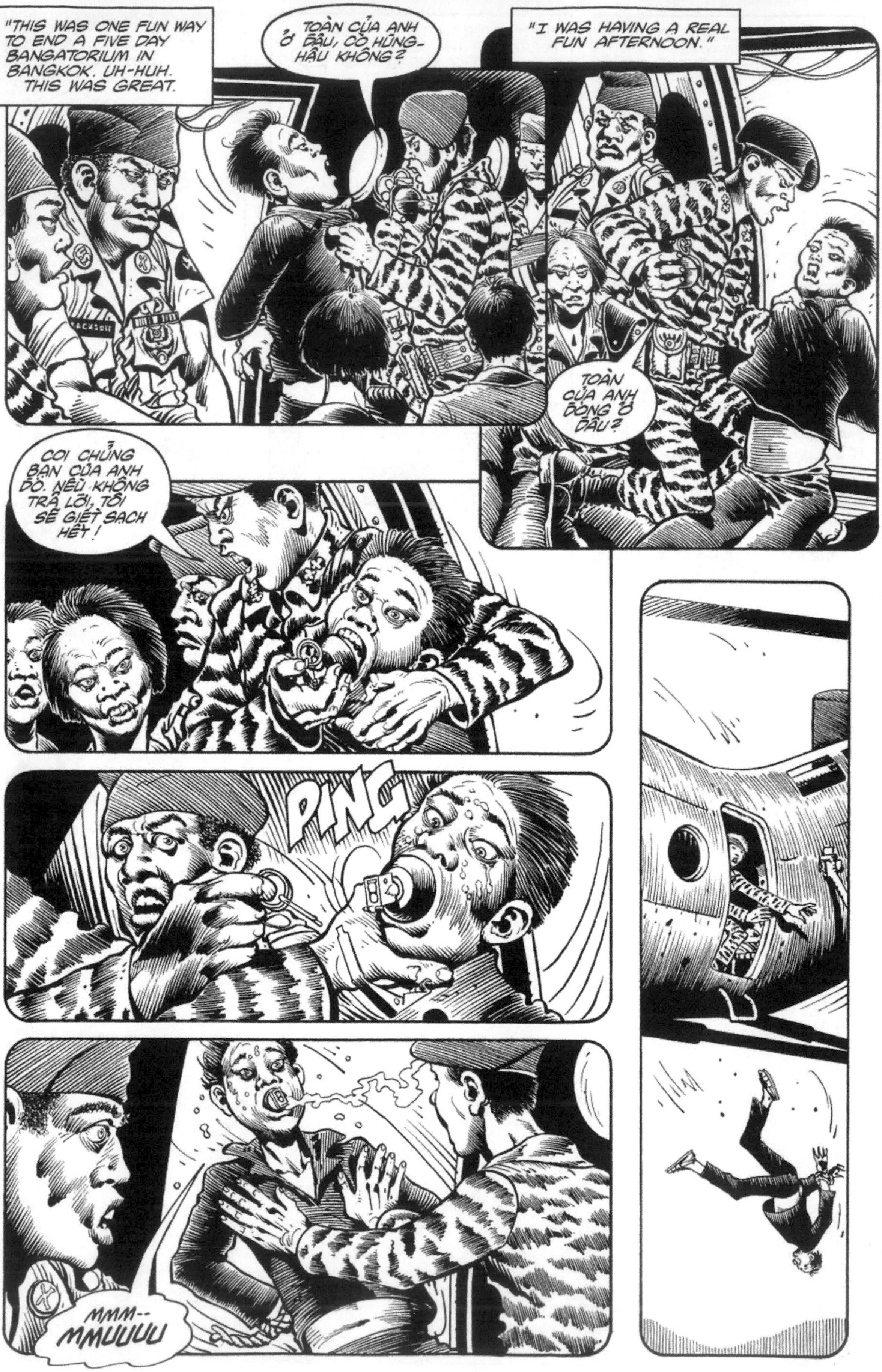
"THIS WAS ONE FUN WAY TO END A FIVE DAY BANGATORIUM IN BANGKOK. UH-HUH. THIS WAS GREAT.
TOÀN CỦA ANH Ở ĐÂU, CÒ HÙNG-HẬU KHÔNG?
"I WAS HAVING A REAL FUN AFTERNOON."
TOÀN CỦA ANH ĐÓNG Ở ĐÂU?
COI CHỪNG BẠN CỦA ANH ĐÓ. NẾU KHÔNG TRẢ LỜI, TÔI SẼ GIẾT SẠCH HẾT!
PING
MMM-- MMUUUU

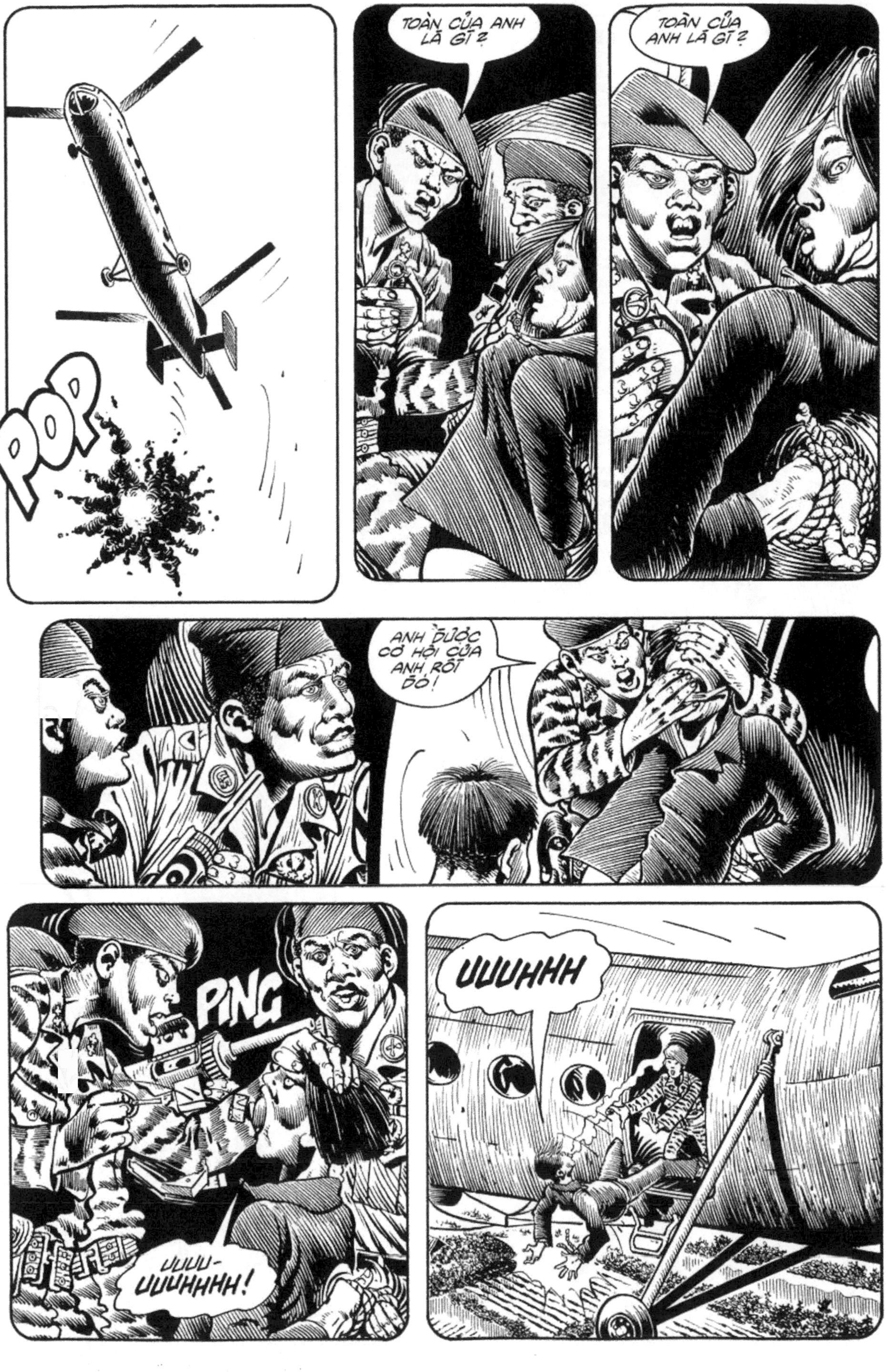
POP
TOÀN CỦA ANH LÀ GÌ?
TOÀN CỦA ANH LÀ GÌ?
ANH ĐƯỢC CƠ HỘI CỦA ANH RỒI ĐÓ!
PING
UUUU-UUUHHHH!
UUUHHH

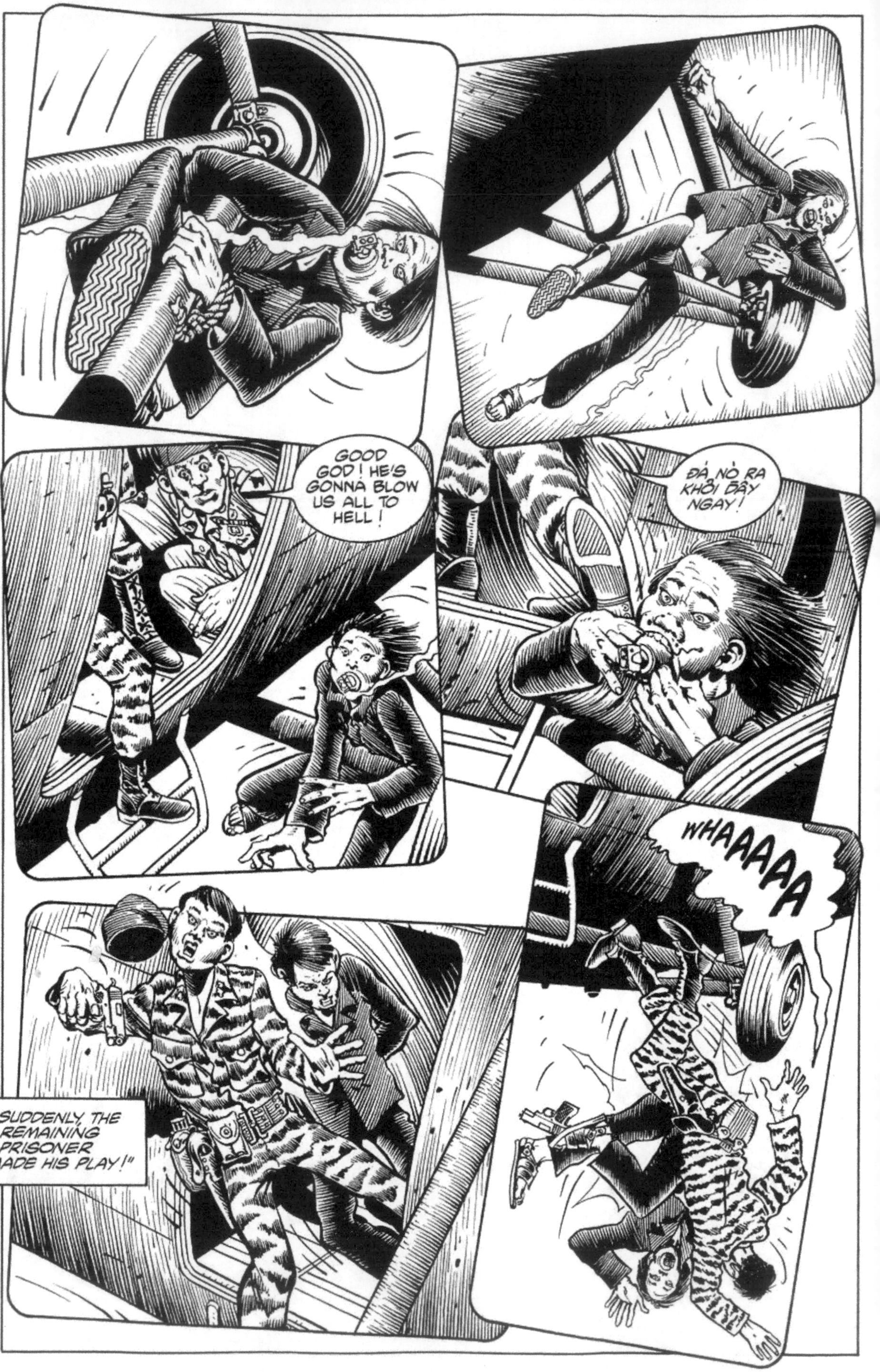
GOOD GOD! HE'S GONNA BLOW US ALL TO HELL!
ĐÁ NÓ RA KHỎI ĐÂY NGAY!
"SUDDENLY, THE REMAINING PRISONER MADE HIS PLAY!"
WHAAAAAA

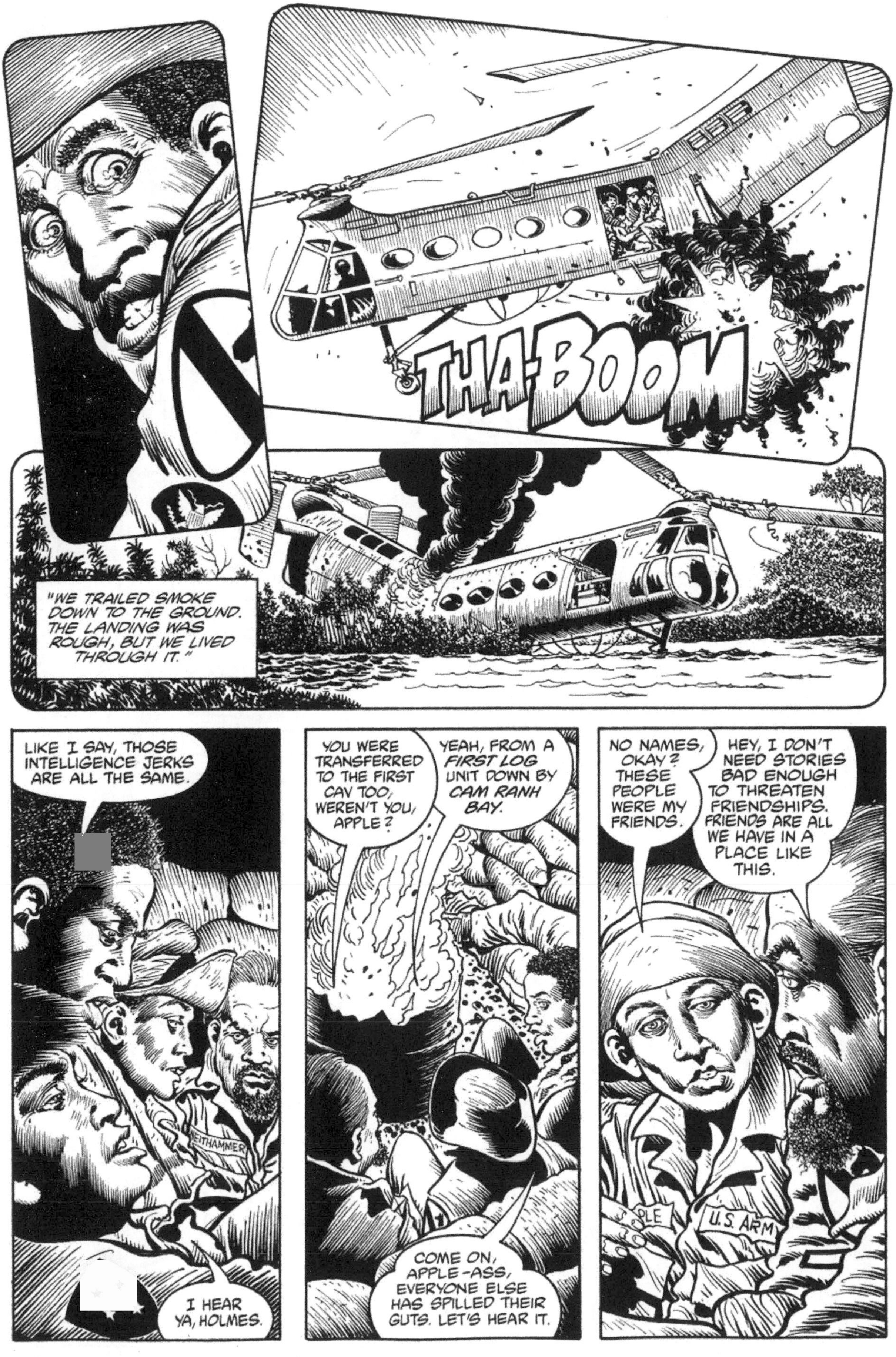

THA-BOOM
"WE TRAILED SMOKE DOWN TO THE GROUND. THE LANDING WAS ROUGH, BUT WE LIVED THROUGH IT."
LIKE I SAY, THOSE INTELLIGENCE JERKS ARE ALL THE SAME.
WEITHAMMER
I HEAR YA, HOLMES.
YOU WERE TRANSFERRED TO THE FIRST CAV TOO, WEREN'T YOU, APPLE?
YEAH, FROM A *FIRST LOG* UNIT DOWN BY *CAM RANH BAY*.
COME ON, APPLE-ASS, EVERYONE ELSE HAS SPILLED THEIR GUTS. LET'S HEAR IT.
NO NAMES, OKAY? THESE PEOPLE WERE MY FRIENDS.
HEY, I DON'T NEED STORIES BAD ENOUGH TO THREATEN FRIENDSHIPS. FRIENDS ARE ALL WE HAVE IN A PLACE LIKE THIS.
U.S. ARMY

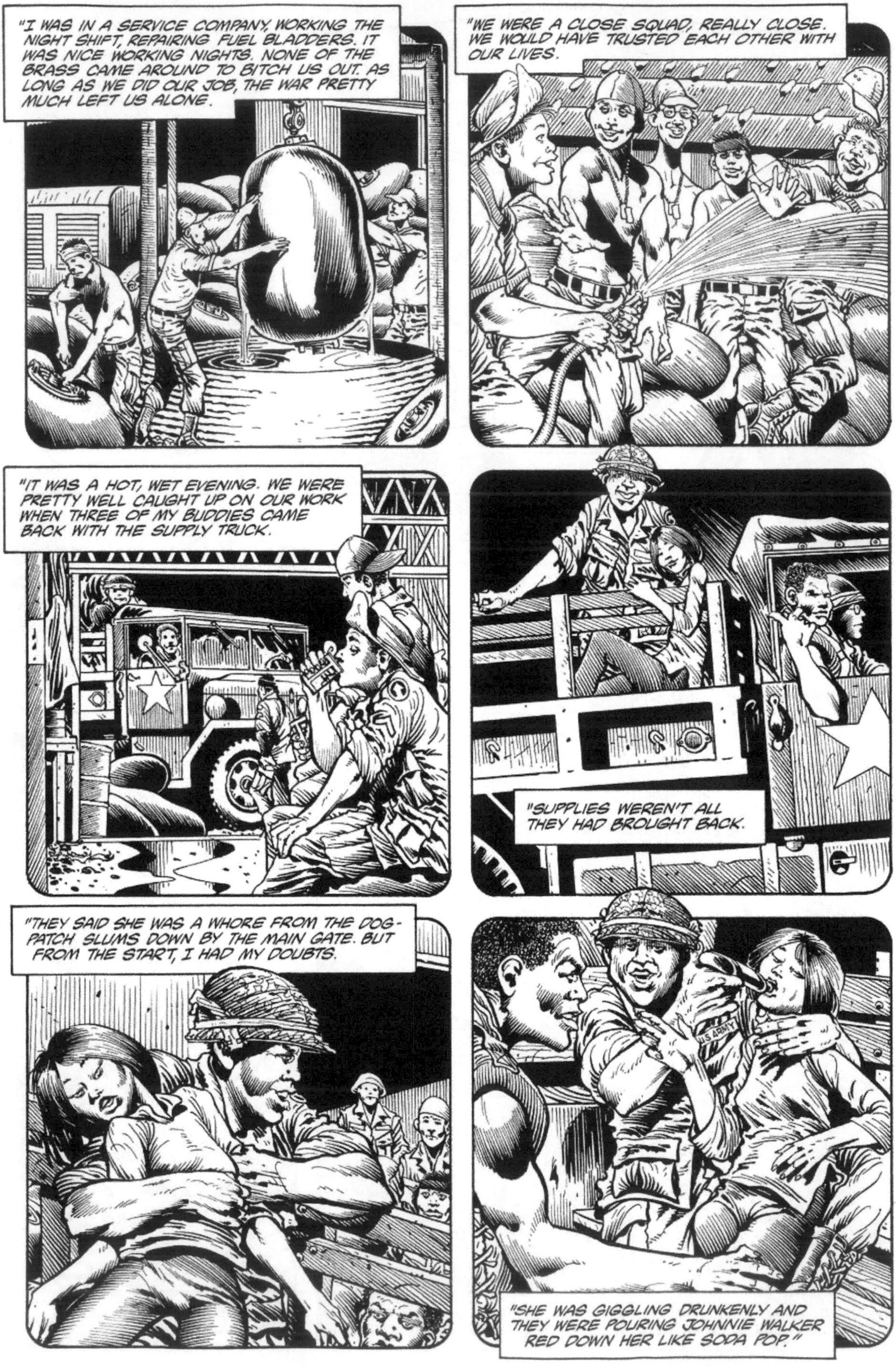
"I WAS IN A SERVICE COMPANY, WORKING THE NIGHT SHIFT, REPAIRING FUEL BLADDERS. IT WAS NICE WORKING NIGHTS. NONE OF THE BRASS CAME AROUND TO BITCH US OUT. AS LONG AS WE DID OUR JOB, THE WAR PRETTY MUCH LEFT US ALONE.
"WE WERE A CLOSE SQUAD, REALLY CLOSE. WE WOULD HAVE TRUSTED EACH OTHER WITH OUR LIVES.
"IT WAS A HOT, WET EVENING. WE WERE PRETTY WELL CAUGHT UP ON OUR WORK WHEN THREE OF MY BUDDIES CAME BACK WITH THE SUPPLY TRUCK.
"SUPPLIES WEREN'T ALL THEY HAD BROUGHT BACK.
"THEY SAID SHE WAS A WHORE FROM THE DOG-PATCH SLUMS DOWN BY THE MAIN GATE. BUT FROM THE START, I HAD MY DOUBTS.
U.S. ARMY
"SHE WAS GIGGLING DRUNKENLY AND THEY WERE POURING JOHNNIE WALKER RED DOWN HER LIKE SODA POP."

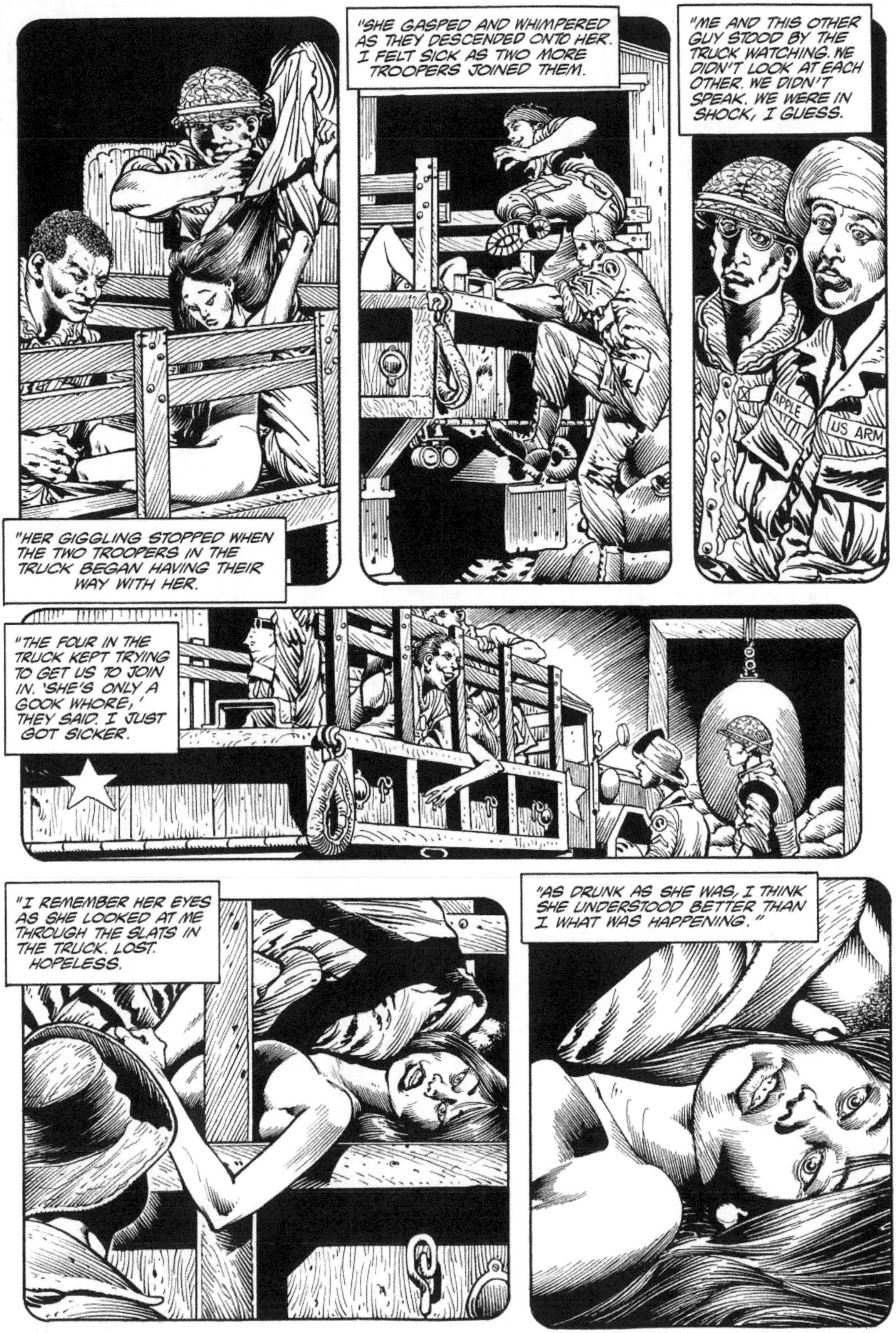
"HER GIGGLING STOPPED WHEN THE TWO TROOPERS IN THE TRUCK BEGAN HAVING THEIR WAY WITH HER.
"SHE GASPED AND WHIMPERED AS THEY DESCENDED ONTO HER. I FELT SICK AS TWO MORE TROOPERS JOINED THEM.
"ME AND THIS OTHER GUY STOOD BY THE TRUCK WATCHING. WE DIDN'T LOOK AT EACH OTHER. WE DIDN'T SPEAK. WE WERE IN SHOCK, I GUESS.
APPLE
US ARM
"THE FOUR IN THE TRUCK KEPT TRYING TO GET US TO JOIN IN. 'SHE'S ONLY A GOOK WHORE,' THEY SAID. I JUST GOT SICKER.
"I REMEMBER HER EYES AS SHE LOOKED AT ME THROUGH THE SLATS IN THE TRUCK. LOST. HOPELESS.
"AS DRUNK AS SHE WAS, I THINK SHE UNDERSTOOD BETTER THAN I WHAT WAS HAPPENING."

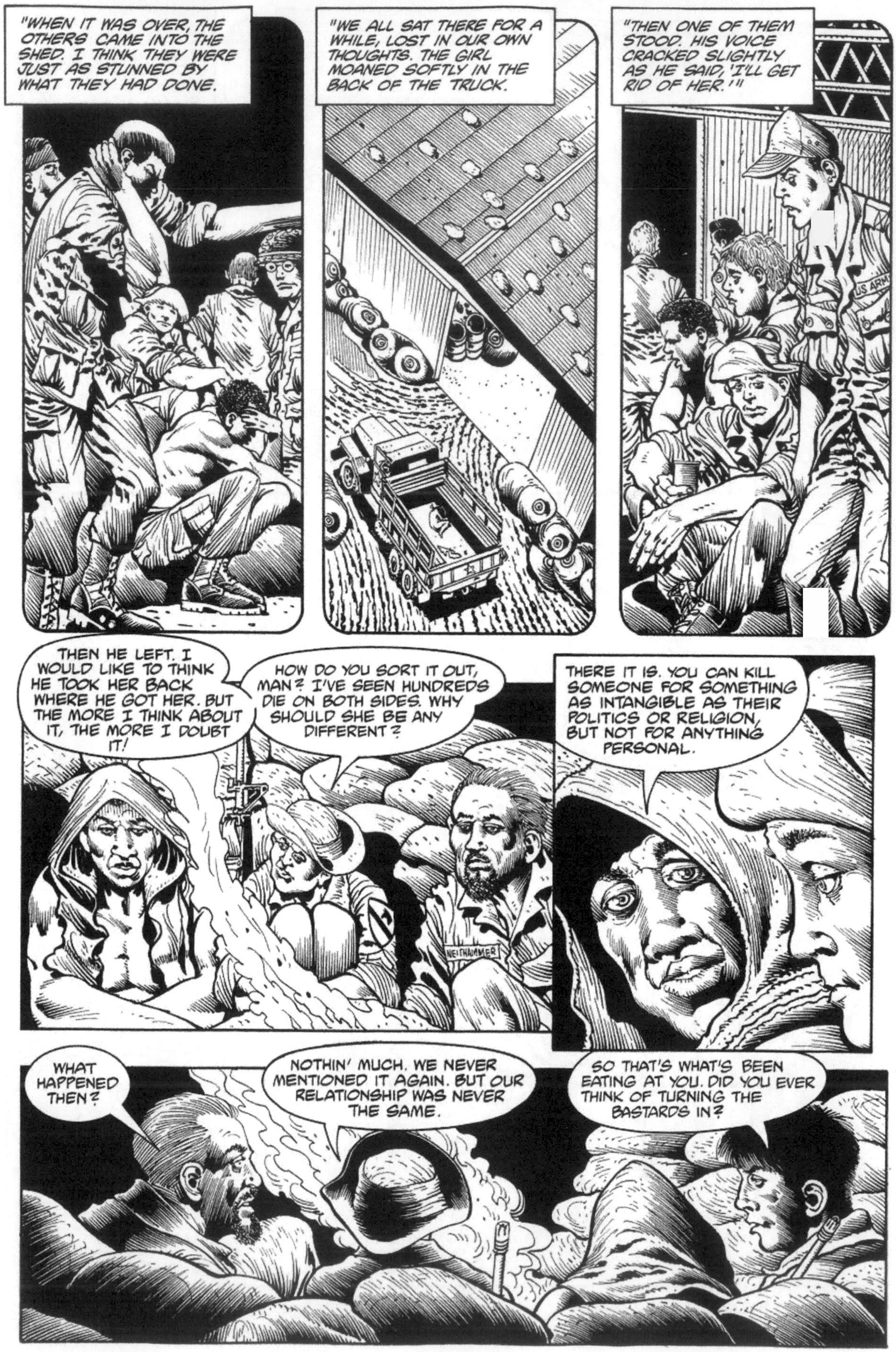
"WHEN IT WAS OVER, THE OTHERS CAME INTO THE SHED. I THINK THEY WERE JUST AS STUNNED BY WHAT THEY HAD DONE.
"WE ALL SAT THERE FOR A WHILE, LOST IN OUR OWN THOUGHTS. THE GIRL MOANED SOFTLY IN THE BACK OF THE TRUCK.
"THEN ONE OF THEM STOOD. HIS VOICE CRACKED SLIGHTLY AS HE SAID, 'I'LL GET RID OF HER.'"
US ARMY
THEN HE LEFT. I WOULD LIKE TO THINK HE TOOK HER BACK WHERE HE GOT HER. BUT THE MORE I THINK ABOUT IT, THE MORE I DOUBT IT!
HOW DO YOU SORT IT OUT, MAN? I'VE SEEN HUNDREDS DIE ON BOTH SIDES. WHY SHOULD SHE BE ANY DIFFERENT?
NEITHAMMER
THERE IT IS. YOU CAN KILL SOMEONE FOR SOMETHING AS INTANGIBLE AS THEIR POLITICS OR RELIGION, BUT NOT FOR ANYTHING PERSONAL.
WHAT HAPPENED THEN?
NOTHIN' MUCH. WE NEVER MENTIONED IT AGAIN. BUT OUR RELATIONSHIP WAS NEVER THE SAME.
SO THAT'S WHAT'S BEEN EATING AT YOU. DID YOU EVER THINK OF TURNING THE BASTARDS IN?

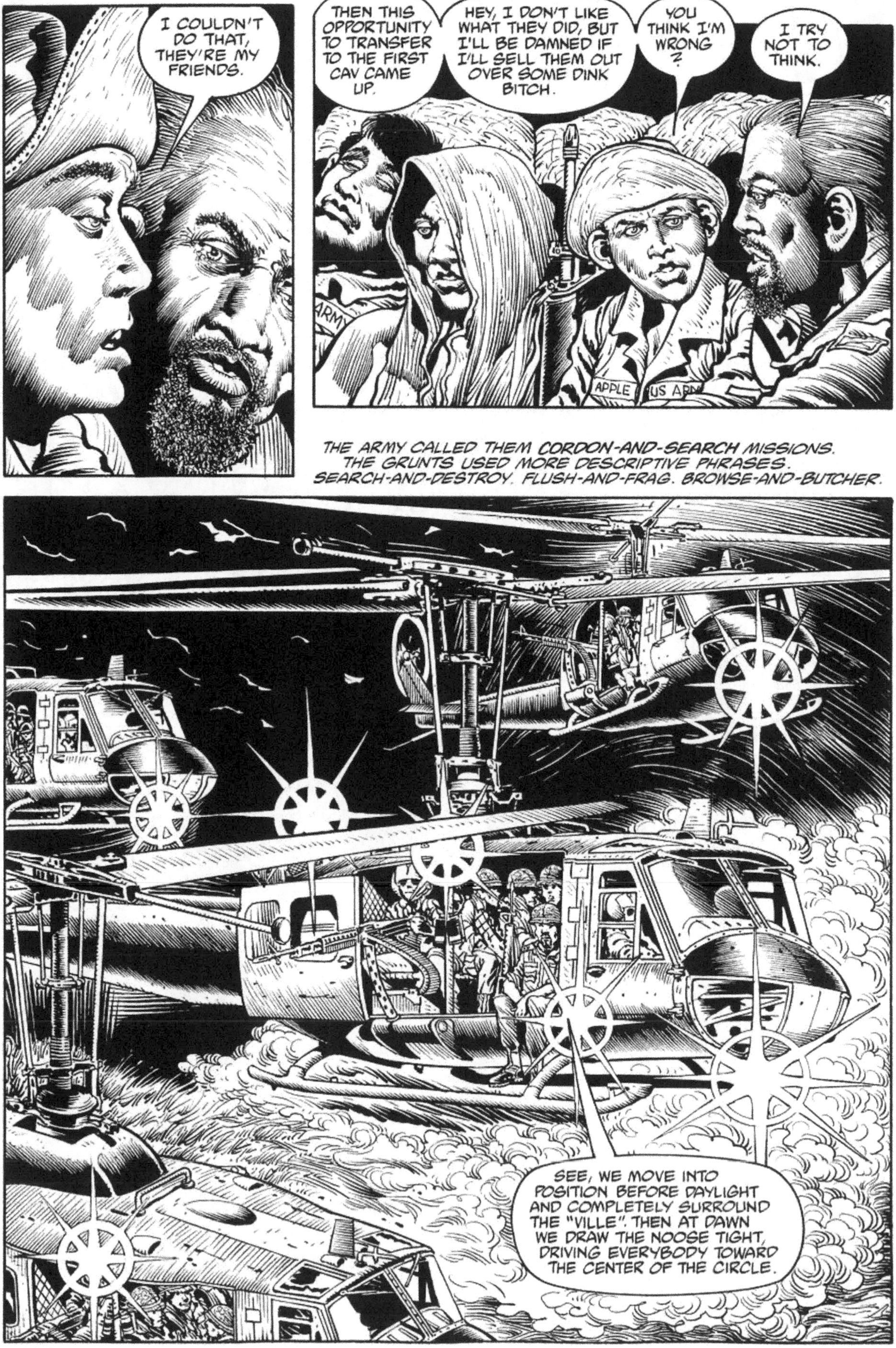

I COULDN'T DO THAT, THEY'RE MY FRIENDS.
THEN THIS OPPORTUNITY TO TRANSFER TO THE FIRST CAV CAME UP.
HEY, I DON'T LIKE WHAT THEY DID, BUT I'LL BE DAMNED IF I'LL SELL THEM OUT OVER SOME DINK BITCH.
YOU THINK I'M WRONG ?
I TRY NOT TO THINK.
ARMY
APPLE
THE ARMY CALLED THEM CORDON-AND-SEARCH MISSIONS. THE GRUNTS USED MORE DESCRIPTIVE PHRASES. SEARCH-AND-DESTROY. FLUSH-AND-FRAG. BROWSE-AND-BUTCHER.
SEE, WE MOVE INTO POSITION BEFORE DAYLIGHT AND COMPLETELY SURROUND THE "VILLE". THEN AT DAWN WE DRAW THE NOOSE TIGHT, DRIVING EVERYBODY TOWARD THE CENTER OF THE CIRCLE.

YEAH, THESE ARE SUPPOSED TO BE JOINT U.S. AND ARVN OPERATIONS.

SURE. WE DO ALL OF THE DANGEROUS WORK. THEN THE ARVN MILITARY POLICE STRUT IN AND BULLY THE LOCALS WITH THEIR "BLACK LISTS".

THE ARVN FIELD POLICE SET UP A SCREENING POINT AND JACK THE INDIGS AROUND--THE RUTHLESS LITTLE BASTARDS.

HEY, MAN, IT'S THEIR COUNTRY. WHO BETTER TO SCREW OVER THE PEASANTS THAN THE GOVERN-MENT?

AT EASE, BEAN.

ANYONE WHO HAS EVER BEEN TO WAR KNOWS THE "SWEATS".

I HAD NOT HAD THEM IN YEARS. THEN, SUDDENLY THEY WERE ALL OVER ME. THE "SWEATS" ARE LIKE THAT. THEY COME OUT OF NOWHERE.

TAKE IT EASY, MAN.

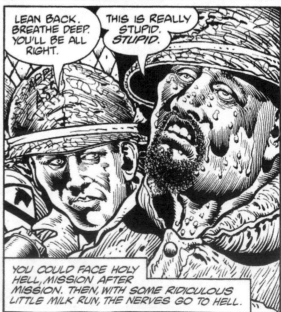

LEAN BACK. BREATHE DEEP. YOU'LL BE ALL RIGHT.

THIS IS REALLY STUPID. STUPID.

YOU COULD FACE HOLY HELL, MISSION AFTER MISSION. THEN, WITH SOME RIDICULOUS LITTLE MILK RUN, THE NERVES GO TO HELL.

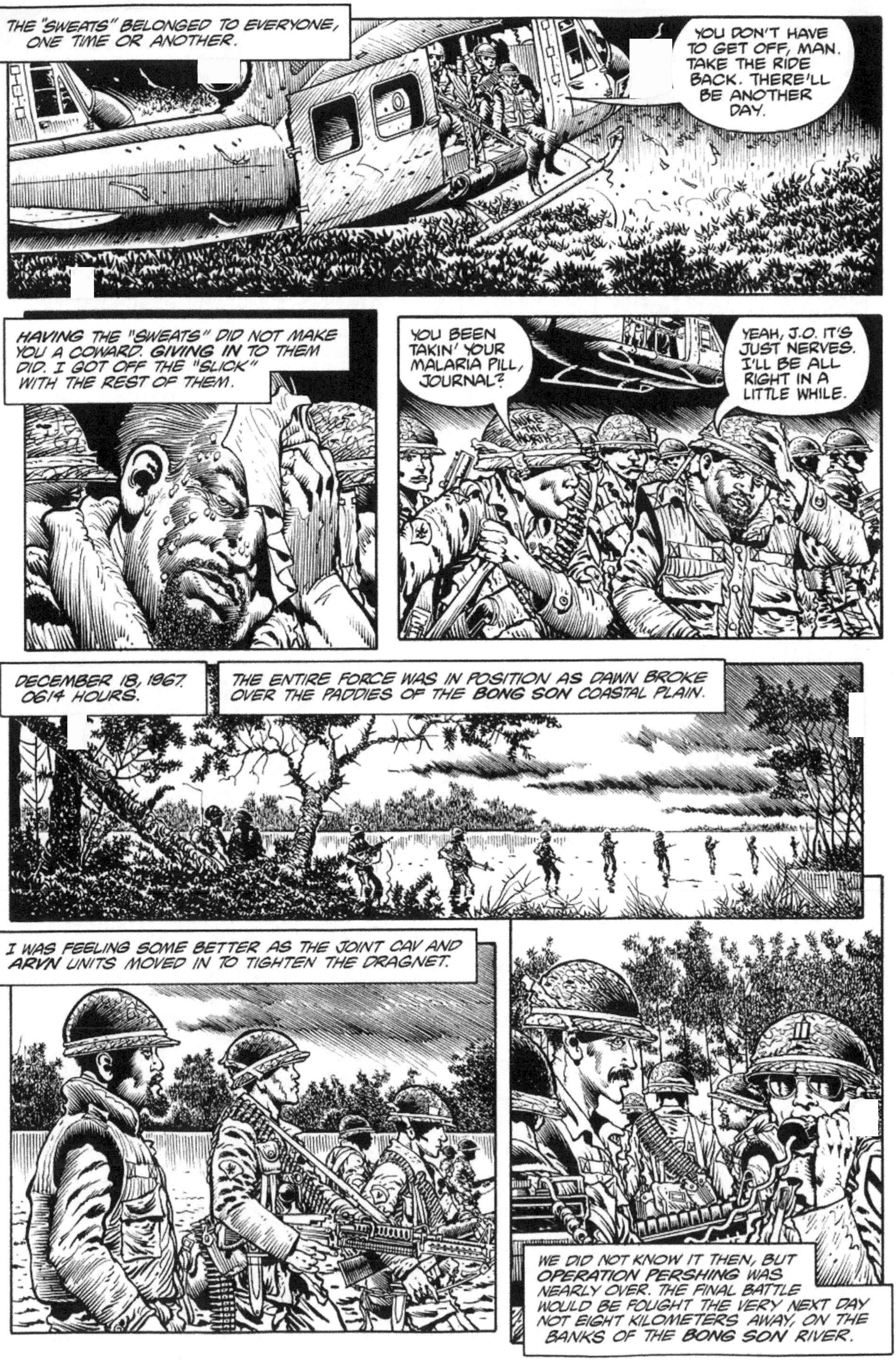
THE "SWEATS" BELONGED TO EVERYONE, ONE TIME OR ANOTHER.
YOU DON'T HAVE TO GET OFF, MAN. TAKE THE RIDE BACK. THERE'LL BE ANOTHER DAY.
HAVING THE "SWEATS" DID NOT MAKE YOU A COWARD. GIVING IN TO THEM DID. I GOT OFF THE "SLICK" WITH THE REST OF THEM.
YOU BEEN TAKIN' YOUR MALARIA PILL, JOURNAL?
YEAH, J.O. IT'S JUST NERVES. I'LL BE ALL RIGHT IN A LITTLE WHILE.
DECEMBER 18, 1967. 0614 HOURS.
THE ENTIRE FORCE WAS IN POSITION AS DAWN BROKE OVER THE PADDIES OF THE BONG SON COASTAL PLAIN.
I WAS FEELING SOME BETTER AS THE JOINT CAV AND ARVN UNITS MOVED IN TO TIGHTEN THE DRAGNET.
WE DID NOT KNOW IT THEN, BUT OPERATION PERSHING WAS NEARLY OVER. THE FINAL BATTLE WOULD BE FOUGHT THE VERY NEXT DAY NOT EIGHT KILOMETERS AWAY, ON THE BANKS OF THE BONG SON RIVER.

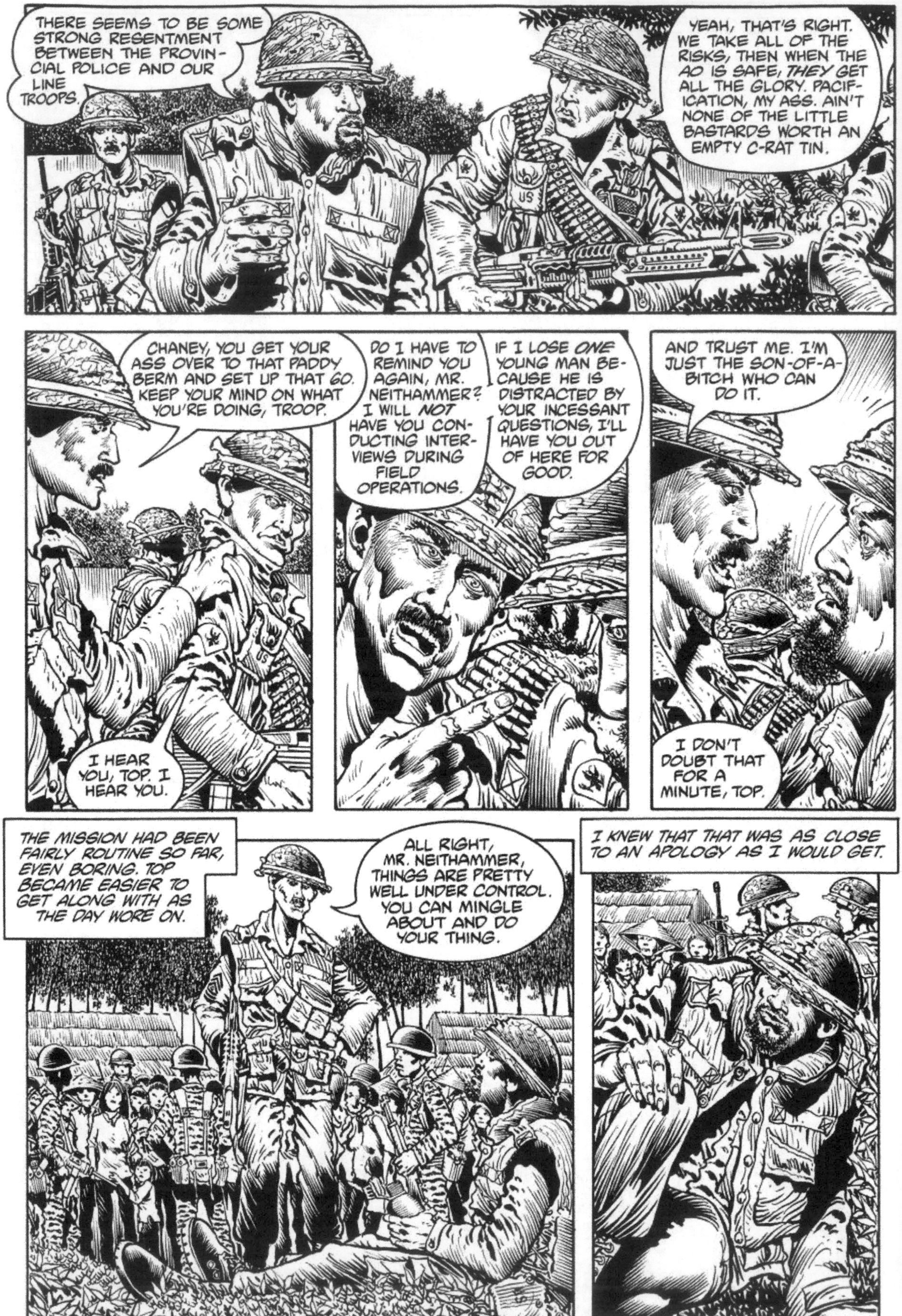
THERE SEEMS TO BE SOME STRONG RESENTMENT BETWEEN THE PROVINCIAL POLICE AND OUR LINE TROOPS.
YEAH, THAT'S RIGHT. WE TAKE ALL OF THE RISKS, THEN WHEN THE AO IS SAFE, *THEY* GET ALL THE GLORY. PACIFICATION, MY ASS. AIN'T NONE OF THE LITTLE BASTARDS WORTH AN EMPTY C-RAT TIN.
CHANEY, YOU GET YOUR ASS OVER TO THAT PADDY BERM AND SET UP THAT 60. KEEP YOUR MIND ON WHAT YOU'RE DOING, TROOP.
I HEAR YOU, TOP. I HEAR YOU.
DO I HAVE TO REMIND YOU AGAIN, MR. NEITHAMMER? I WILL *NOT* HAVE YOU CONDUCTING INTERVIEWS DURING FIELD OPERATIONS.
IF I LOSE *ONE* YOUNG MAN BECAUSE HE IS DISTRACTED BY YOUR INCESSANT QUESTIONS, I'LL HAVE YOU OUT OF HERE FOR GOOD.
AND TRUST ME. I'M JUST THE SON-OF-A-BITCH WHO CAN DO IT.
I DON'T DOUBT THAT FOR A MINUTE, TOP.
THE MISSION HAD BEEN FAIRLY ROUTINE SO FAR, EVEN BORING. TOP BECAME EASIER TO GET ALONG WITH AS THE DAY WORE ON.
ALL RIGHT, MR. NEITHAMMER, THINGS ARE PRETTY WELL UNDER CONTROL. YOU CAN MINGLE ABOUT AND DO YOUR THING.
I KNEW THAT THAT WAS AS CLOSE TO AN APOLOGY AS I WOULD GET.
I COULD LIVE WITH IT.

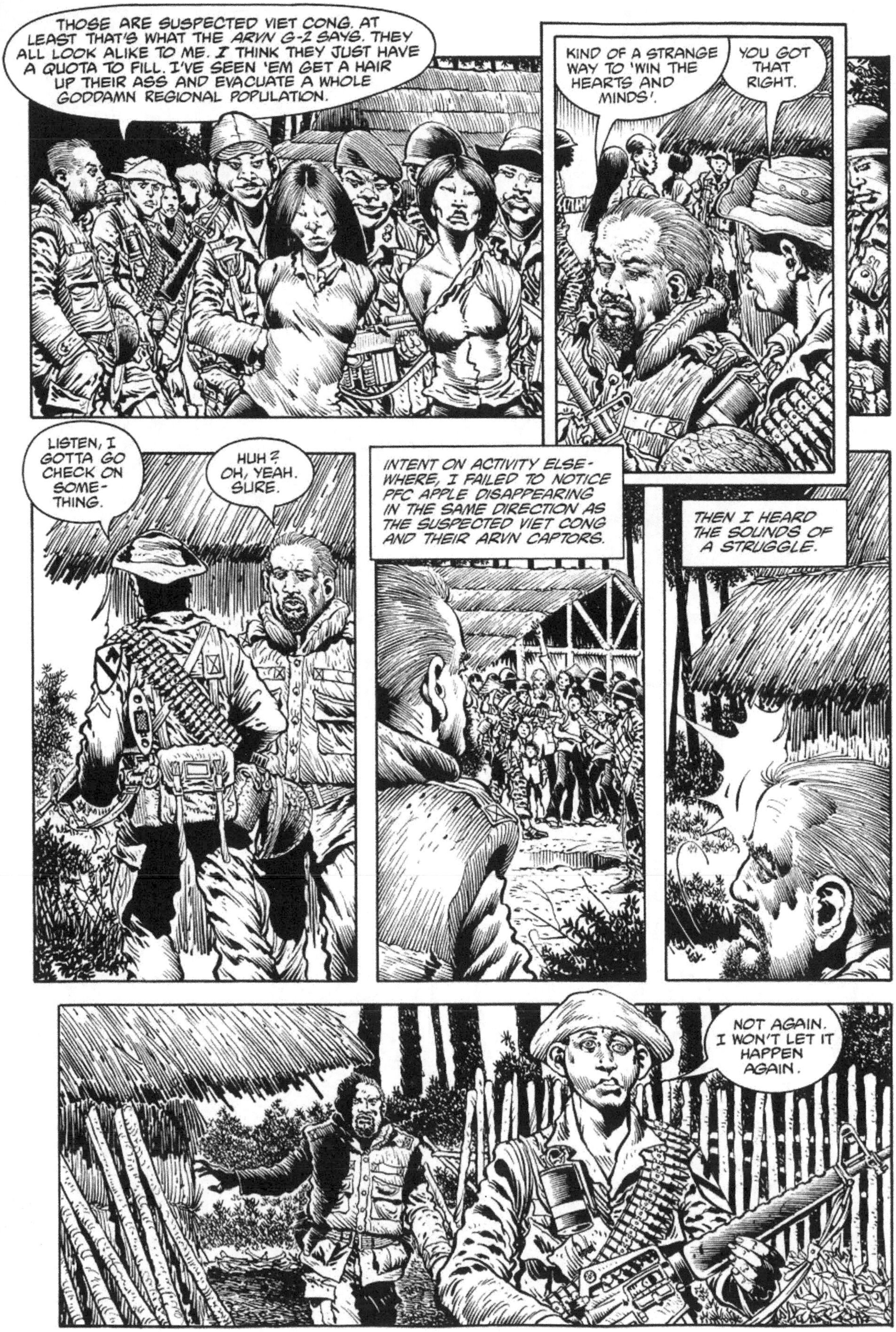
THOSE ARE SUSPECTED VIET CONG. AT LEAST THAT'S WHAT THE ARVN G-2 SAYS. THEY ALL LOOK ALIKE TO ME. I THINK THEY JUST HAVE A QUOTA TO FILL. I'VE SEEN 'EM GET A HAIR UP THEIR ASS AND EVACUATE A WHOLE GODDAMN REGIONAL POPULATION.
KIND OF A STRANGE WAY TO 'WIN THE HEARTS AND MINDS'.
YOU GOT THAT RIGHT.
LISTEN, I GOTTA GO CHECK ON SOME-THING.
HUH? OH, YEAH. SURE.
INTENT ON ACTIVITY ELSE-WHERE, I FAILED TO NOTICE PFC APPLE DISAPPEARING IN THE SAME DIRECTION AS THE SUSPECTED VIET CONG AND THEIR ARVN CAPTORS.
THEN I HEARD THE SOUNDS OF A STRUGGLE.
NOT AGAIN. I WON'T LET IT HAPPEN AGAIN.

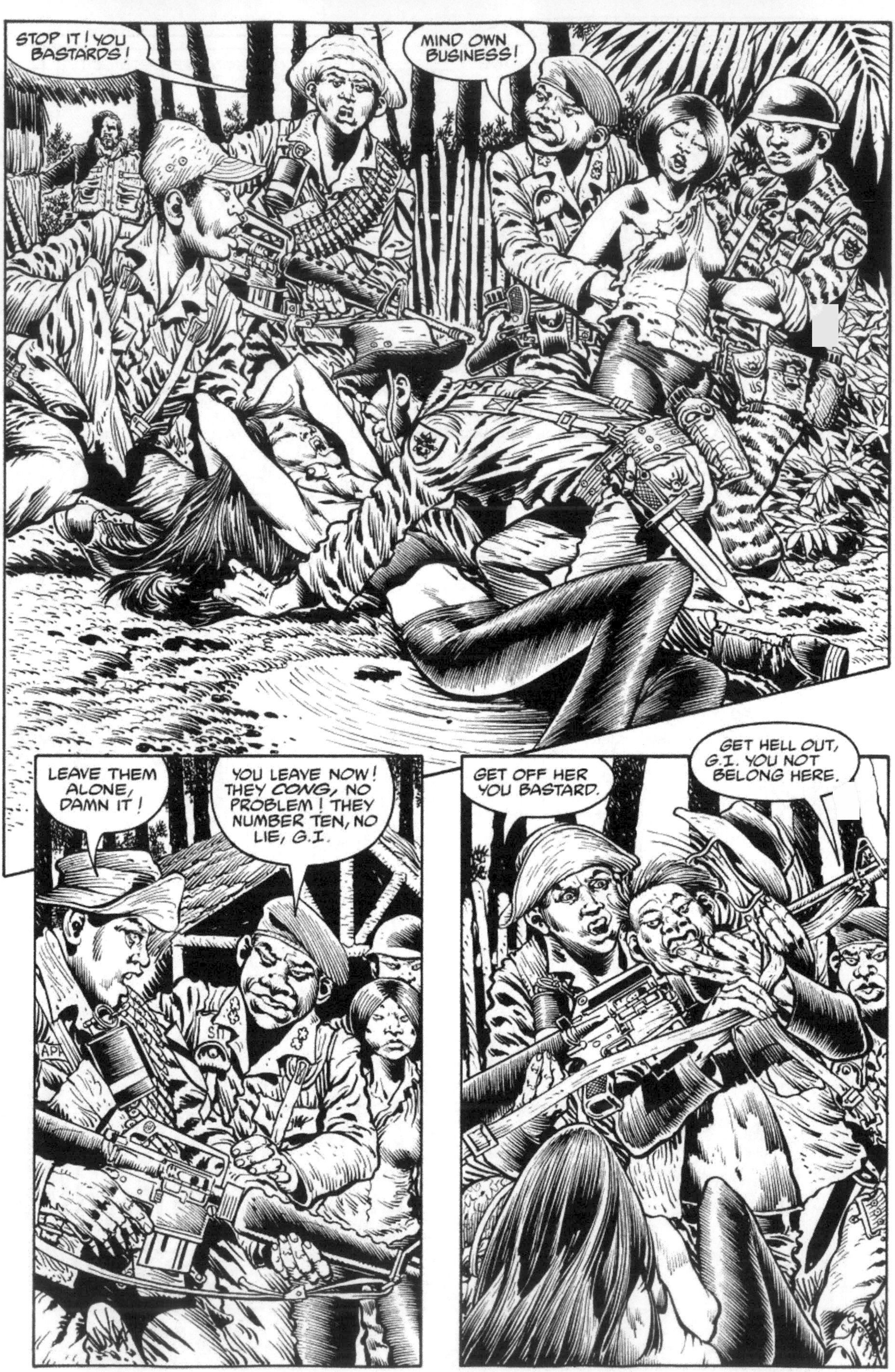
STOP IT! YOU BASTARDS!
MIND OWN BUSINESS!
LEAVE THEM ALONE, DAMN IT!
YOU LEAVE NOW! THEY *CONG*, NO PROBLEM! THEY NUMBER TEN, NO LIE, G.I.
GET OFF HER YOU BASTARD.
GET HELL OUT, G.I. YOU NOT BELONG HERE.

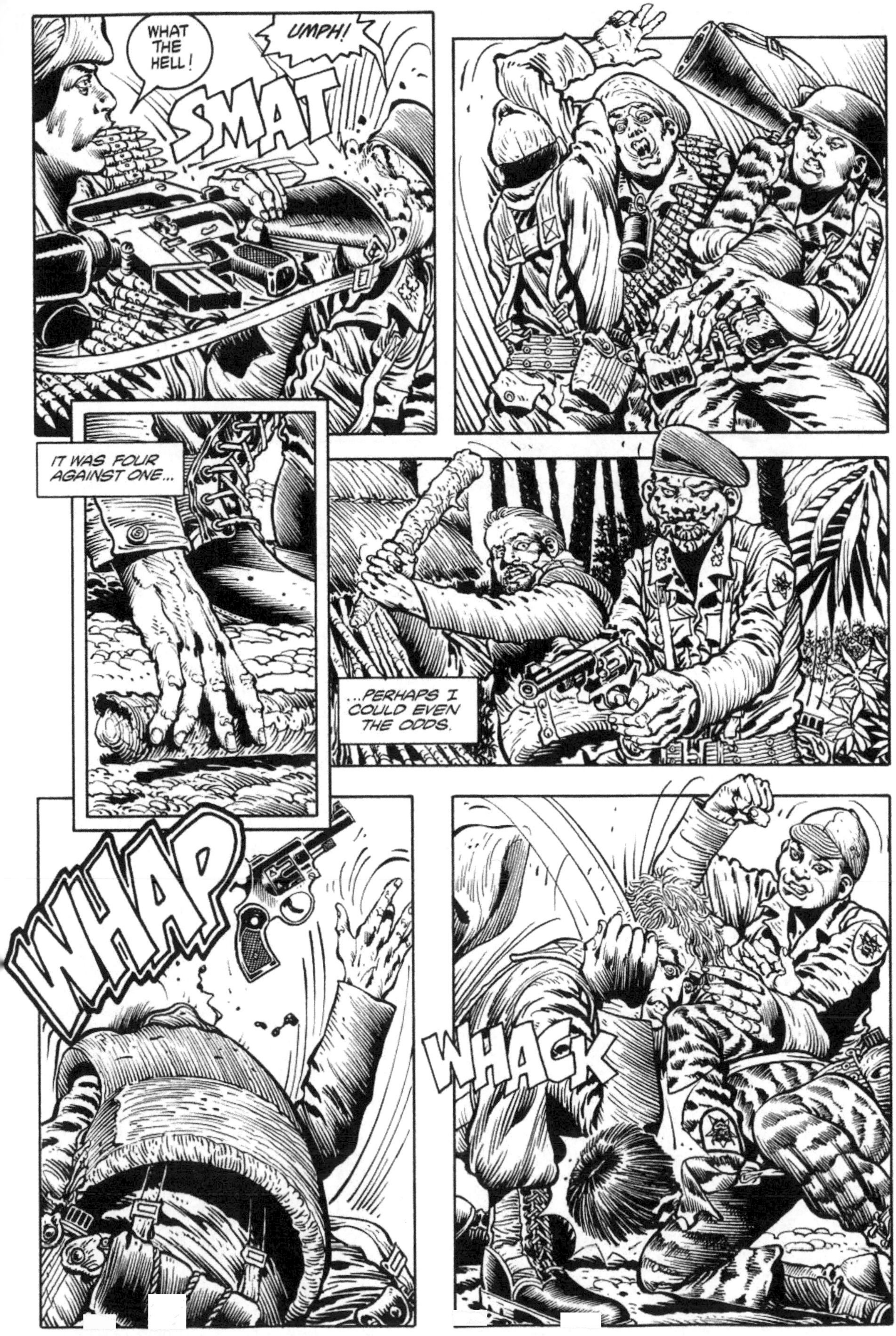
WHAT THE HELL!
UMPH!
SMAT
IT WAS FOUR AGAINST ONE...
...PERHAPS I COULD EVEN THE ODDS.
WHAP
WHACK

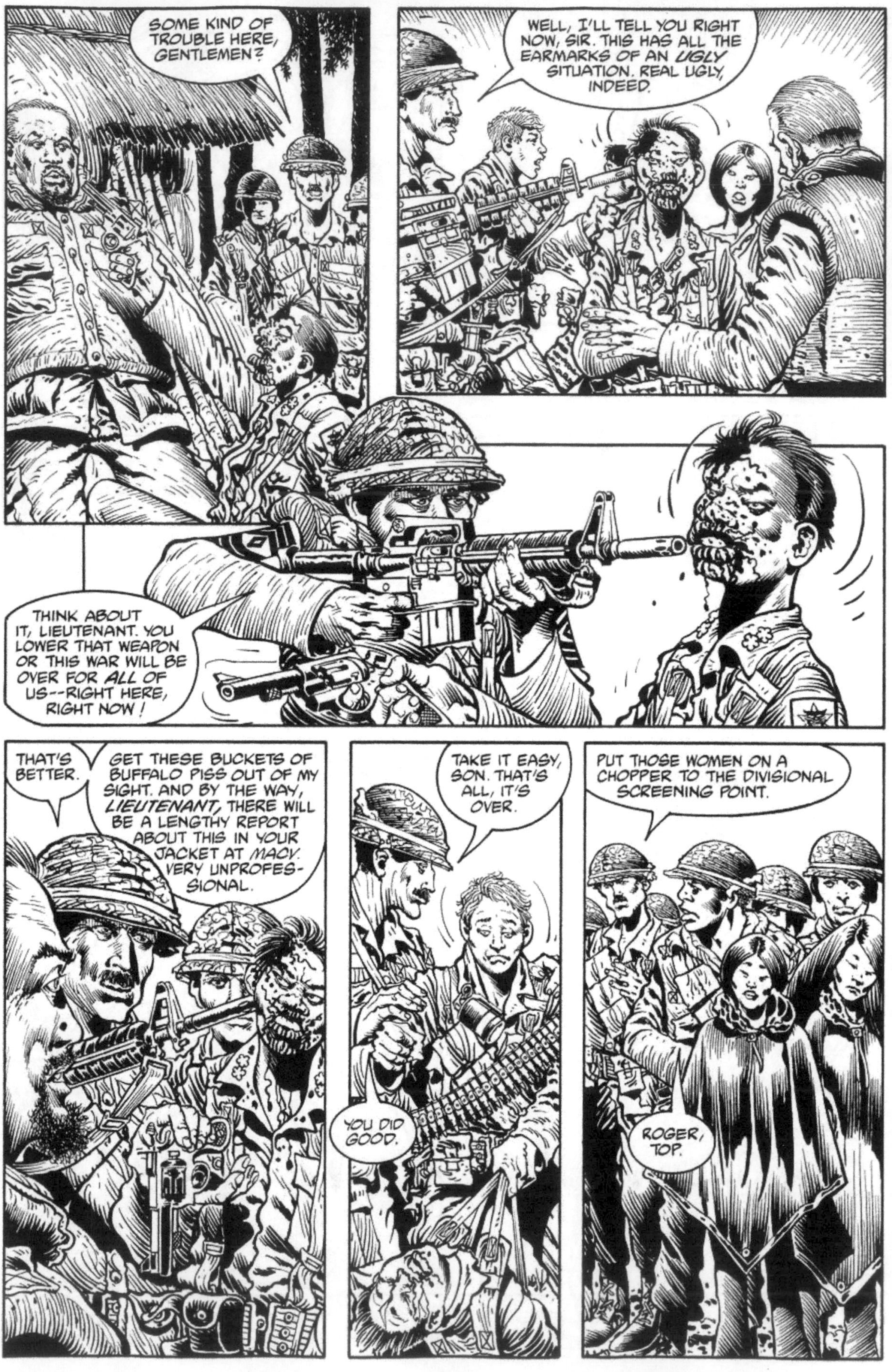
SOME KIND OF TROUBLE HERE, GENTLEMEN?
WELL, I'LL TELL YOU RIGHT NOW, SIR. THIS HAS ALL THE EARMARKS OF AN UGLY SITUATION. REAL UGLY, INDEED.
THINK ABOUT IT, LIEUTENANT. YOU LOWER THAT WEAPON OR THIS WAR WILL BE OVER FOR ALL OF US--RIGHT HERE, RIGHT NOW!
THAT'S BETTER.
GET THESE BUCKETS OF BUFFALO PISS OUT OF MY SIGHT. AND BY THE WAY, LIEUTENANT, THERE WILL BE A LENGTHY REPORT ABOUT THIS IN YOUR JACKET AT MACV. VERY UNPROFES-SIONAL.
TAKE IT EASY, SON. THAT'S ALL, IT'S OVER.
YOU DID GOOD.
PUT THOSE WOMEN ON A CHOPPER TO THE DIVISIONAL SCREENING POINT.
ROGER, TOP.

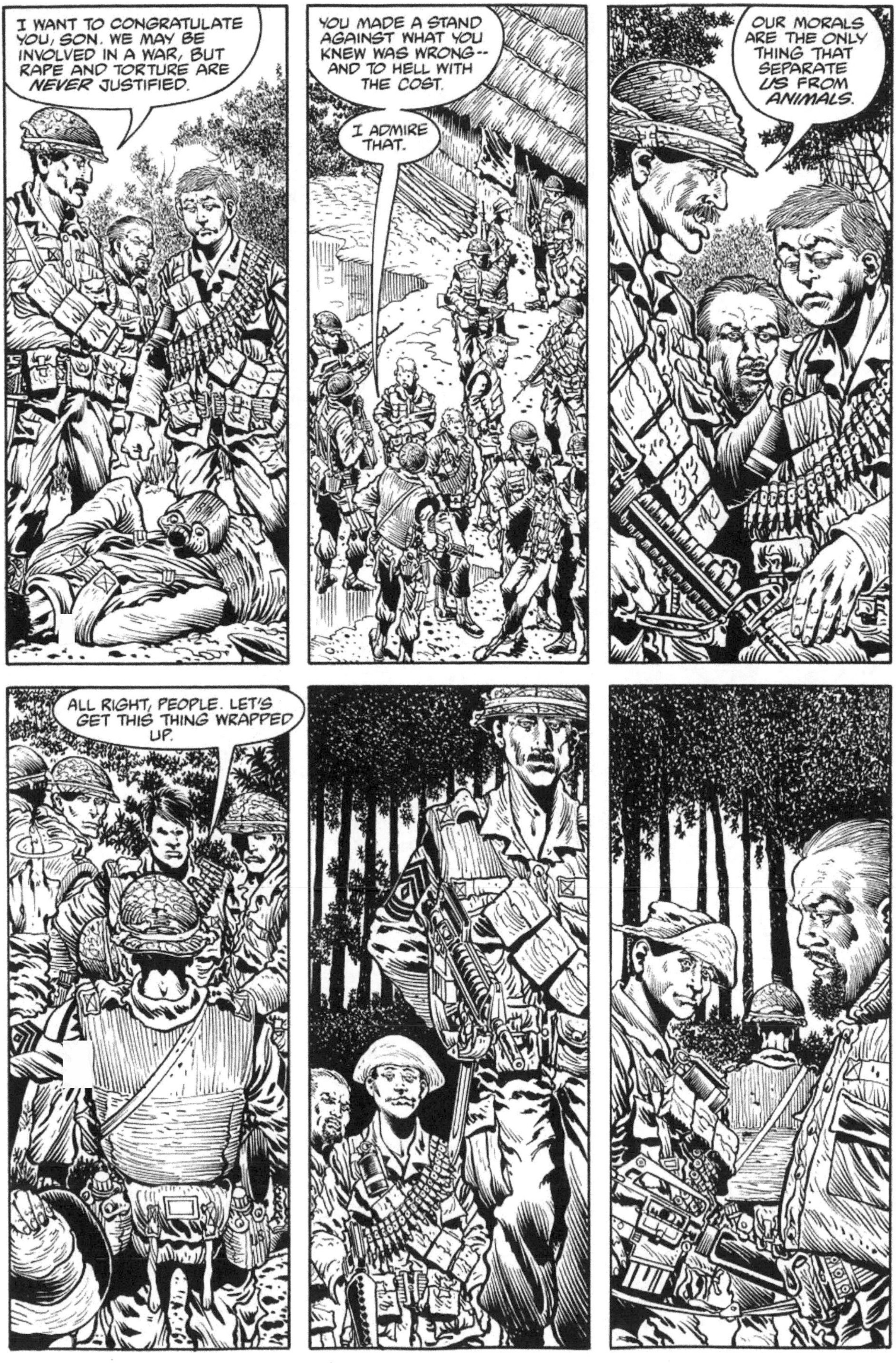
I WANT TO CONGRATULATE YOU, SON. WE MAY BE INVOLVED IN A WAR, BUT RAPE AND TORTURE ARE NEVER JUSTIFIED.
YOU MADE A STAND AGAINST WHAT YOU KNEW WAS WRONG-- AND TO HELL WITH THE COST.
I ADMIRE THAT.
OUR MORALS ARE THE ONLY THING THAT SEPARATE US FROM ANIMALS.
ALL RIGHT, PEOPLE. LET'S GET THIS THING WRAPPED UP.

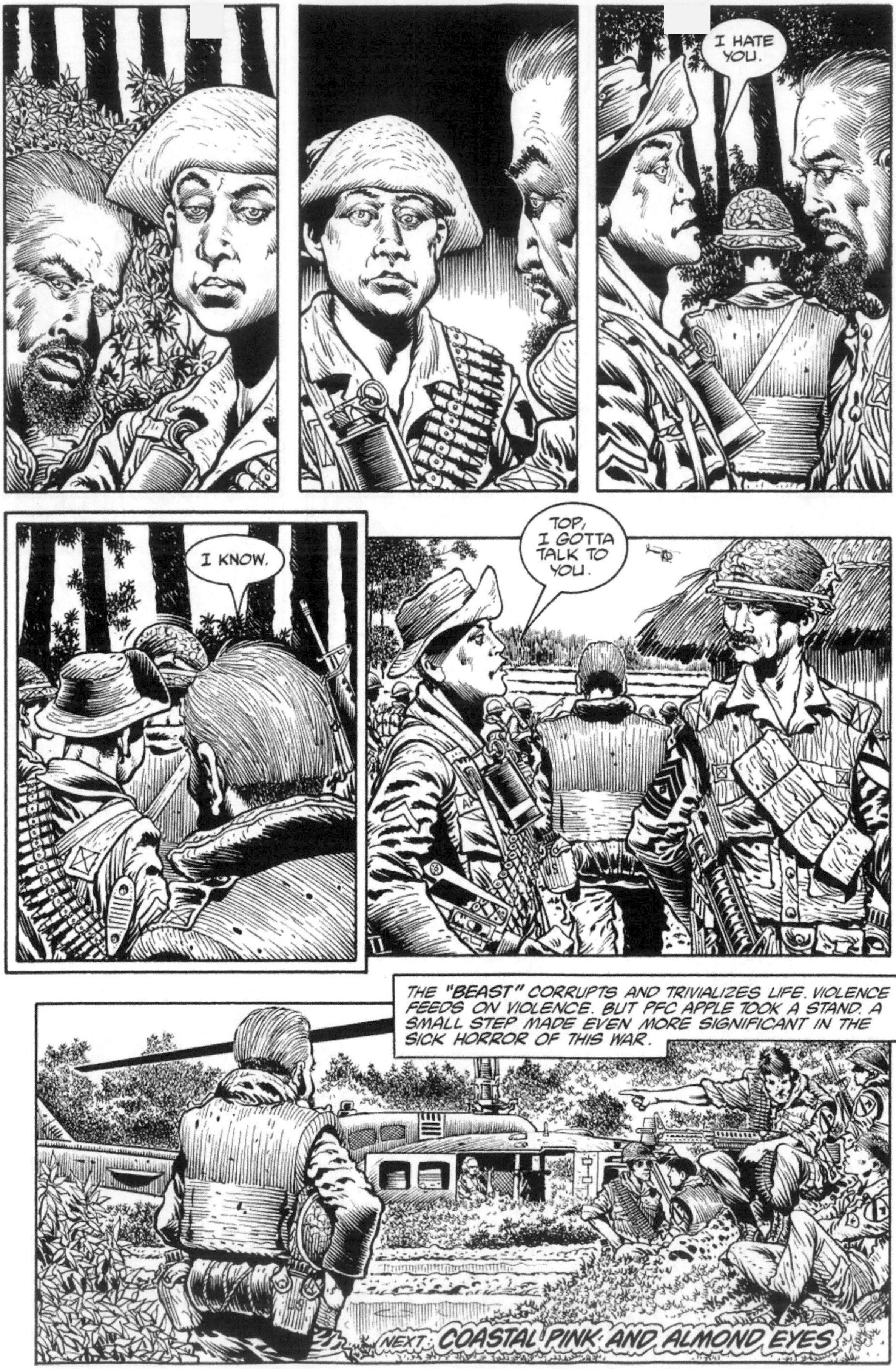
I HATE YOU.
I KNOW.
TOP, I GOTTA TALK TO YOU.
THE "BEAST" CORRUPTS AND TRIVIALIZES LIFE. VIOLENCE FEEDS ON VIOLENCE. BUT PFC APPLE TOOK A STAND. A SMALL STEP MADE EVEN MORE SIGNIFICANT IN THE SICK HORROR OF THIS WAR.
NEXT: COASTAL PINK AND ALMOND EYES

Missing Americans™

POW Forum: Robert Garwood's story, bugging a friendly diplomat, Tony Po's letter

On February 1, 1988, The Connecticut chapter of the National Forget-Me-Not Association sponsored a Prisoner-of-War Forum at Western Connecticut State University in Danbury, Connecticut.

Participants included Bill Paul, a reporter for The Wall Street Journal, *and U.S. Rep. John Rowland (R-Conn.). The Departments of Defense and State were invited to send representatives to participate, but declined.*

In part 4 of our edited transcript of those proceedings, Mr. Paul continues his historical overview of the issue...

In 1984, Robert Garwood told me that he had seen a minimum of 75 men. Now Bob Garwood, in case you don't know, was convicted of collaboration with the enemy. He came back, he was exonerated of charges of treason. But there's no question about it — he stayed on after the war and he was more than their prisoner. He was a party to what was going on.

Does that disqualify him? You tell me. [Former Reagan Secretary of Defense Caspar] "Cap" Weinberger told former Representative William Hendon [R-NC, 1981-1982] that he'd never believe a traitor — which Garwood wasn't, by the way.

What does Bob Garwood say? "I saw a minimum of 75 men." Some he worked with, some he guarded, some he saw on a train one night when the boxcar opened right in front of him and out they tumbled. He could tell us what they looked like, what they spoke, everything.

The day after my story appeared, a White House official was quoted in the *Washington Times* as saying, "We already know that a lot of what he told *The Wall Street Journal* is true." They never said what was true and what was not. All I know is that they could never seem to figure out what to do with Bob Garwood, so they did absolutely nothing.

Let's move on. After the war, the CIA bugged a diplomat's office. We're not supposed to know this — but we bugged a friendly diplomat just back from Vietnam. Our bug picked up conversation where he's saying, "You know, those Vietnamese took me aside and said 'How do we get rid of these Americans? We want money for them, how can we get rid of them?'"

Well *that* provoked a flurry at Langley. But it [the CIA] didn't do anything because to reveal the source of this information would be too great an admission. So we sat on it. Needless to say, the opportunity, if one was there, was gone.

Let's talk about Tony Po. Tony Po was a CIA operative in Laos. Strange man. He was ruthless to the point of cutting off his opponents' ears and sticking them in formaldehyde in a jar next to his bed. Unfor-

"[The U.S. government] could never seem to figure out what to do ... so they did ... nothing." — Bill Paul
Photo by Carol Kaliff. Copyright ©1990 The Danbury (Ct.) News-Times

tunately, though — as I think some veterans might nod with me — that's how you fight a war sometimes and win.

Tony Po wrote two letters — one to Jeff Donahue of Connecticut, another to a gentleman in New Hampshire — around Christmas, 1984. He said, "I know where there's a Navy Lt. Col. He's just outside of Tchepone. Kinda take the bend here, go up there, and you'll find him tilling the soil. With his wife. When they let him out of prison, they married him off to a local woman."

He was that specific. He went further. He said, the man doesn't dare come out. Apparently he made a propaganda broadcast during the war and he's afraid the U.S. government might turn on him.

I can understand that fear. What I can't understand is when Assistant Secretary of Defense Richard Armitage, in 1983, told ABC's national security correspondent that anybody who came out of Laos today would be tainted — that he would have to be at least a collaborator. In other words, guilty until proven innocent.

Needless to say, this man has never come out. You just have to ask yourself, how many times did the Vietnamese play *that* videotape for this poor guy. So now he sits there. I think he's still there.

Coastal Pink and Almond Eyes

APPLE COMICS
"... the best war comic book in more than 35 years."
— Don Thompson, The Comics Buyer's Guide
POW★MIA
No. 15
$2.25
$2.75 in Canada
VIETNAM JOURNAL
by Don Lomax
UNITED STATES ARMY
ALMOND EYES
Coastal Pink and Almond Eyes

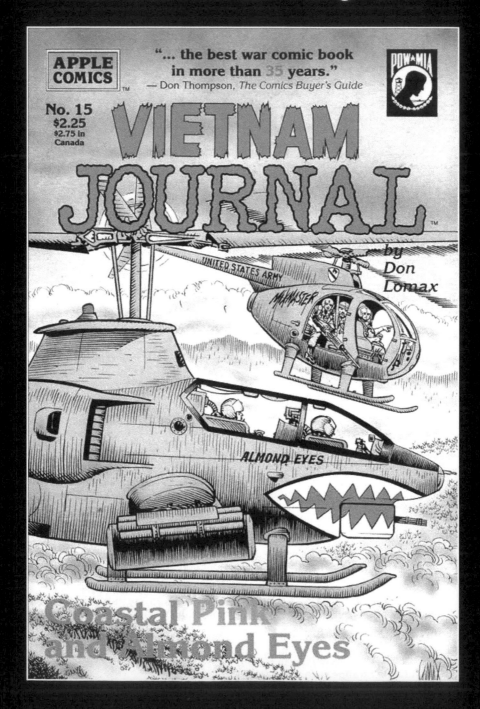

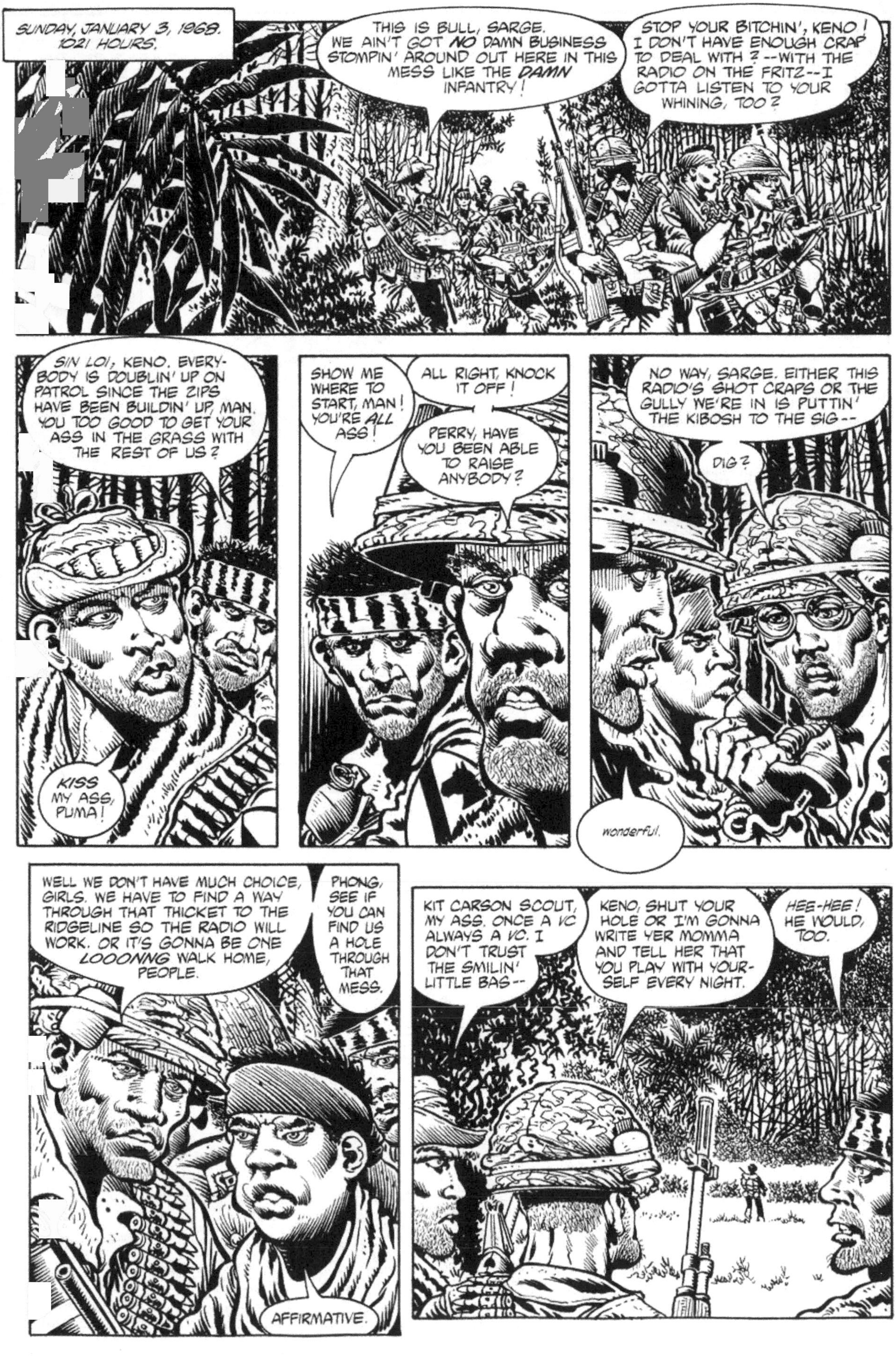
SUNDAY, JANUARY 3, 1968. 1021 HOURS.
THIS IS BULL, SARGE. WE AIN'T GOT NO DAMN BUSINESS STOMPIN' AROUND OUT HERE IN THIS MESS LIKE THE DAMN INFANTRY!
STOP YOUR BITCHIN', KENO! I DON'T HAVE ENOUGH CRAP TO DEAL WITH ? --WITH THE RADIO ON THE FRITZ--I GOTTA LISTEN TO YOUR WHINING, TOO?
SIN LOI, KENO. EVERYBODY IS DOUBLIN' UP ON PATROL SINCE THE ZIPS HAVE BEEN BUILDIN' UP, MAN. YOU TOO GOOD TO GET YOUR ASS IN THE GRASS WITH THE REST OF US?
KISS MY ASS, PUMA!
SHOW ME WHERE TO START, MAN! YOU'RE ALL ASS!
ALL RIGHT, KNOCK IT OFF!
PERRY, HAVE YOU BEEN ABLE TO RAISE ANYBODY?
NO WAY, SARGE. EITHER THIS RADIO'S SHOT CRAPS OR THE GULLY WE'RE IN IS PUTTIN' THE KIBOSH TO THE SIG--
DIG?
wonderful.
WELL WE DON'T HAVE MUCH CHOICE, GIRLS. WE HAVE TO FIND A WAY THROUGH THAT THICKET TO THE RIDGELINE SO THE RADIO WILL WORK. OR IT'S GONNA BE ONE LOOONNG WALK HOME, PEOPLE.
PHONG, SEE IF YOU CAN FIND US A HOLE THROUGH THAT MESS.
AFFIRMATIVE.
KIT CARSON SCOUT, MY ASS. ONCE A VC ALWAYS A VC. I DON'T TRUST THE SMILIN' LITTLE BAS--
KENO, SHUT YOUR HOLE OR I'M GONNA WRITE YER MOMMA AND TELL HER THAT YOU PLAY WITH YOURSELF EVERY NIGHT.
HEE-HEE! HE WOULD, TOO.

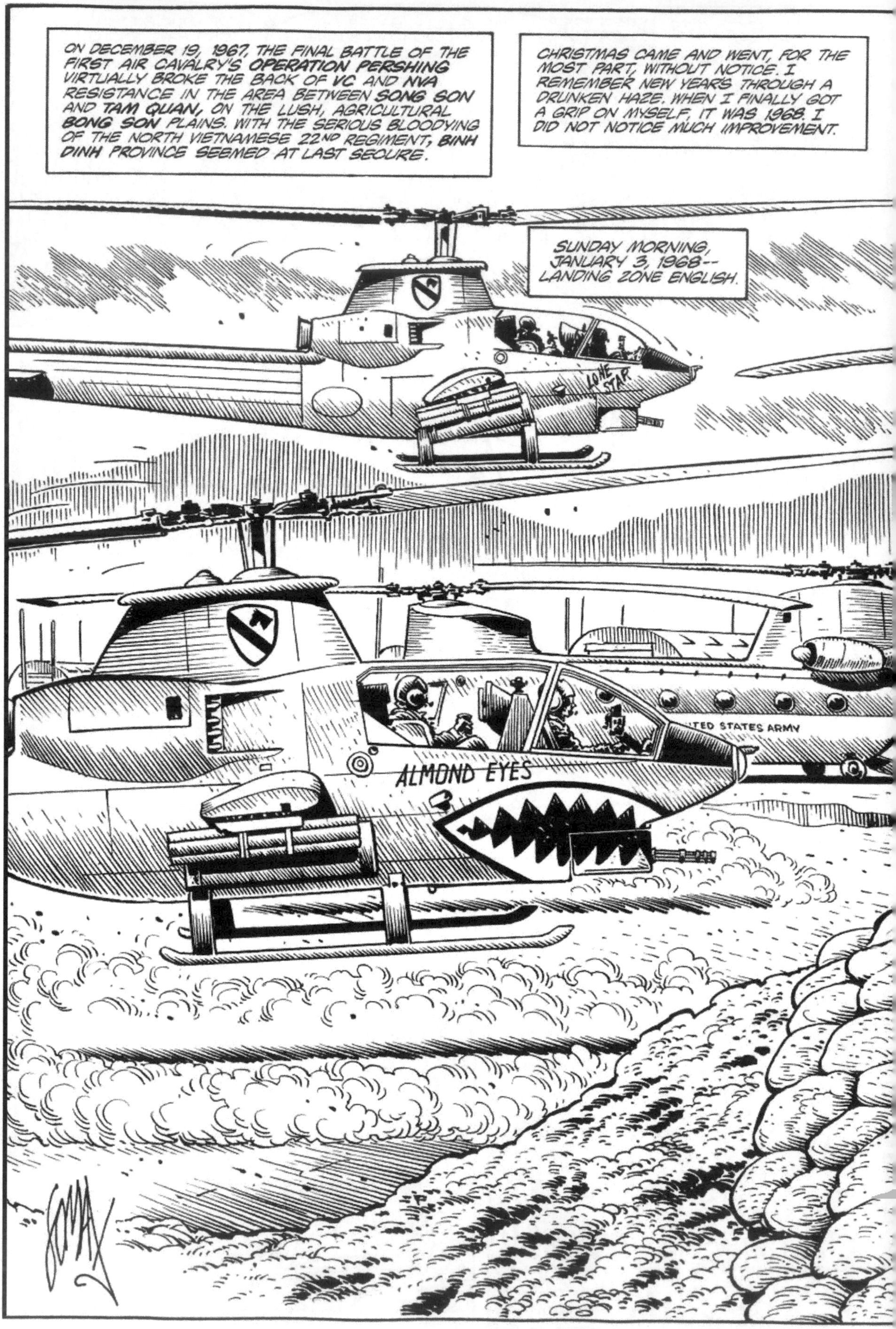
ON DECEMBER 19, 1967, THE FINAL BATTLE OF THE FIRST AIR CAVALRY'S OPERATION PERSHING VIRTUALLY BROKE THE BACK OF VC AND NVA RESISTANCE IN THE AREA BETWEEN SONG SON AND TAM QUAN, ON THE LUSH, AGRICULTURAL BONG SON PLAINS. WITH THE SERIOUS BLOODYING OF THE NORTH VIETNAMESE 22ND REGIMENT, BINH DINH PROVINCE SEEMED AT LAST SECURE.
CHRISTMAS CAME AND WENT, FOR THE MOST PART, WITHOUT NOTICE. I REMEMBER NEW YEAR'S THROUGH A DRUNKEN HAZE. WHEN I FINALLY GOT A GRIP ON MYSELF, IT WAS 1968. I DID NOT NOTICE MUCH IMPROVEMENT.
SUNDAY MORNING, JANUARY 3, 1968-- LANDING ZONE ENGLISH.
LONE STAR
ALMOND EYES

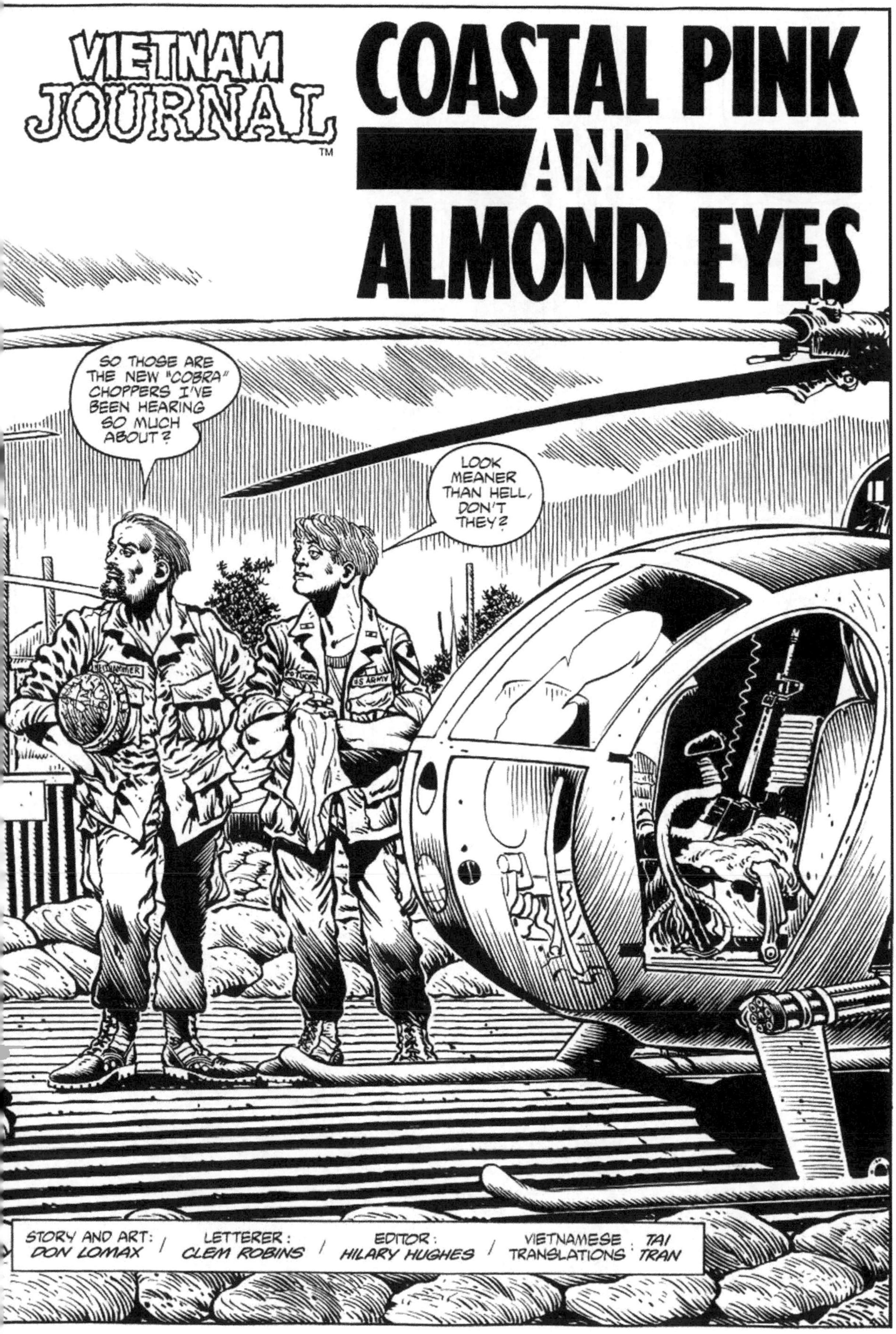
VIETNAM JOURNAL™
COASTAL PINK AND ALMOND EYES
SO THOSE ARE THE NEW "COBRA" CHOPPERS I'VE BEEN HEARING SO MUCH ABOUT?
LOOK MEANER THAN HELL, DON'T THEY?
STORY AND ART: DON LOMAX / LETTERER: CLEM ROBINS / EDITOR: HILARY HUGHES / VIETNAMESE TRANSLATIONS: TAI TRAN

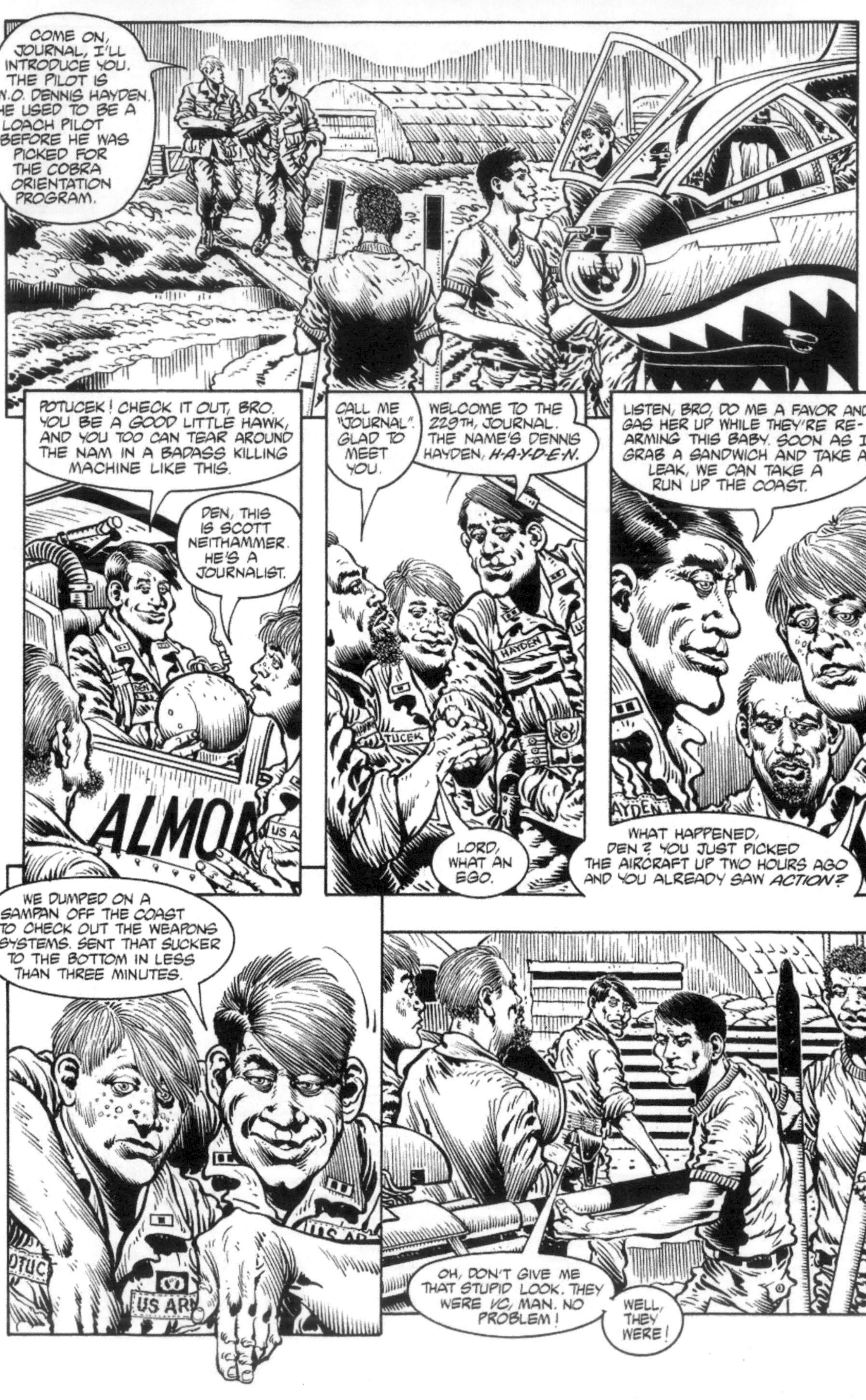

COME ON, JOURNAL, I'LL INTRODUCE YOU. THE PILOT IS W.O. DENNIS HAYDEN. HE USED TO BE A LOACH PILOT BEFORE HE WAS PICKED FOR THE COBRA ORIENTATION PROGRAM.
POTUCEK! CHECK IT OUT, BRO. YOU BE A GOOD LITTLE HAWK, AND YOU TOO CAN TEAR AROUND THE NAM IN A BADASS KILLING MACHINE LIKE THIS.
DEN, THIS IS SCOTT NEITHAMMER. HE'S A JOURNALIST.
ALMOA
CALL ME "JOURNAL". GLAD TO MEET YOU.
WELCOME TO THE 229TH, JOURNAL. THE NAME'S DENNIS HAYDEN, H-A-Y-D-E-N.
HAYDEN
TUCEK
LORD, WHAT AN EGO.
LISTEN, BRO, DO ME A FAVOR AND GAS HER UP WHILE THEY'RE RE-ARMING THIS BABY. SOON AS I GRAB A SANDWICH AND TAKE A LEAK, WE CAN TAKE A RUN UP THE COAST.
HAYDEN
WHAT HAPPENED, DEN? YOU JUST PICKED THE AIRCRAFT UP TWO HOURS AGO AND YOU ALREADY SAW ACTION?
WE DUMPED ON A SAMPAN OFF THE COAST TO CHECK OUT THE WEAPONS SYSTEMS. SENT THAT SUCKER TO THE BOTTOM IN LESS THAN THREE MINUTES.
OTUC
US AR
OH, DON'T GIVE ME THAT STUPID LOOK. THEY WERE VC, MAN. NO PROBLEM!
WELL, THEY WERE!

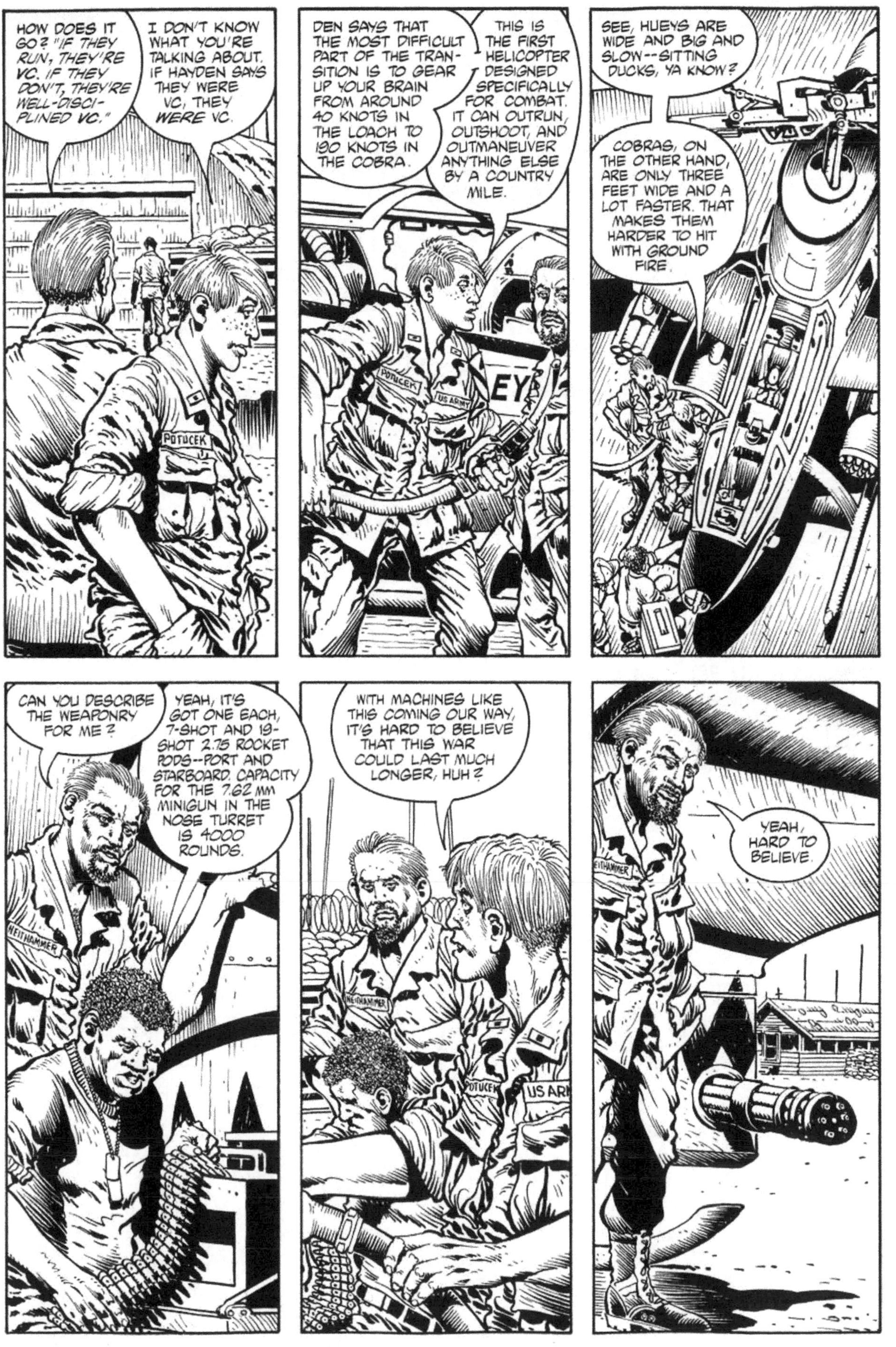
HOW DOES IT GO? "IF THEY RUN, THEY'RE VC. IF THEY DON'T, THEY'RE WELL-DISCIPLINED VC."
I DON'T KNOW WHAT YOU'RE TALKING ABOUT. IF HAYDEN SAYS THEY WERE VC, THEY WERE VC.
POTUCEK
DEN SAYS THAT THE MOST DIFFICULT PART OF THE TRANSITION IS TO GEAR UP YOUR BRAIN FROM AROUND 40 KNOTS IN THE LOACH TO 190 KNOTS IN THE COBRA.
THIS IS THE FIRST HELICOPTER DESIGNED SPECIFICALLY FOR COMBAT. IT CAN OUTRUN, OUTSHOOT, AND OUTMANEUVER ANYTHING ELSE BY A COUNTRY MILE.
POTUCEK
US ARMY
EY
SEE, HUEYS ARE WIDE AND BIG AND SLOW--SITTING DUCKS, YA KNOW?
COBRAS, ON THE OTHER HAND, ARE ONLY THREE FEET WIDE AND A LOT FASTER. THAT MAKES THEM HARDER TO HIT WITH GROUND FIRE.
CAN YOU DESCRIBE THE WEAPONRY FOR ME?
YEAH, IT'S GOT ONE EACH, 7-SHOT AND 19-SHOT 2.75 ROCKET PODS--PORT AND STARBOARD. CAPACITY FOR THE 7.62 MM MINIGUN IN THE NOSE TURRET IS 4000 ROUNDS.
NEITHAMMER
WITH MACHINES LIKE THIS COMING OUR WAY, IT'S HARD TO BELIEVE THAT THIS WAR COULD LAST MUCH LONGER, HUH?
NEITHAMMER
POTUCEK
US ARM
YEAH, HARD TO BELIEVE.
NEITHAMMER

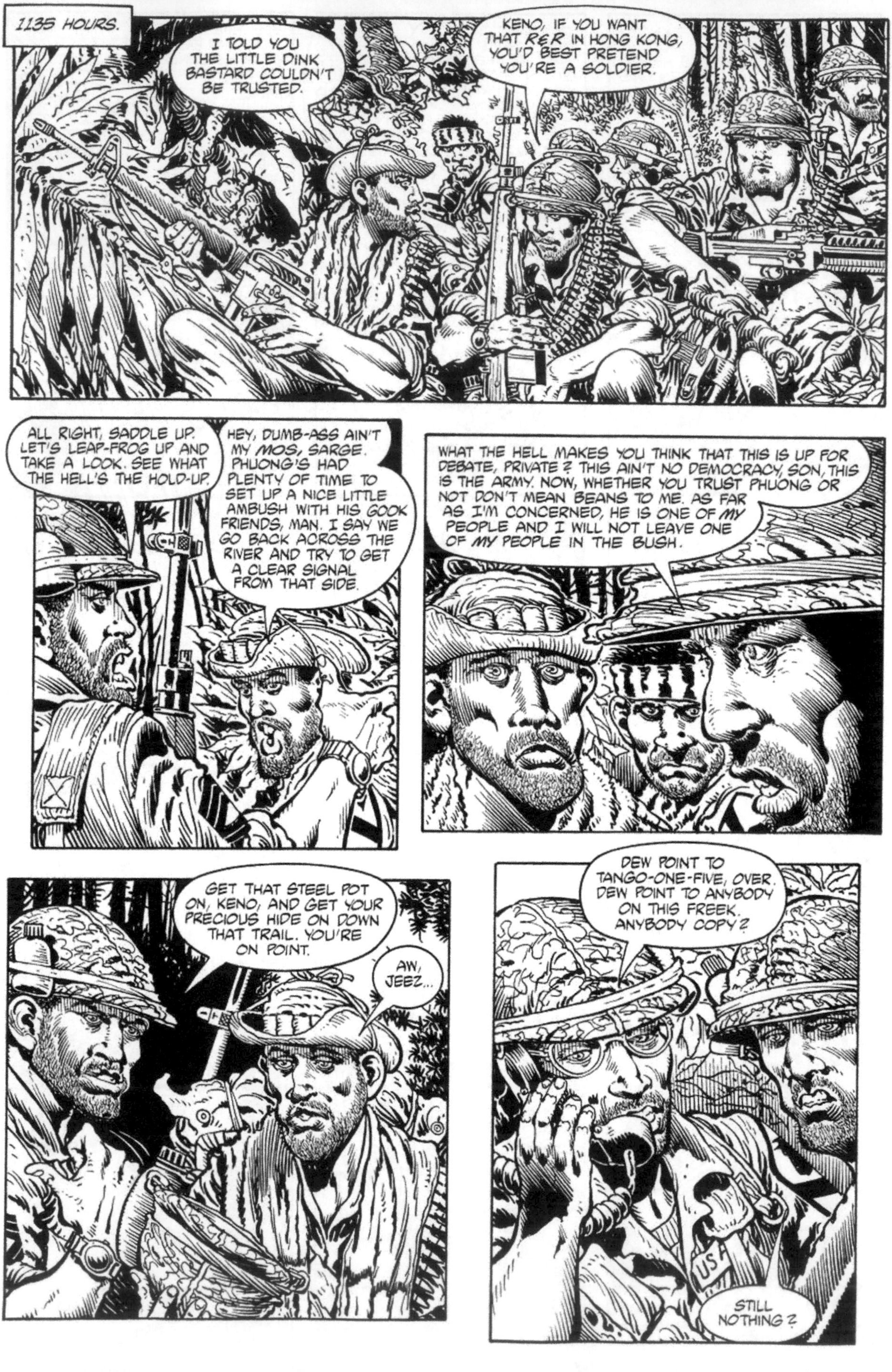
1135 HOURS.
I TOLD YOU THE LITTLE DINK BASTARD COULDN'T BE TRUSTED.
KENO, IF YOU WANT THAT R&R IN HONG KONG, YOU'D BEST PRETEND YOU'RE A SOLDIER.
ALL RIGHT, SADDLE UP. LET'S LEAP-FROG UP AND TAKE A LOOK. SEE WHAT THE HELL'S THE HOLD-UP.
HEY, DUMB-ASS AIN'T MY MOS, SARGE. PHUONG'S HAD PLENTY OF TIME TO SET UP A NICE LITTLE AMBUSH WITH HIS GOOK FRIENDS, MAN. I SAY WE GO BACK ACROSS THE RIVER AND TRY TO GET A CLEAR SIGNAL FROM THAT SIDE.
WHAT THE HELL MAKES YOU THINK THAT THIS IS UP FOR DEBATE, PRIVATE? THIS AIN'T NO DEMOCRACY, SON, THIS IS THE ARMY. NOW, WHETHER YOU TRUST PHUONG OR NOT DON'T MEAN BEANS TO ME. AS FAR AS I'M CONCERNED, HE IS ONE OF MY PEOPLE AND I WILL NOT LEAVE ONE OF MY PEOPLE IN THE BUSH.
GET THAT STEEL POT ON, KENO, AND GET YOUR PRECIOUS HIDE ON DOWN THAT TRAIL. YOU'RE ON POINT.
AW, JEEZ...
DEW POINT TO TANGO-ONE-FIVE, OVER. DEW POINT TO ANYBODY ON THIS FREEK. ANYBODY COPY?
USA
STILL NOTHING?

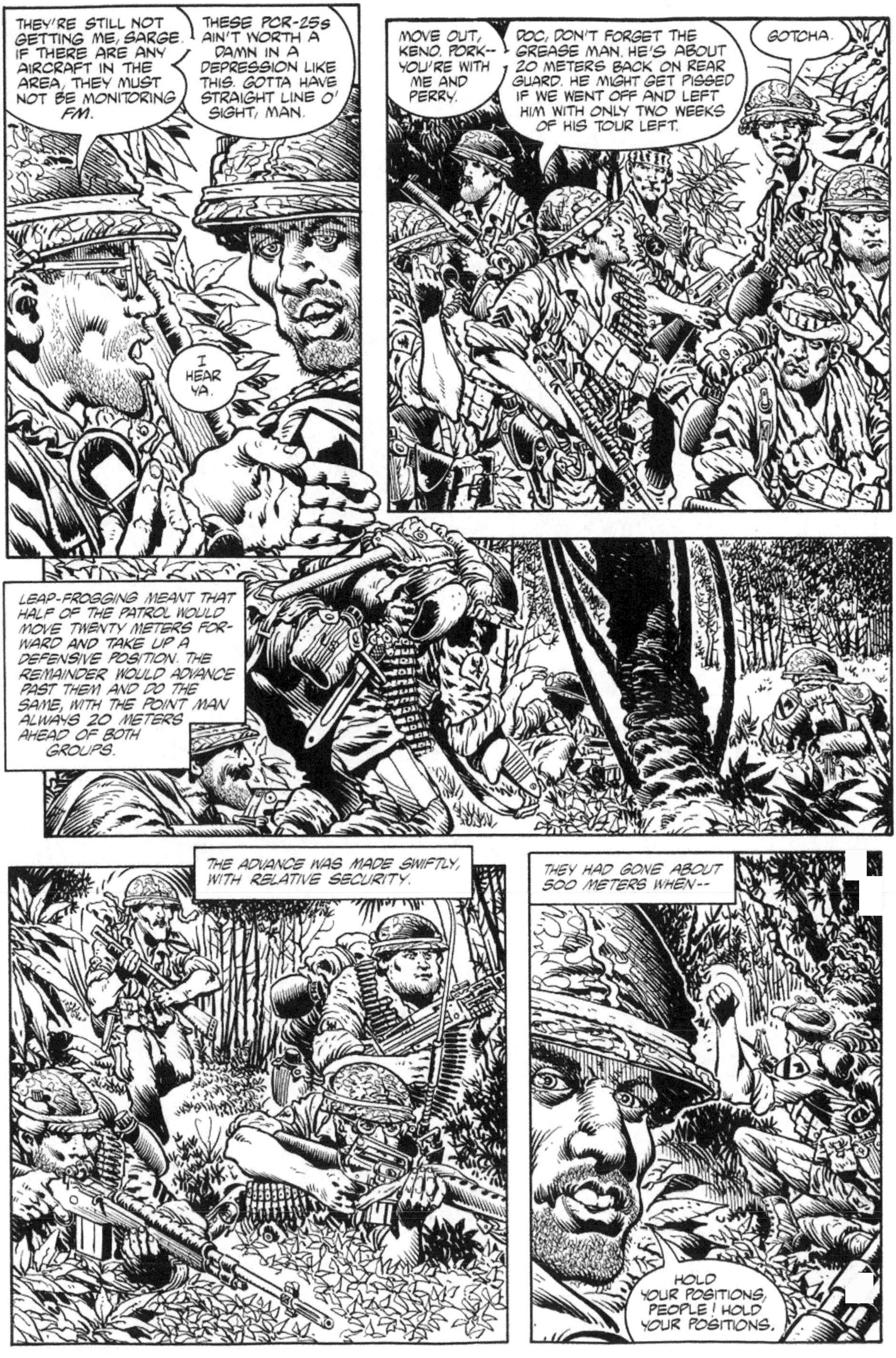
THEY'RE STILL NOT GETTING ME, SARGE. IF THERE ARE ANY AIRCRAFT IN THE AREA, THEY MUST NOT BE MONITORING FM.
THESE PCR-25s AIN'T WORTH A DAMN IN A DEPRESSION LIKE THIS. GOTTA HAVE STRAIGHT LINE O' SIGHT, MAN.
I HEAR YA.
MOVE OUT, KENO. PORK-- YOU'RE WITH ME AND PERRY.
DOC, DON'T FORGET THE GREASE MAN. HE'S ABOUT 20 METERS BACK ON REAR GUARD. HE MIGHT GET PISSED IF WE WENT OFF AND LEFT HIM WITH ONLY TWO WEEKS OF HIS TOUR LEFT.
GOTCHA.
LEAP-FROGGING MEANT THAT HALF OF THE PATROL WOULD MOVE TWENTY METERS FORWARD AND TAKE UP A DEFENSIVE POSITION. THE REMAINDER WOULD ADVANCE PAST THEM AND DO THE SAME, WITH THE POINT MAN ALWAYS 20 METERS AHEAD OF BOTH GROUPS.
THE ADVANCE WAS MADE SWIFTLY, WITH RELATIVE SECURITY.
THEY HAD GONE ABOUT 500 METERS WHEN--
HOLD YOUR POSITIONS, PEOPLE! HOLD YOUR POSITIONS.

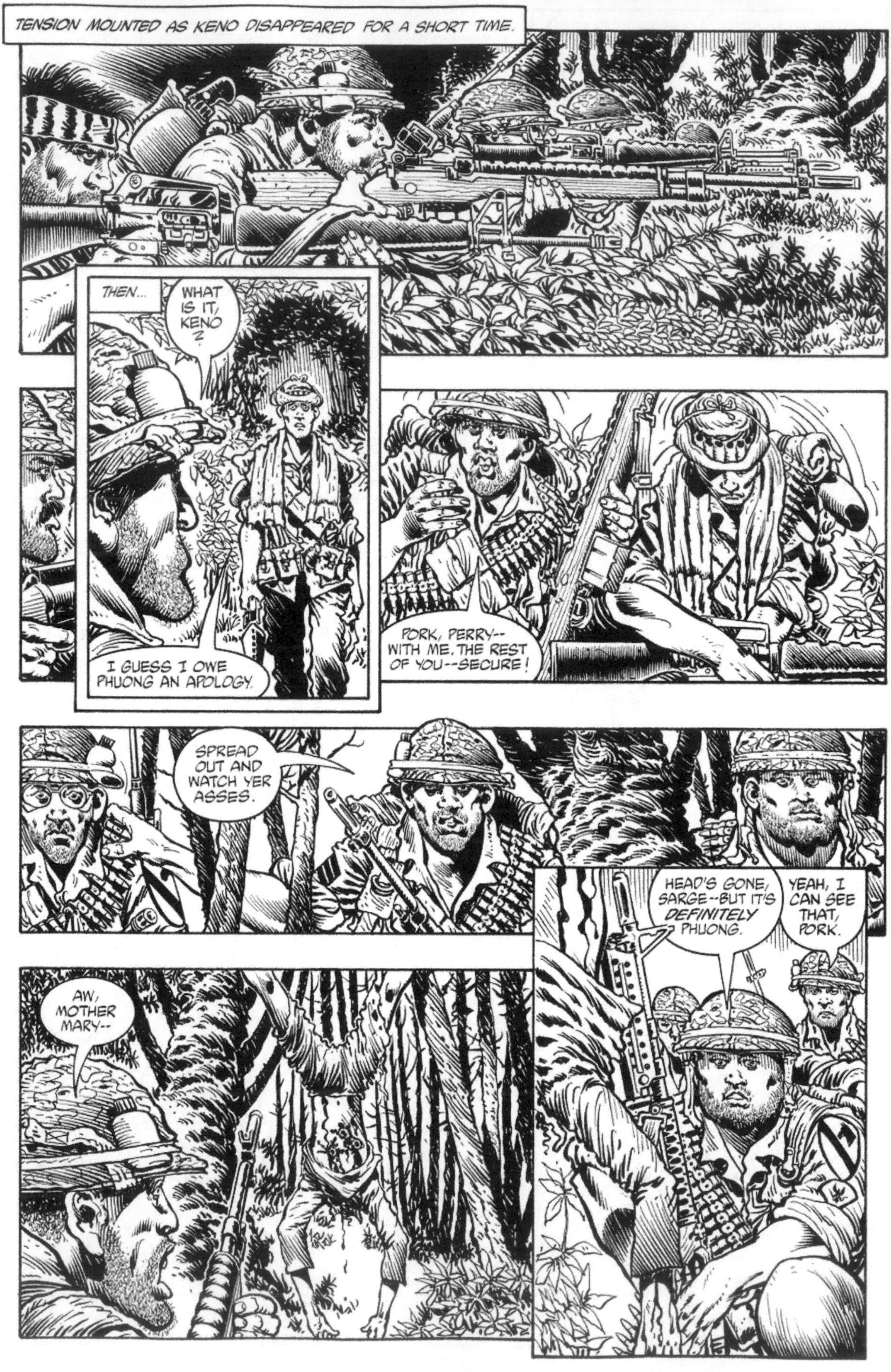
TENSION MOUNTED AS KENO DISAPPEARED FOR A SHORT TIME.
THEN...
WHAT IS IT, KENO ?
I GUESS I OWE PHUONG AN APOLOGY.
PORK, PERRY-- WITH ME. THE REST OF YOU--SECURE!
SPREAD OUT AND WATCH YER ASSES.
AW, MOTHER MARY--
HEAD'S GONE, SARGE--BUT IT'S *DEFINITELY* PHUONG.
YEAH, I CAN SEE THAT, PORK.

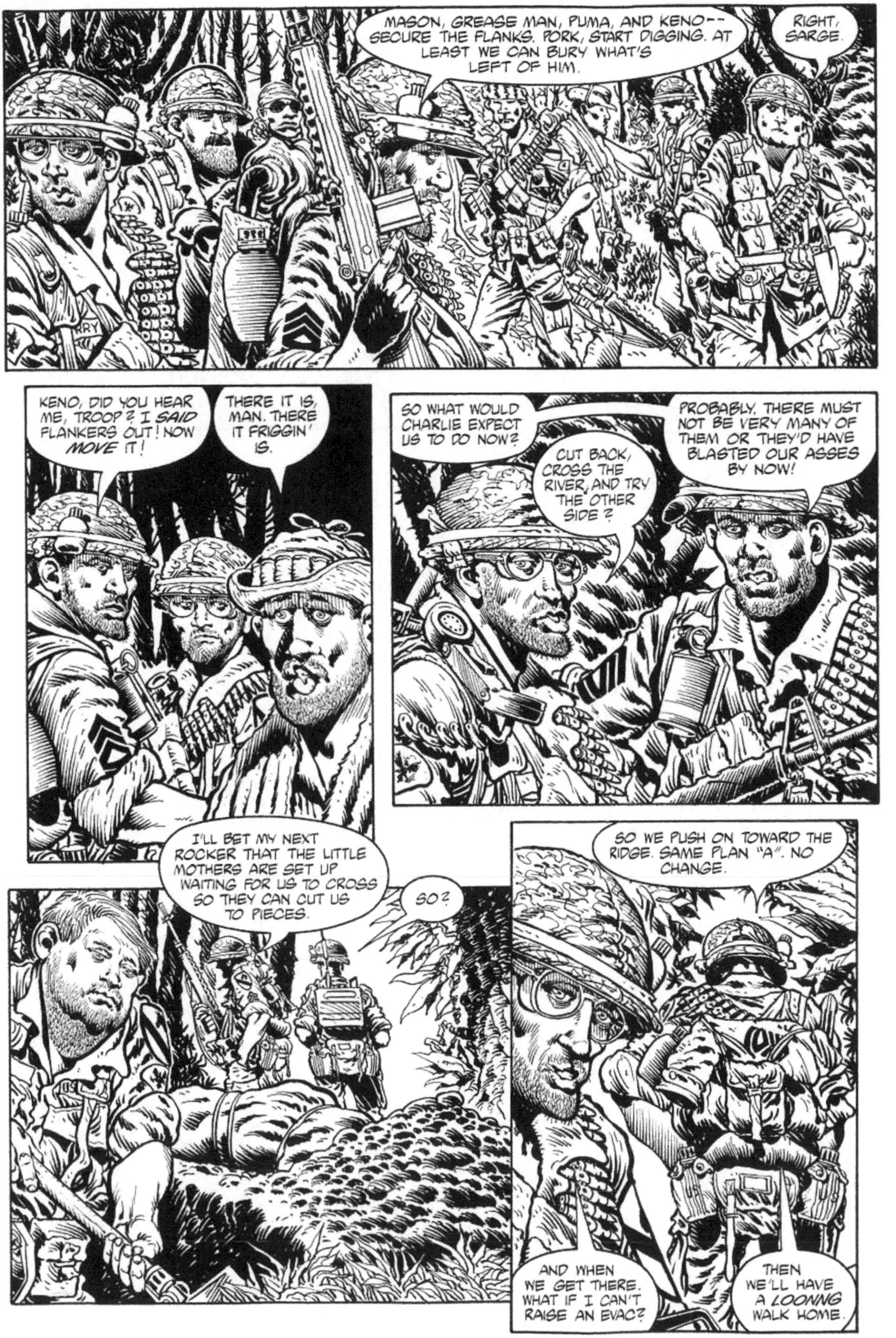
MASON, GREASE MAN, PUMA, AND KENO-- SECURE THE FLANKS. PORK, START DIGGING. AT LEAST WE CAN BURY WHAT'S LEFT OF HIM.
RIGHT, SARGE.
KENO, DID YOU HEAR ME, TROOP? I SAID FLANKERS OUT! NOW MOVE IT!
THERE IT IS, MAN. THERE IT FRIGGIN' IS.
SO WHAT WOULD CHARLIE EXPECT US TO DO NOW?
CUT BACK, CROSS THE RIVER, AND TRY THE OTHER SIDE?
PROBABLY. THERE MUST NOT BE VERY MANY OF THEM OR THEY'D HAVE BLASTED OUR ASSES BY NOW!
I'LL BET MY NEXT ROCKER THAT THE LITTLE MOTHERS ARE SET UP WAITING FOR US TO CROSS SO THEY CAN CUT US TO PIECES.
SO?
SO WE PUSH ON TOWARD THE RIDGE. SAME PLAN "A". NO CHANGE.
AND WHEN WE GET THERE. WHAT IF I CAN'T RAISE AN EVAC?
THEN WE'LL HAVE A LOONNG WALK HOME.

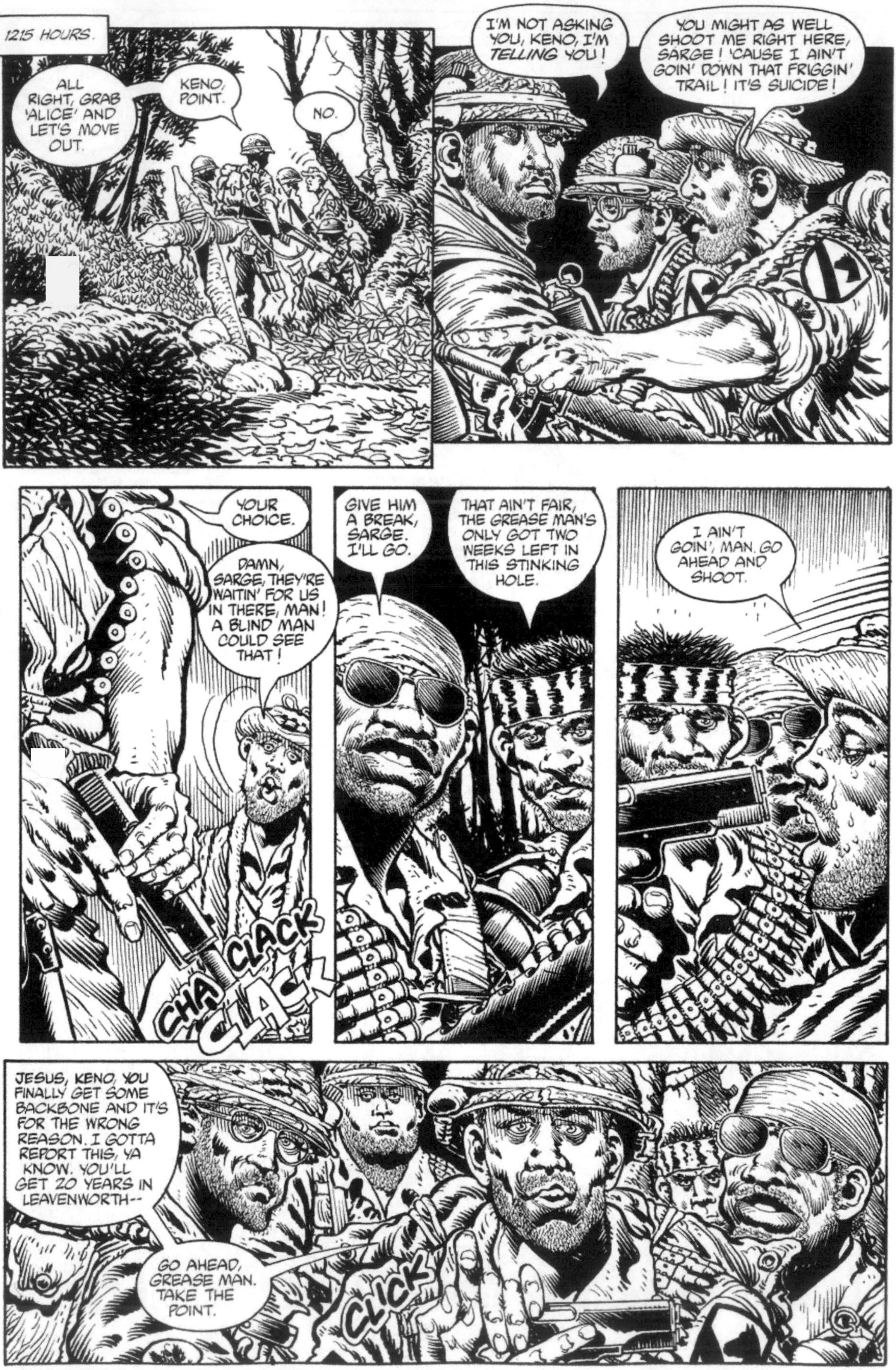

1215 HOURS.
ALL RIGHT, GRAB 'ALICE' AND LET'S MOVE OUT.
KENO, POINT.
NO.
I'M NOT ASKING YOU, KENO, I'M TELLING YOU!
YOU MIGHT AS WELL SHOOT ME RIGHT HERE, SARGE! 'CAUSE I AIN'T GOIN' DOWN THAT FRIGGIN' TRAIL! IT'S SUICIDE!
YOUR CHOICE.
DAMN, SARGE, THEY'RE WAITIN' FOR US IN THERE, MAN! A BLIND MAN COULD SEE THAT!
CHA CLACK CLACK
GIVE HIM A BREAK, SARGE. I'LL GO.
THAT AIN'T FAIR, THE GREASE MAN'S ONLY GOT TWO WEEKS LEFT IN THIS STINKING HOLE.
I AIN'T GOIN', MAN. GO AHEAD AND SHOOT.
JESUS, KENO, YOU FINALLY GET SOME BACKBONE AND IT'S FOR THE WRONG REASON. I GOTTA REPORT THIS, YA KNOW. YOU'LL GET 20 YEARS IN LEAVENWORTH--
GO AHEAD, GREASE MAN. TAKE THE POINT.
CLICK

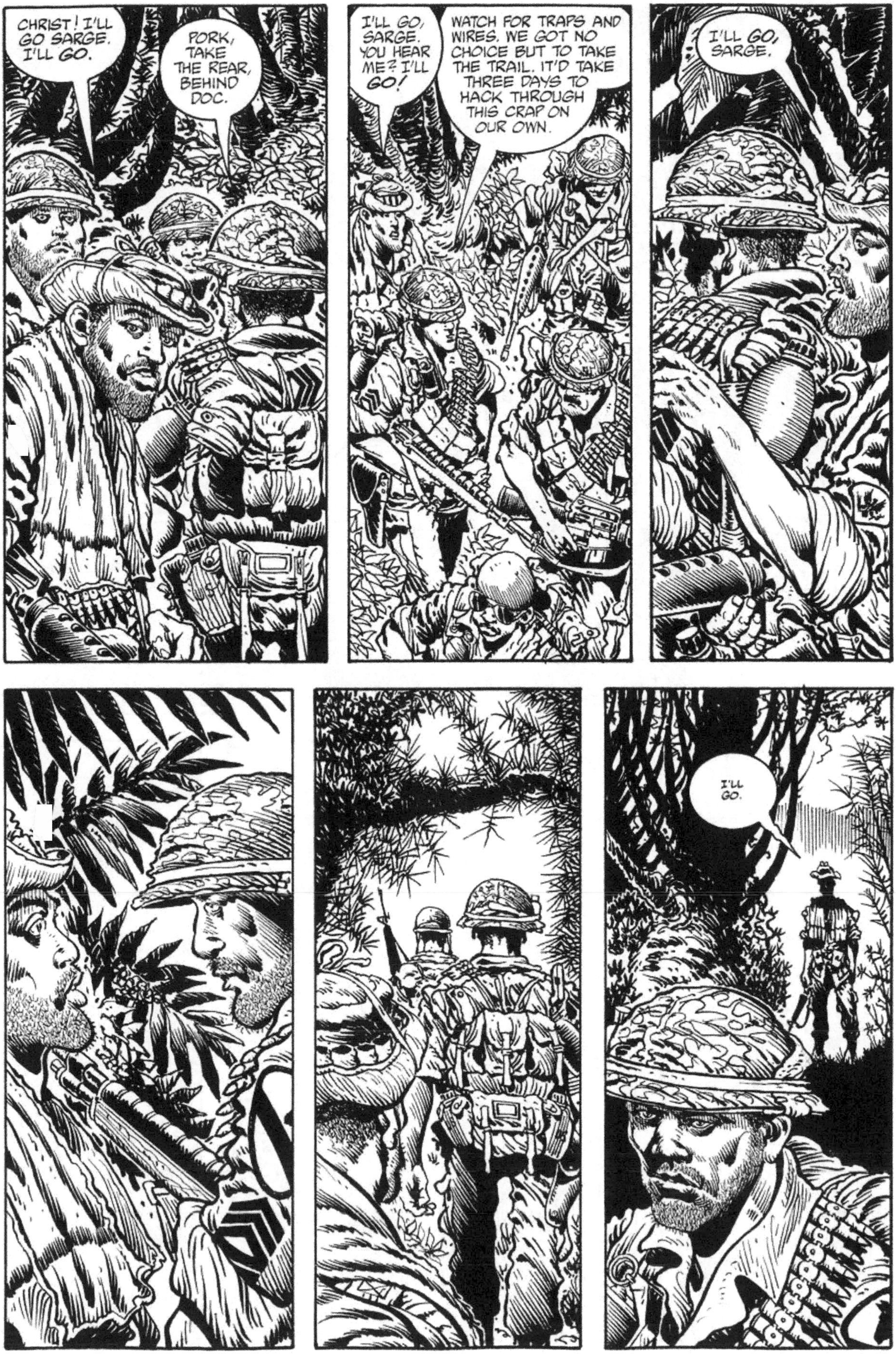
CHRIST! I'LL GO SARGE. I'LL GO.
PORK, TAKE THE REAR, BEHIND DOC.
I'LL GO, SARGE. YOU HEAR ME? I'LL GO!
WATCH FOR TRAPS AND WIRES. WE GOT NO CHOICE BUT TO TAKE THE TRAIL. IT'D TAKE THREE DAYS TO HACK THROUGH THIS CRAP ON OUR OWN.
I'LL GO, SARGE.
I'LL GO.

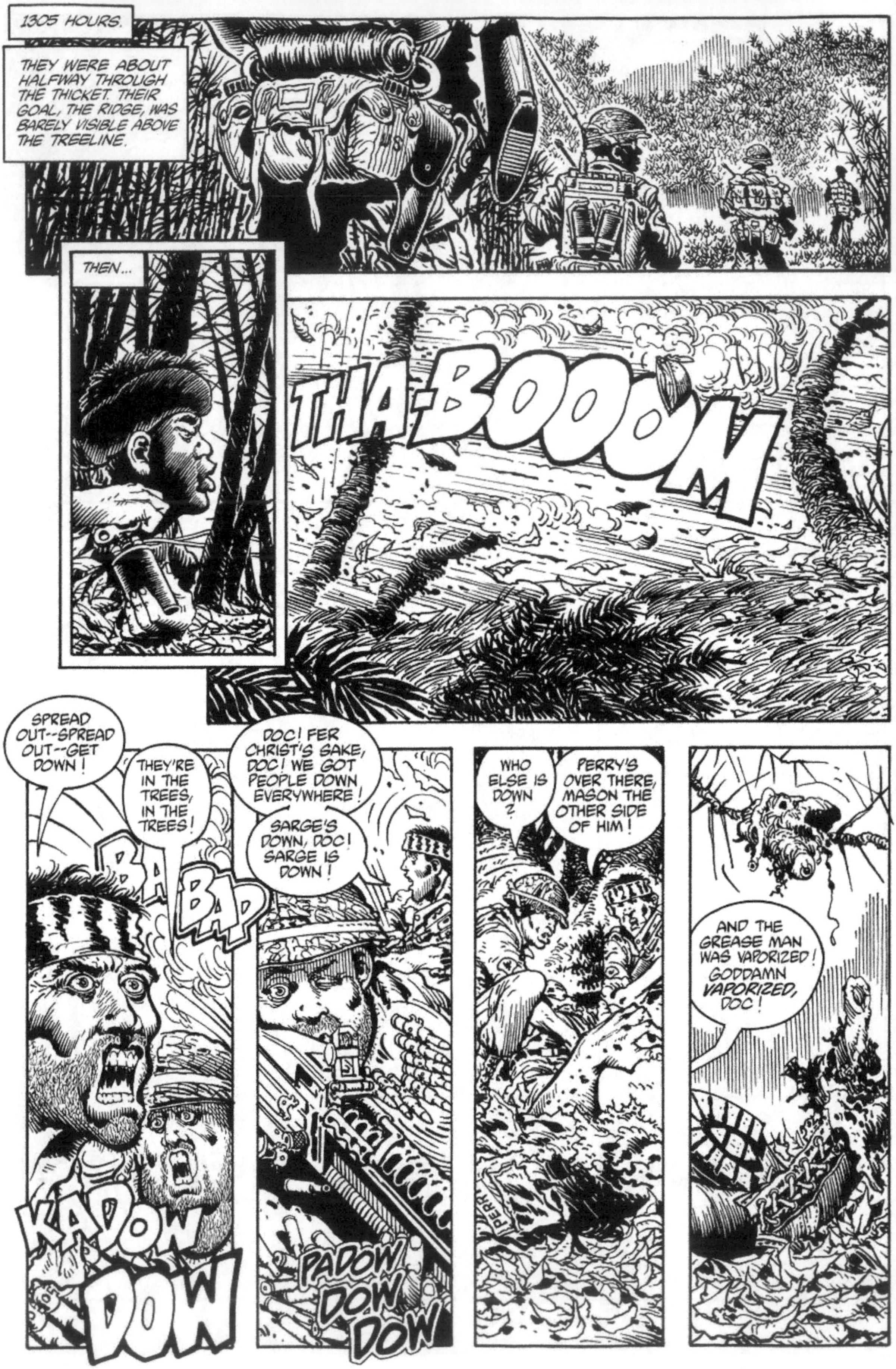
1305 HOURS.
THEY WERE ABOUT HALFWAY THROUGH THE THICKET. THEIR GOAL, THE RIDGE, WAS BARELY VISIBLE ABOVE THE TREELINE.
THEN...
THA-BOOOOM
SPREAD OUT--SPREAD OUT--GET DOWN!
THEY'RE IN THE TREES, IN THE TREES!
BA
BAP
KADOW
DOW
DOC! FER CHRIST'S SAKE, DOC! WE GOT PEOPLE DOWN EVERYWHERE!
SARGE'S DOWN, DOC! SARGE IS DOWN!
PADOW DOW DOW
WHO ELSE IS DOWN?
PERRY'S OVER THERE, MASON THE OTHER SIDE OF HIM!
PERRY
AND THE GREASE MAN WAS VAPORIZED! GODDAMN *VAPORIZED,* DOC!

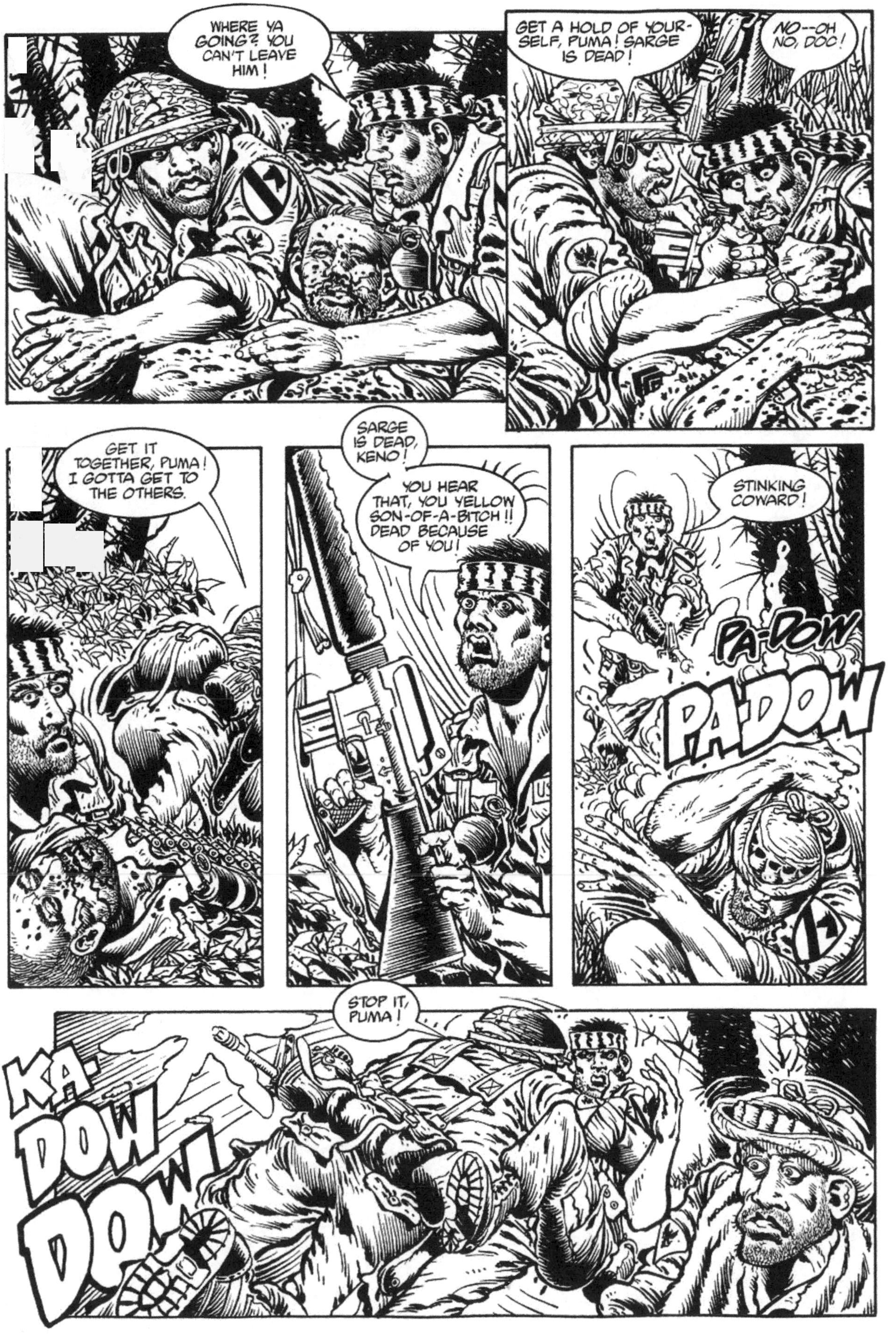
WHERE YA GOING? YOU CAN'T LEAVE HIM!
GET A HOLD OF YOURSELF, PUMA! SARGE IS DEAD!
NO--OH NO, DOC!
GET IT TOGETHER, PUMA! I GOTTA GET TO THE OTHERS.
SARGE IS DEAD, KENO!
YOU HEAR THAT, YOU YELLOW SON-OF-A-BITCH!! DEAD BECAUSE OF YOU!
STINKING COWARD!
PA-DOW
PA-DOW
STOP IT, PUMA!
KA-DOW DOW DOW

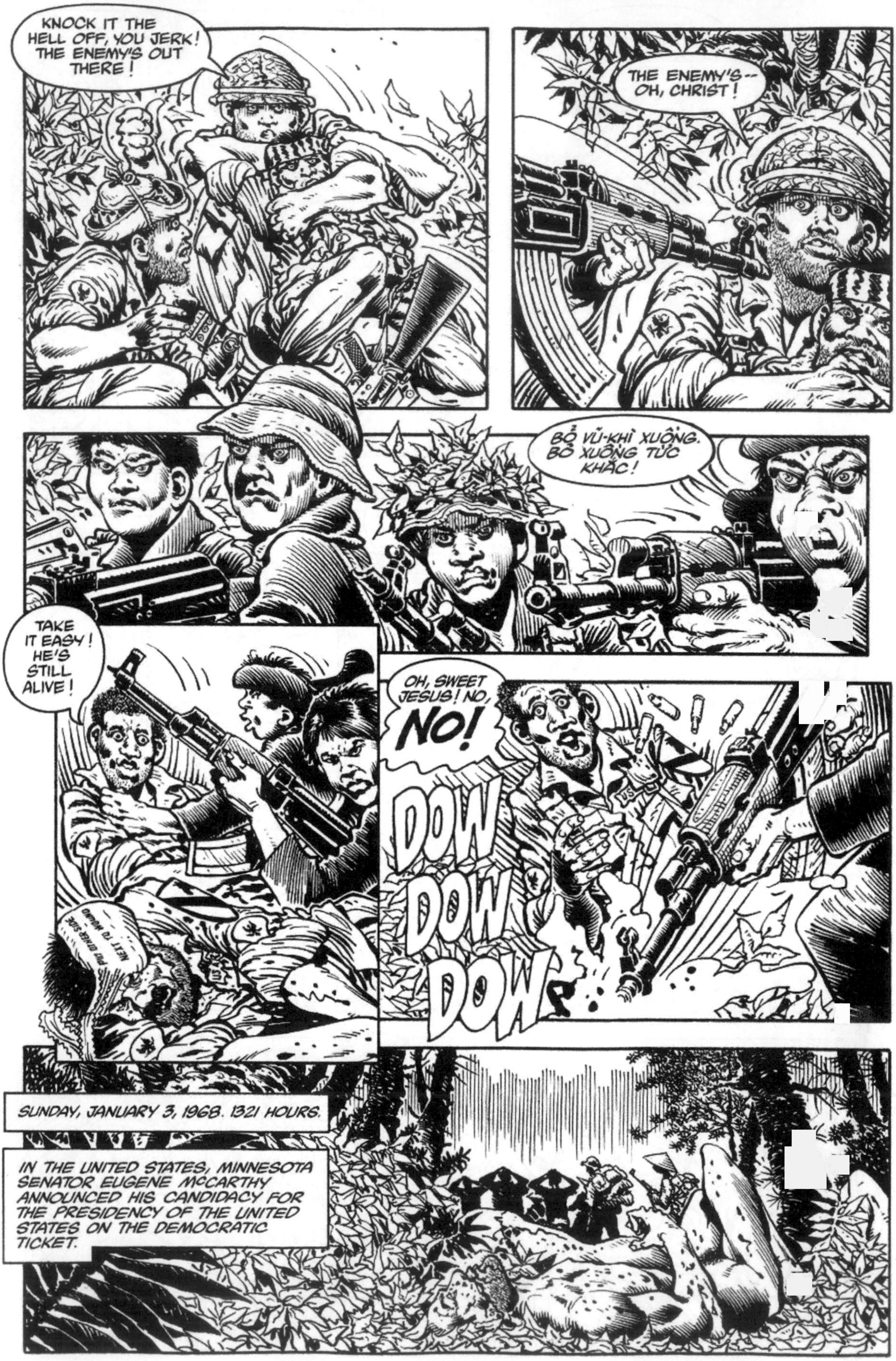
KNOCK IT THE HELL OFF, YOU JERK! THE ENEMY'S OUT THERE!
THE ENEMY'S-- OH, CHRIST!
BỎ VŨ-KHÌ XUỘNG. BỎ XUỘNG TỨC KHẮC!
TAKE IT EASY! HE'S STILL ALIVE!
OH, SWEET JESUS! NO, NO!
DOW DOW DOW
SUNDAY, JANUARY 3, 1968. 1321 HOURS.
IN THE UNITED STATES, MINNESOTA SENATOR EUGENE McCARTHY ANNOUNCED HIS CANDIDACY FOR THE PRESIDENCY OF THE UNITED STATES ON THE DEMOCRATIC TICKET.

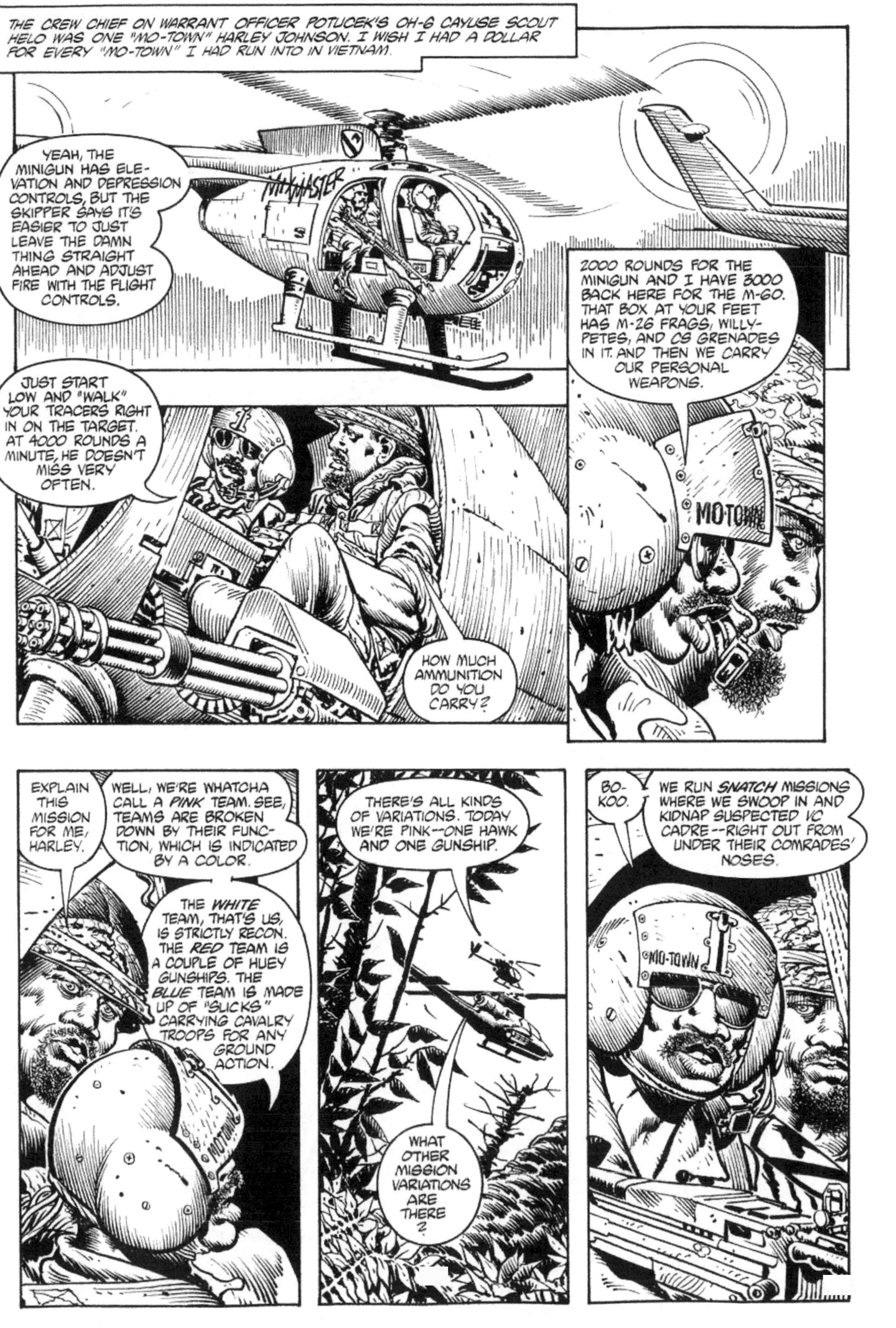
THE CREW CHIEF ON WARRANT OFFICER POTUCEK'S OH-6 CAYUSE SCOUT HELO WAS ONE "MO-TOWN" HARLEY JOHNSON. I WISH I HAD A DOLLAR FOR EVERY "MO-TOWN" I HAD RUN INTO IN VIETNAM.
MIXMASTER
YEAH, THE MINIGUN HAS ELEVATION AND DEPRESSION CONTROLS, BUT THE SKIPPER SAYS IT'S EASIER TO JUST LEAVE THE DAMN THING STRAIGHT AHEAD AND ADJUST FIRE WITH THE FLIGHT CONTROLS.
JUST START LOW AND "WALK" YOUR TRACERS RIGHT IN ON THE TARGET. AT 4000 ROUNDS A MINUTE, HE DOESN'T MISS VERY OFTEN.
HOW MUCH AMMUNITION DO YOU CARRY?
2000 ROUNDS FOR THE MINIGUN AND I HAVE 3000 BACK HERE FOR THE M-60. THAT BOX AT YOUR FEET HAS M-26 FRAGS, WILLY-PETES, AND CS GRENADES IN IT. AND THEN WE CARRY OUR PERSONAL WEAPONS.
MO-TOWN
EXPLAIN THIS MISSION FOR ME, HARLEY.
WELL, WE'RE WHATCHA CALL A *PINK* TEAM. SEE, TEAMS ARE BROKEN DOWN BY THEIR FUNCTION, WHICH IS INDICATED BY A COLOR.
THE *WHITE* TEAM, THAT'S US, IS STRICTLY RECON. THE *RED* TEAM IS A COUPLE OF HUEY GUNSHIPS. THE *BLUE* TEAM IS MADE UP OF "SLICKS" CARRYING CAVALRY TROOPS FOR ANY GROUND ACTION.
THERE'S ALL KINDS OF VARIATIONS. TODAY WE'RE PINK--ONE HAWK AND ONE GUNSHIP.
WHAT OTHER MISSION VARIATIONS ARE THERE?
BO-KOO.
WE RUN *SNATCH* MISSIONS WHERE WE SWOOP IN AND KIDNAP SUSPECTED VC CADRE--RIGHT OUT FROM UNDER THEIR COMRADES' NOSES.
MO-TOWN

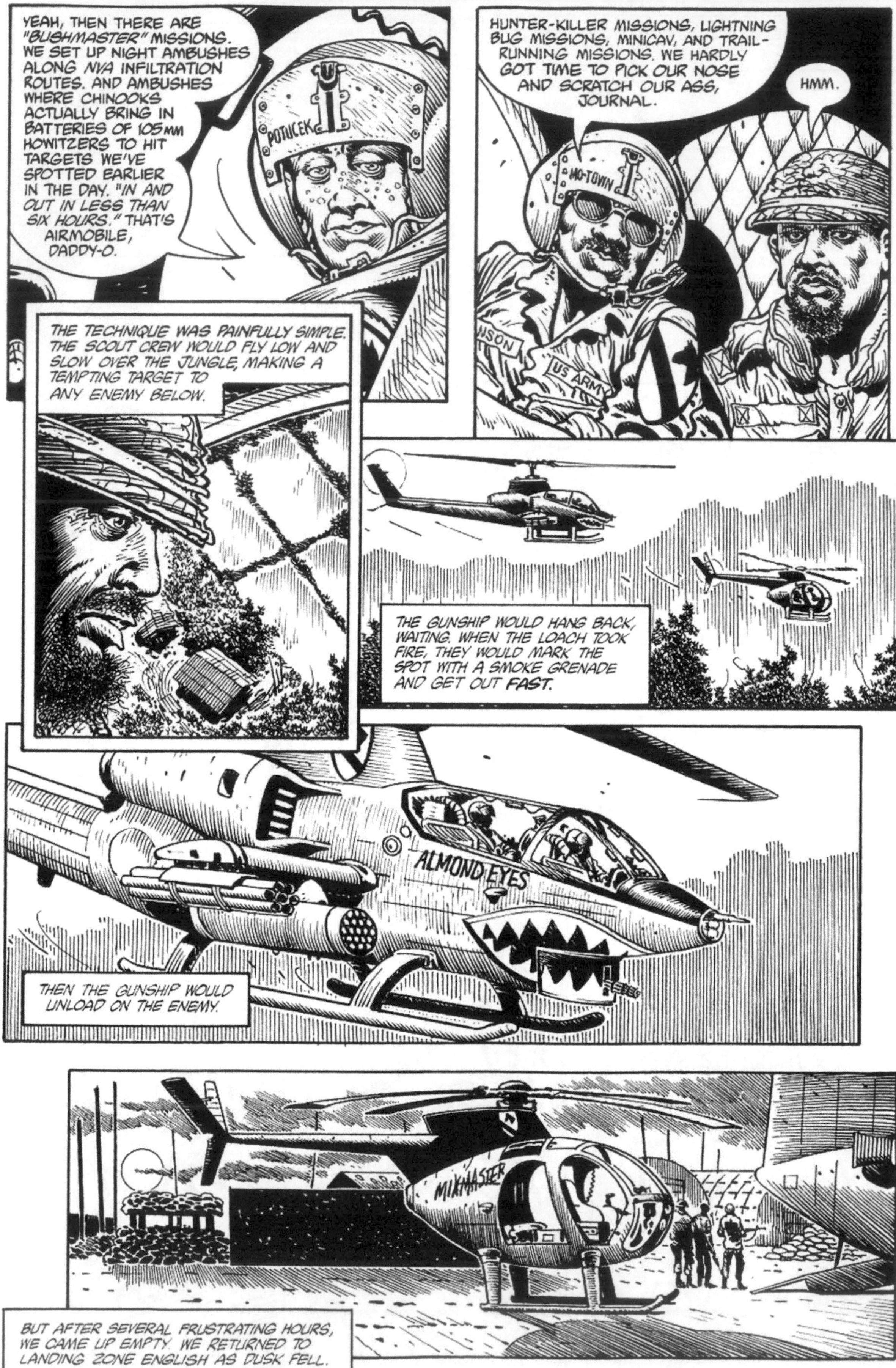
YEAH, THEN THERE ARE "BUSHMASTER" MISSIONS. WE SET UP NIGHT AMBUSHES ALONG NVA INFILTRATION ROUTES. AND AMBUSHES WHERE CHINOOKS ACTUALLY BRING IN BATTERIES OF 105MM HOWITZERS TO HIT TARGETS WE'VE SPOTTED EARLIER IN THE DAY. "IN AND OUT IN LESS THAN SIX HOURS." THAT'S AIRMOBILE, DADDY-O.
POTUCEK
HUNTER-KILLER MISSIONS, LIGHTNING BUG MISSIONS, MINICAV, AND TRAIL-RUNNING MISSIONS. WE HARDLY GOT TIME TO PICK OUR NOSE AND SCRATCH OUR ASS, JOURNAL.
HMM.
MO-TOWN
US ARMY
THE TECHNIQUE WAS PAINFULLY SIMPLE. THE SCOUT CREW WOULD FLY LOW AND SLOW OVER THE JUNGLE, MAKING A TEMPTING TARGET TO ANY ENEMY BELOW.
THE GUNSHIP WOULD HANG BACK, WAITING. WHEN THE LOACH TOOK FIRE, THEY WOULD MARK THE SPOT WITH A SMOKE GRENADE AND GET OUT FAST.
ALMOND EYES
THEN THE GUNSHIP WOULD UNLOAD ON THE ENEMY.
MIXMASTER
BUT AFTER SEVERAL FRUSTRATING HOURS, WE CAME UP EMPTY. WE RETURNED TO LANDING ZONE ENGLISH AS DUSK FELL.

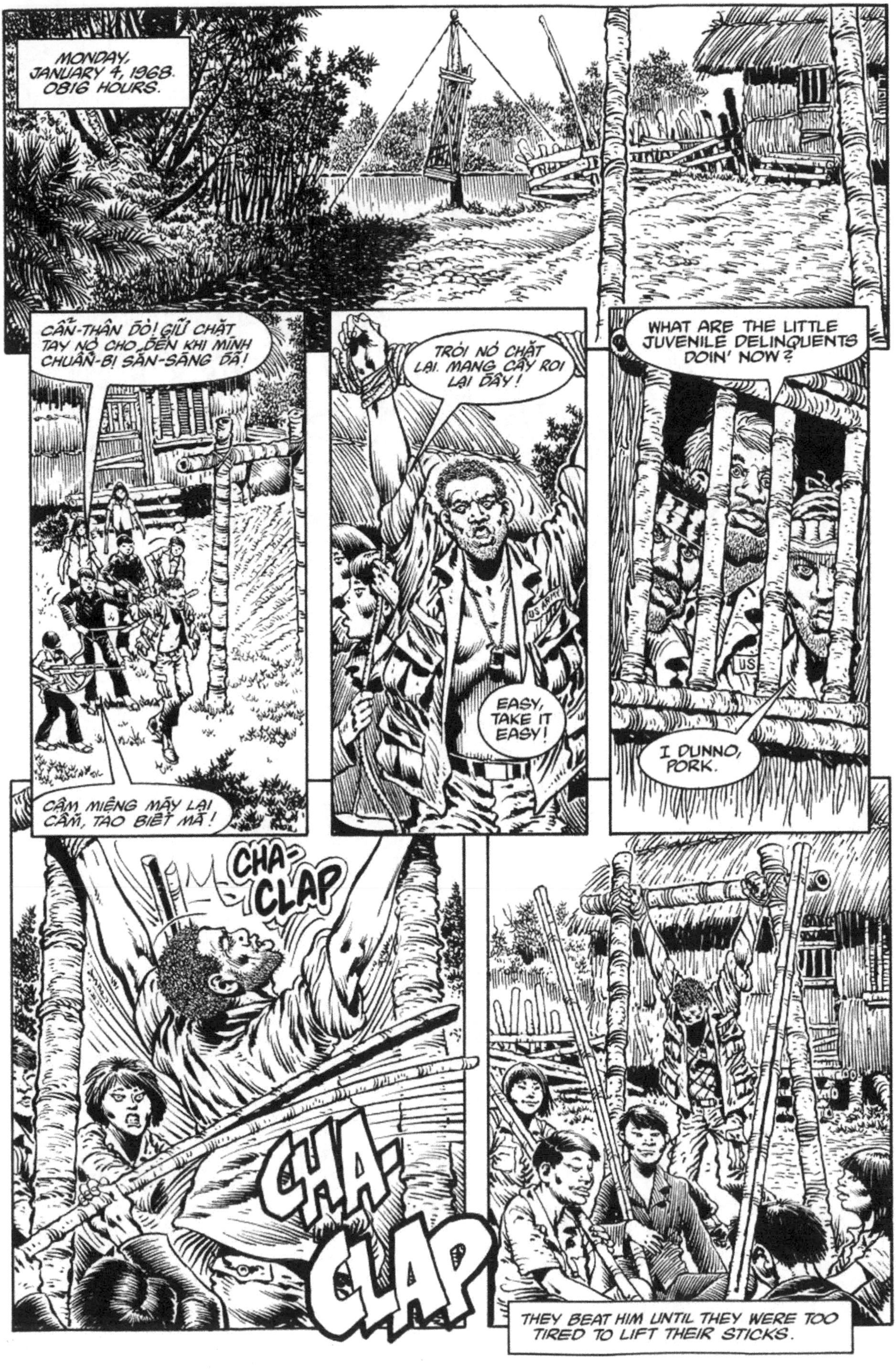
MONDAY, JANUARY 4, 1968. 0816 HOURS.
CẨN-THẬN ĐÓ! GIỮ CHẶT TAY NÓ CHO ĐẾN KHI MÌNH CHUẨN-BỊ SẴN-SÀNG ĐÃ!
CÂM MIỆNG MÀY LẠI CÂM, TAO BIẾT MÀ!
TRÓI NÓ CHẶT LẠI. MANG CÂY ROI LẠI ĐÂY!
EASY, TAKE IT EASY!
WHAT ARE THE LITTLE JUVENILE DELINQUENTS DOIN' NOW?
I DUNNO, PORK.
CHA-CLAP
CHA-CLAP
THEY BEAT HIM UNTIL THEY WERE TOO TIRED TO LIFT THEIR STICKS.

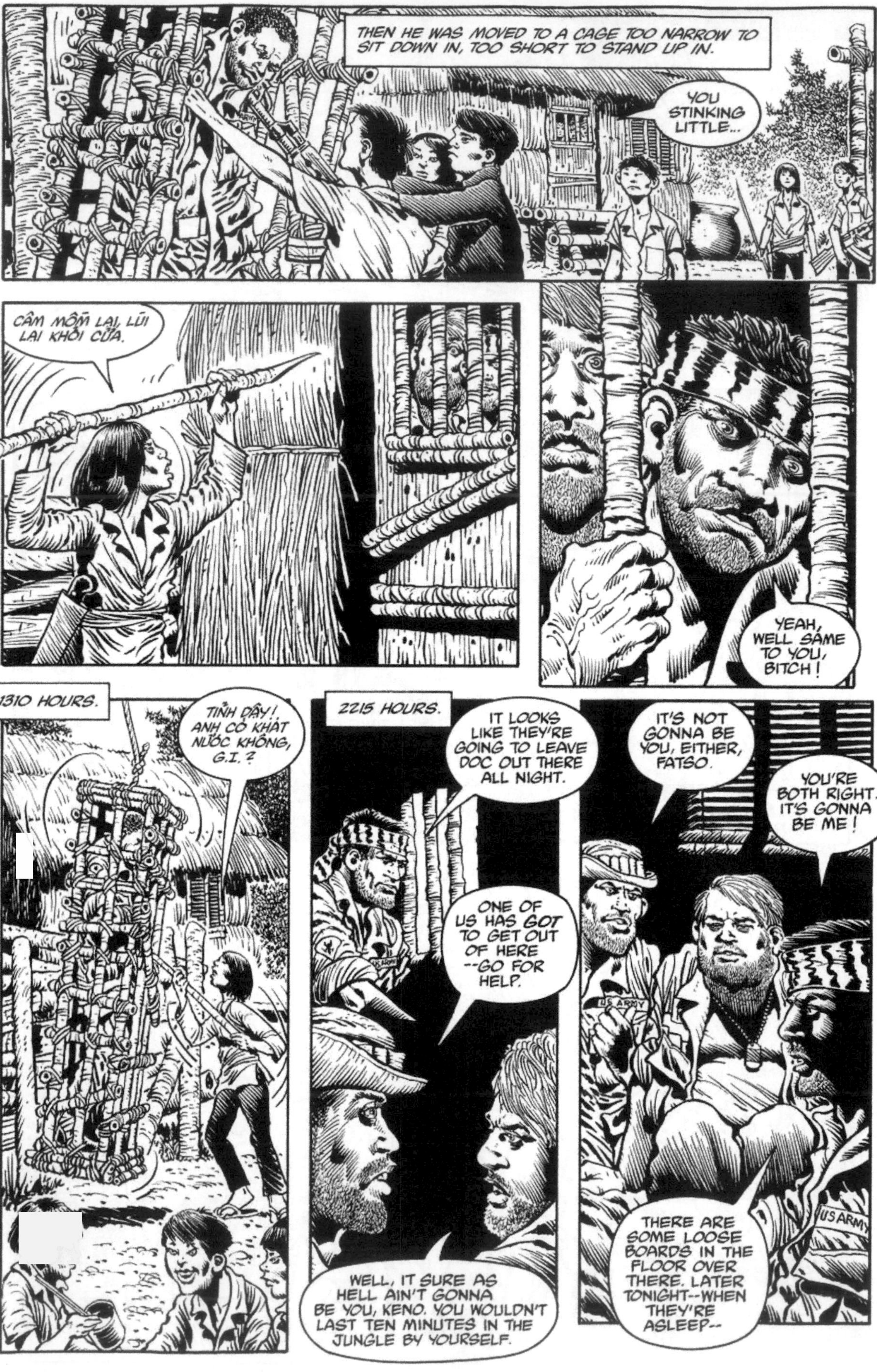
THEN HE WAS MOVED TO A CAGE TOO NARROW TO SIT DOWN IN, TOO SHORT TO STAND UP IN.
YOU STINKING LITTLE...
CÂM MỒM LẠI, LŨI LẠI KHỎI CỬA.
YEAH, WELL SAME TO YOU, BITCH!
1310 HOURS.
TỈNH DẬY! ANH CÓ KHÁT NƯỚC KHÔNG, G.I.?
2215 HOURS.
IT LOOKS LIKE THEY'RE GOING TO LEAVE DOC OUT THERE ALL NIGHT.
ONE OF US HAS GOT TO GET OUT OF HERE --GO FOR HELP.
WELL, IT SURE AS HELL AIN'T GONNA BE YOU, KENO. YOU WOULDN'T LAST TEN MINUTES IN THE JUNGLE BY YOURSELF.
IT'S NOT GONNA BE YOU, EITHER, FATSO.
YOU'RE BOTH RIGHT. IT'S GONNA BE ME!
THERE ARE SOME LOOSE BOARDS IN THE FLOOR OVER THERE. LATER TONIGHT--WHEN THEY'RE ASLEEP--

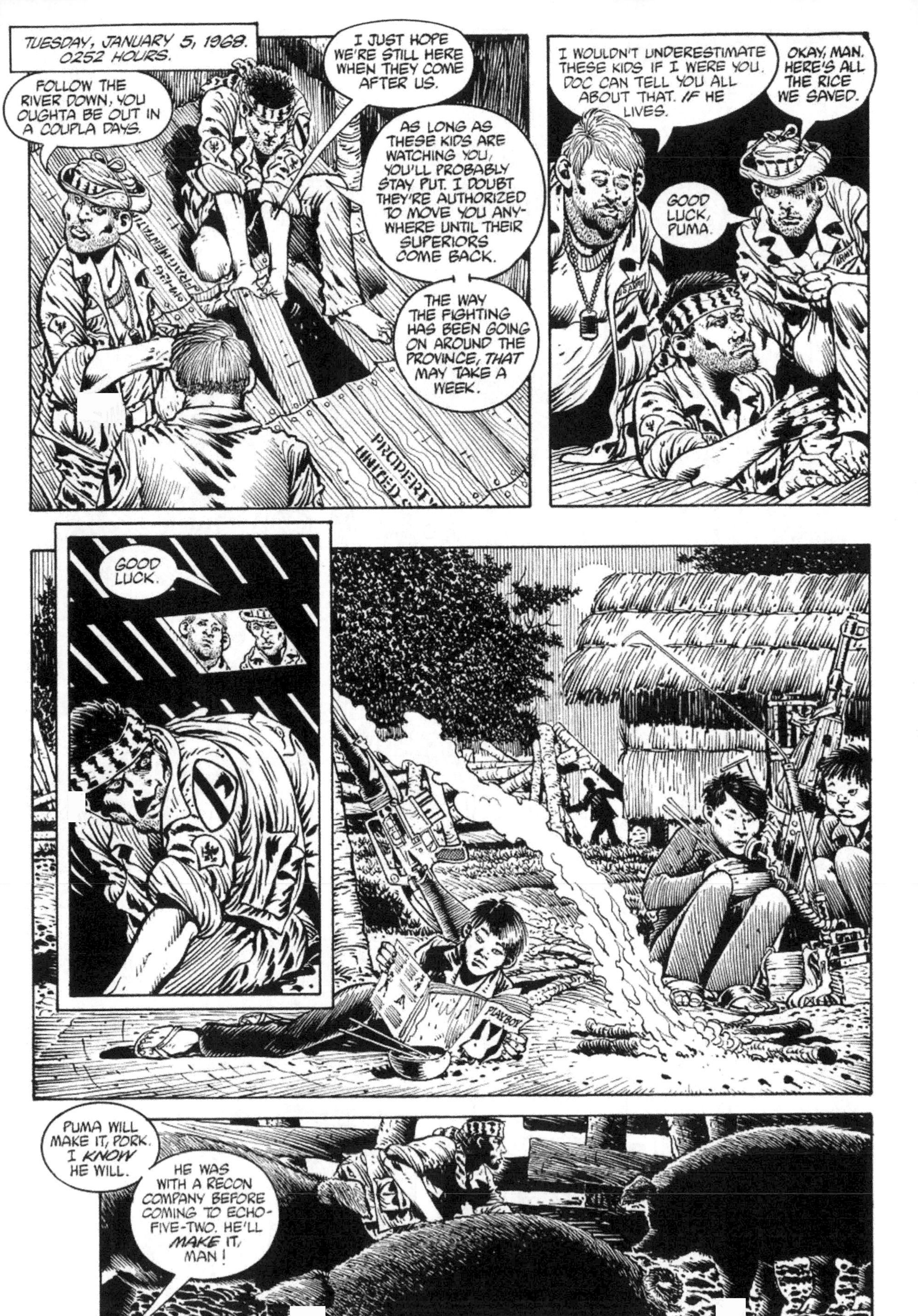
TUESDAY, JANUARY 5, 1968. 0252 HOURS.
FOLLOW THE RIVER DOWN, YOU OUGHTA BE OUT IN A COUPLA DAYS.
I JUST HOPE WE'RE STILL HERE WHEN THEY COME AFTER US.
AS LONG AS THESE KIDS ARE WATCHING YOU, YOU'LL PROBABLY STAY PUT. I DOUBT THEY'RE AUTHORIZED TO MOVE YOU ANY-WHERE UNTIL THEIR SUPERIORS COME BACK.
THE WAY THE FIGHTING HAS BEEN GOING ON AROUND THE PROVINCE, *THAT* MAY TAKE A WEEK.
I WOULDN'T UNDERESTIMATE THESE KIDS IF I WERE YOU. DOC CAN TELL YOU ALL ABOUT THAT. *IF* HE LIVES.
OKAY, MAN. HERE'S ALL THE RICE WE SAVED.
GOOD LUCK, PUMA.
GOOD LUCK.
PUMA WILL MAKE IT, PORK. I *KNOW* HE WILL.
HE WAS WITH A RECON COMPANY BEFORE COMING TO ECHO-FIVE-TWO. HE'LL *MAKE* IT, MAN!

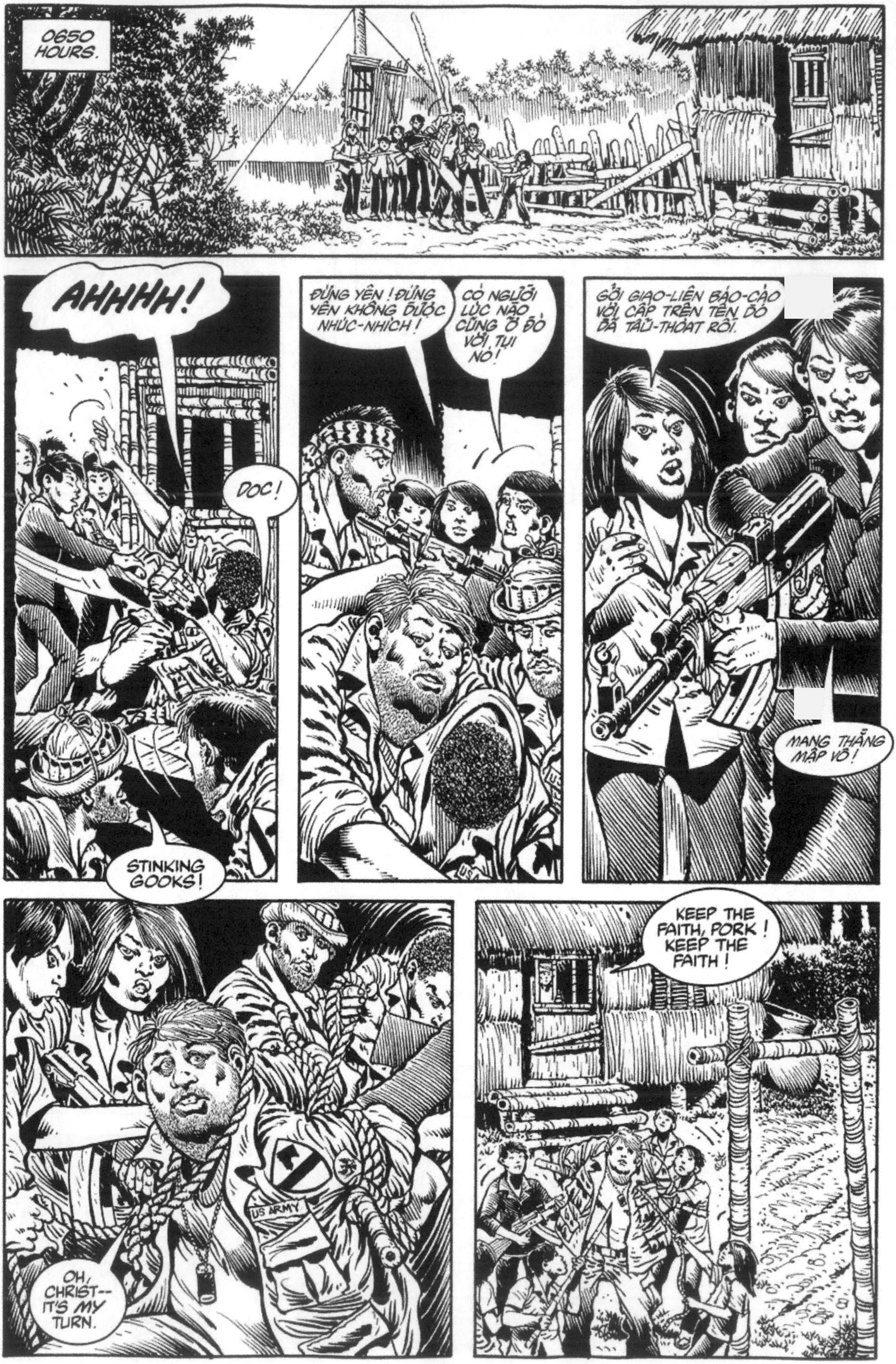
0650 HOURS.
AHHHH!
DOC!
STINKING GOOKS!
ĐỪNG YÊN! ĐỪNG YÊN KHÔNG ĐƯỢC NHÚC-NHÍCH!
CÓ NGƯỜI LÚC NÀO CŨNG Ở ĐÓ VỚI TỤI NÓ!
GỞI GIAO-LIÊN BÁO-CÁO VỚI CẤP TRÊN TÊN ĐÓ ĐÃ TẨU-THOÁT RỒI.
MANG THẰNG MẬP VÔ!
US ARMY
OH, CHRIST-- IT'S MY TURN.
KEEP THE FAITH, PORK! KEEP THE FAITH!

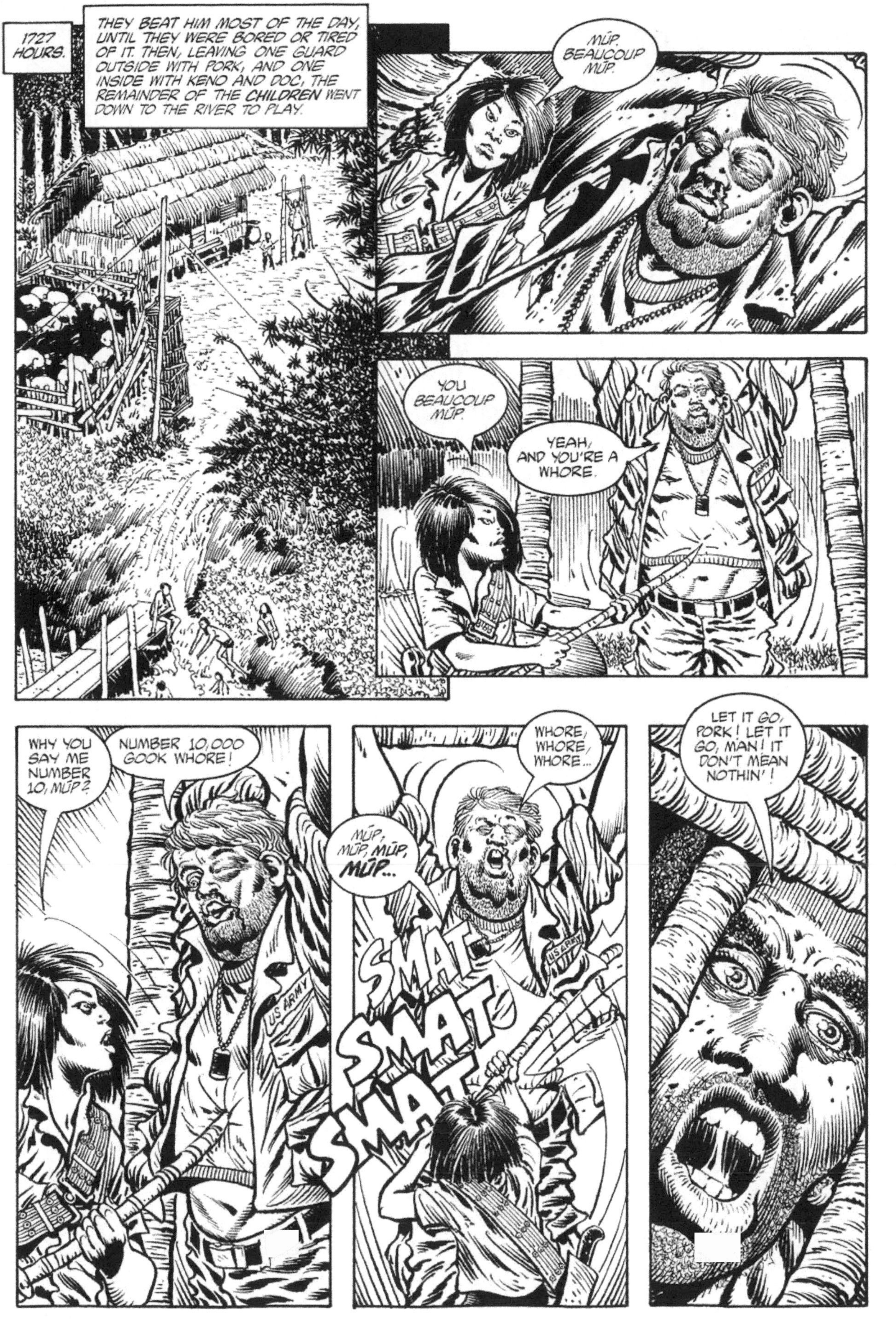
1727 HOURS.
THEY BEAT HIM MOST OF THE DAY, UNTIL THEY WERE BORED OR TIRED OF IT. THEN, LEAVING ONE GUARD OUTSIDE WITH PORK, AND ONE INSIDE WITH KENO AND DOC, THE REMAINDER OF THE CHILDREN WENT DOWN TO THE RIVER TO PLAY.
MŨP. BEAUCOUP MŨP.
YOU BEAUCOUP MŨP.
YEAH, AND YOU'RE A WHORE.
WHY YOU SAY ME NUMBER 10, MŨP?
NUMBER 10,000 GOOK WHORE!
WHORE, WHORE, WHORE...
MŨP, MŨP, MŨP, MŨP...
SMAT
SMAT
SMAT
LET IT GO, PORK! LET IT GO, MAN! IT DON'T MEAN NOTHIN'!

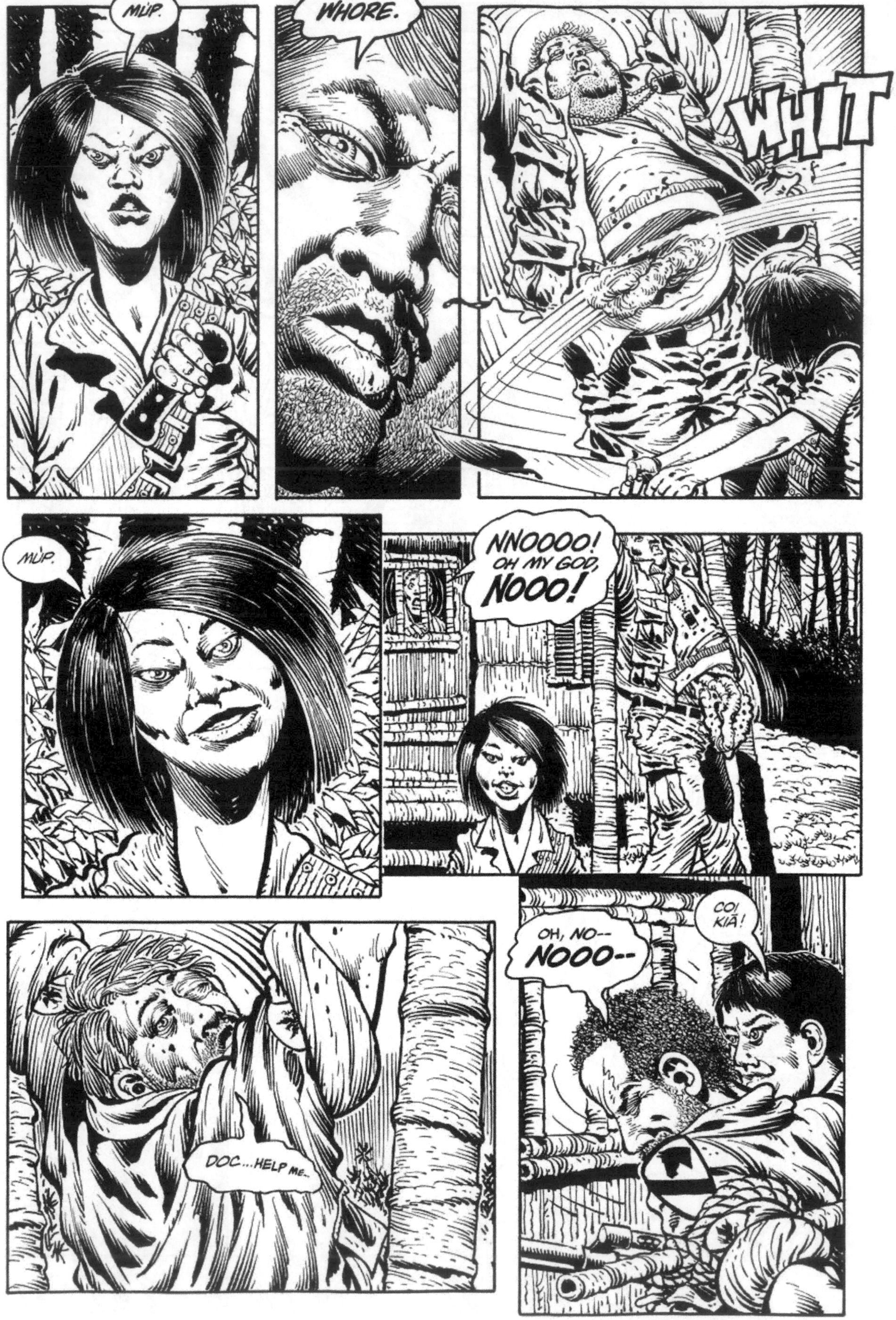
MÚP.
WHORE.
WHIT
MÚP.
NNOOOO! OH MY GOD, NOOO!
DOC...HELP ME..
OH, NO-- NOOO--
CO! KIÃ!

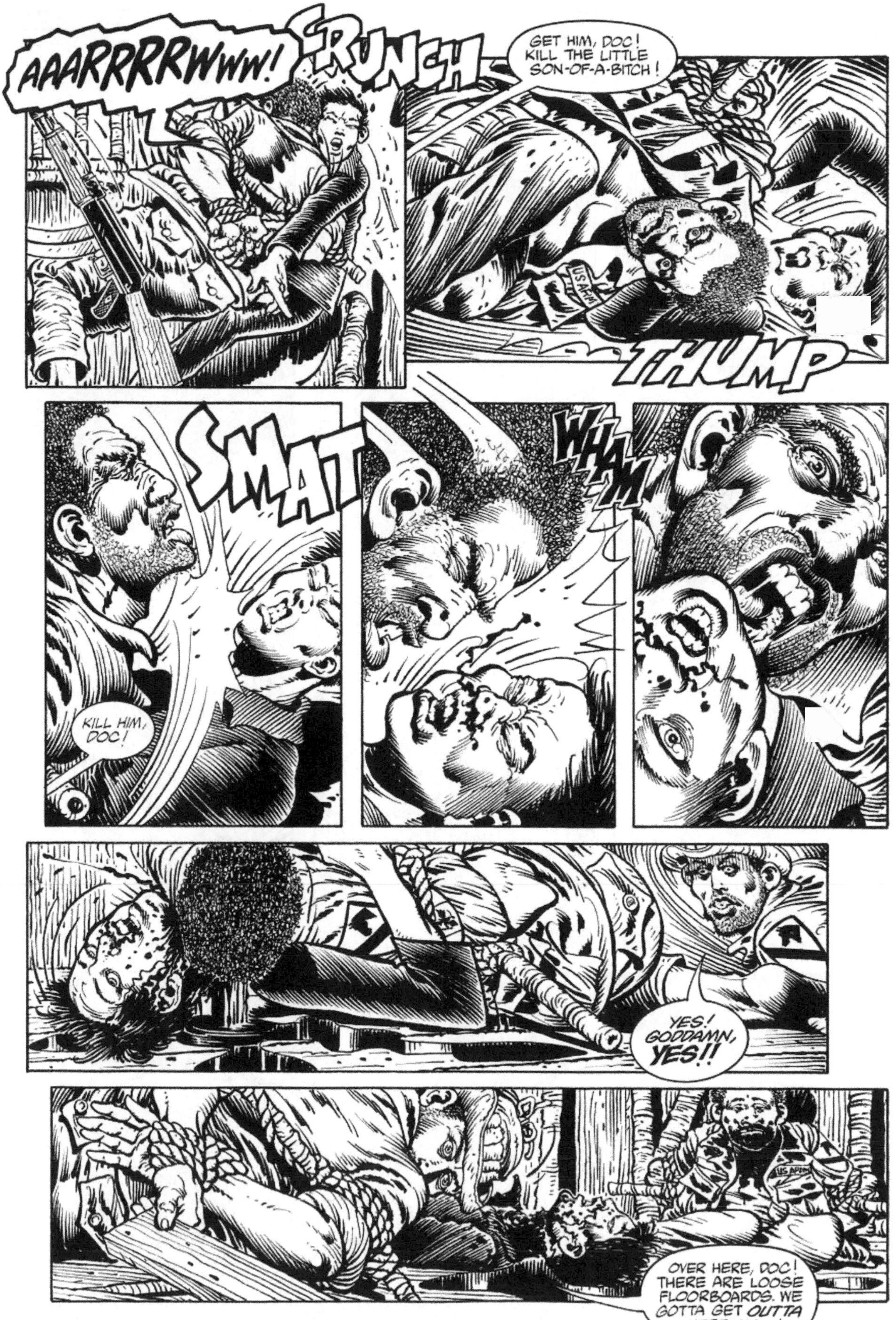
AAARRRRWWW!
CRUNCH
GET HIM, DOC! KILL THE LITTLE SON-OF-A-BITCH!
THUMP
SMAT
KILL HIM, DOC!
WHAM
YES! GODDAMN, YES!!
OVER HERE, DOC! THERE ARE LOOSE FLOORBOARDS. WE GOTTA GET OUTTA HERE, MAN!

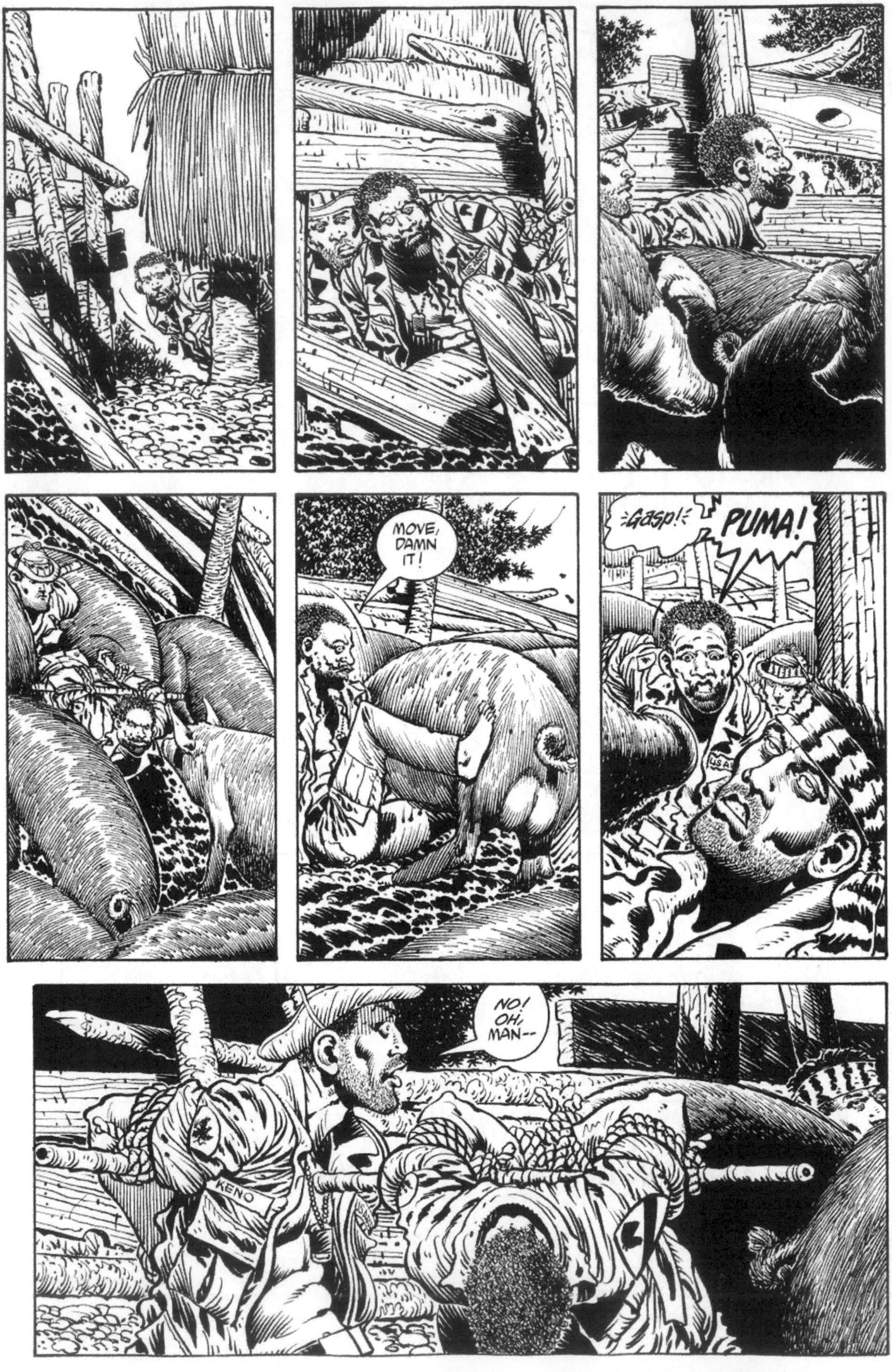
MOVE, DAMN IT!
GASP!
PUMA!
NO! OH, MAN--
KENO

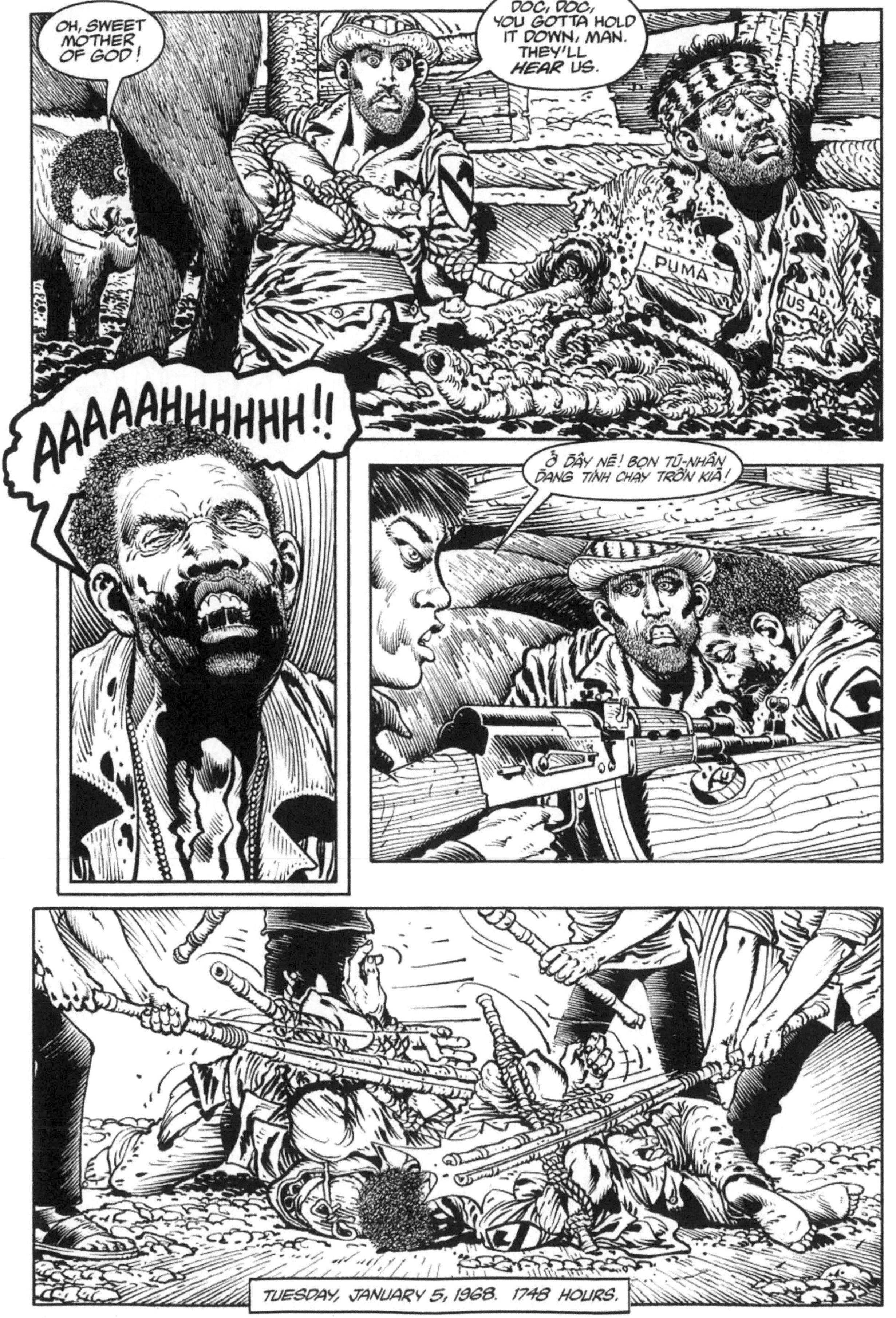
OH, SWEET MOTHER OF GOD!
DOC, DOC, YOU GOTTA HOLD IT DOWN, MAN. THEY'LL HEAR US.
PUMA
US ARMY
AAAAAHHHHHH!!
Ở ĐÂY NÈ! BỌN TÙ-NHÂN ĐANG TÍNH CHẠY TRỐN KIÀ!
TUESDAY, JANUARY 5, 1968. 1748 HOURS.

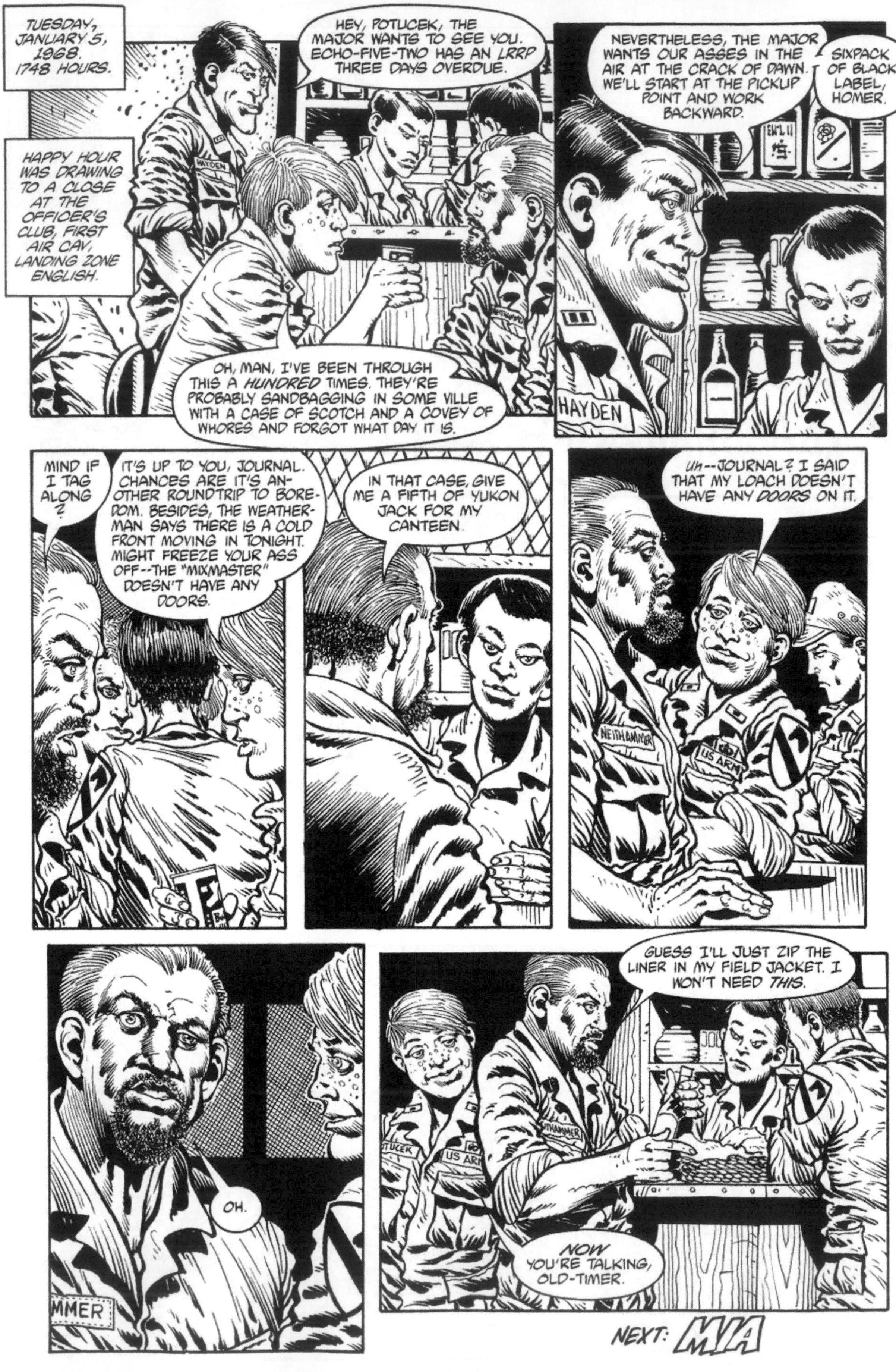

TUESDAY, JANUARY 5, 1968. 1748 HOURS.
HAPPY HOUR WAS DRAWING TO A CLOSE AT THE OFFICER'S CLUB, FIRST AIR CAV, LANDING ZONE ENGLISH.
HEY, POTUCEK, THE MAJOR WANTS TO SEE YOU. ECHO-FIVE-TWO HAS AN LRRP THREE DAYS OVERDUE.
OH, MAN, I'VE BEEN THROUGH THIS A HUNDRED TIMES. THEY'RE PROBABLY SANDBAGGING IN SOME VILLE WITH A CASE OF SCOTCH AND A COVEY OF WHORES AND FORGOT WHAT DAY IT IS.
HAYDEN
NEVERTHELESS, THE MAJOR WANTS OUR ASSES IN THE AIR AT THE CRACK OF DAWN. WE'LL START AT THE PICKUP POINT AND WORK BACKWARD.
SIXPACK OF BLACK LABEL, HOMER.
HAYDEN
MIND IF I TAG ALONG?
IT'S UP TO YOU, JOURNAL. CHANCES ARE IT'S ANOTHER ROUNDTRIP TO BOREDOM. BESIDES, THE WEATHERMAN SAYS THERE IS A COLD FRONT MOVING IN TONIGHT. MIGHT FREEZE YOUR ASS OFF--THE "MIXMASTER" DOESN'T HAVE ANY DOORS.
IN THAT CASE, GIVE ME A FIFTH OF YUKON JACK FOR MY CANTEEN.
UH--JOURNAL? I SAID THAT MY LOACH DOESN'T HAVE ANY DOORS ON IT.
NEITHAMMER
US ARMY
OH.
MMER
GUESS I'LL JUST ZIP THE LINER IN MY FIELD JACKET. I WON'T NEED THIS.
POTUCEK
US ARM
THAMMER
NOW YOU'RE TALKING, OLD-TIMER.
NEXT: MIA

POW Forum: The story of Potato John and the bank vice-president that got away

On February 1, 1988, The Connecticut chapter of the National Forget-Me-Not Association sponsored a Prisoner-of-War Forum at Western Connecticut State University in Danbury, Connecticut.

Participants included Bill Paul, a reporter for The Wall Street Journal, *and U.S. Rep. John Rowland (R-Conn.), a leader in Congress on the issue of POWs abandoned in Vietnam. The Departments of Defense and State were invited to send representatives to participate, but declined, saying no one was available.*

In part 5 of our edited transcript of those proceedings, Mr. Paul continues his historical overview of the issue...

In 1980, a retired Air Force intelligence man went back to Thailand. During the war, he had served as an advisor to the Royal Lao — those were our guys — to their Police Force in Vientiane, Laos — the capital city.

He went to one of the refugee camps near the Thai-Lao border. He met someone who had been a police assistant deputy chief or something. He had known this guy, worked with him, knew him cold. Remember now, this is a trained Air Force intelligence officer talking to someone he knows well.

The Lao says, "I know him, him, him, and him. They all say they've seen [Americans]. We ought to debrief them." So the guy says "Great! Let's do it right here." And his buddy says, "No, there are too many Communist spies in this camp. They will kill these people." So they go across the street, the guy buys them a cup of tea, and they tell their stories.

He goes back to Bangkok, to the American embassy, and needless to say, he's a bit excited. Among other things, he has found an educated Lao who had been a bank vice president in Vientiane before the war. This bank vice president tells him about having been in a work camp in Laos, how every day, without fail, his work contingent would pass an American work contingent.

He said, "we used to pass notes." They used to take potato leaves, harden them, write on them. One note said "potato from John, Camp #3," dropped, you know — the [American] drops the note and the Lao scoops it up before the Vietnamese guard sees him. He could tell you the trail, the date, what John looked like. That specific.

What do we do with this information? First we castigate it because this retired Air Force intelligence officer took them out of the camp, which means they have something to hide. Their evidence is no good, and they probably wanted money anyway.

They kept telling this Air Force guy, "They probably wanted money, didn't they?" He said, "No, they didn't want any money. They wanted to stay alive, which is why they left the camp." It takes a week before somebody gets on a train and goes the 12 hours up to this camp — by which point these men are gone. Gone. Not to be seen again — or so we think.

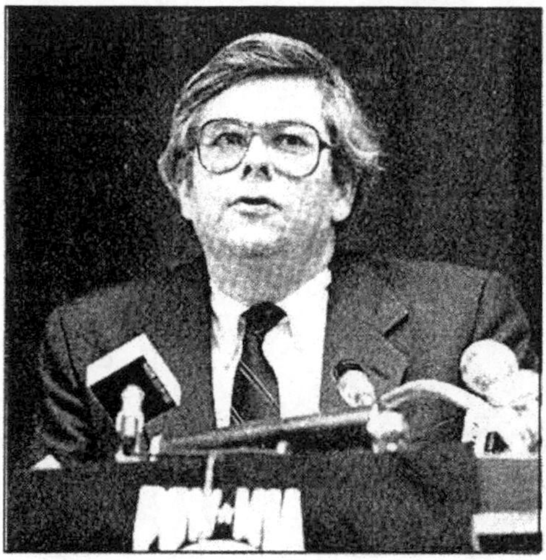

"...there was no convincing DIA they had the wrong guy. To this day, they say they had [him]." — Bill Paul
Photo by Carol Kaliff. Copyright ©1990 The Danbury (Ct.) News-Times

Three years later, former Congressman Hendon is in the Pentagon. Congressman Hendon is a leading opponent of the Reagan Administration. He believes that we have the evidence, [but] we don't do anything about it because it's not part of our overall agenda.

He sees this story and says, "We gotta find this bank vice president." To make a long story short, they find the guy who they say is the bank vice president. "They" is the Pentagon, the Defense Intelligence Agency. They bring him to suburban Washington, where, according to this man, they came damn near [to] brutalizing him.

It was the wrong guy. It wasn't the bank vice president, it was one of the other guys that the Air Force intelligence officer had debriefed. But there was no convincing DIA that they had the wrong guy. To this day, they say they had that bank vice president.

And I'm here to tell you I know the name of the guy who was in the camp — the vice president. I know the name of the guy they took to Washington. It's not the same guy. I don't know where the bank vice president is. I don't know how to confirm the Potato John story. DIA doesn't want to know.

M.I.A.

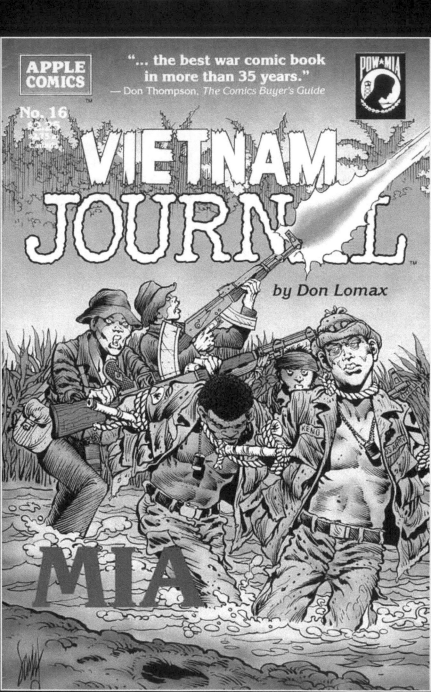

APPLE COMICS

POW★MIA

"... the best war comic book in more than 35 years."
— Don Thompson, *The Comics Buyer's Guide*

No. 16
$2.25
$2.75

VIETNAM JOURNAL

by Don Lomax

MIA

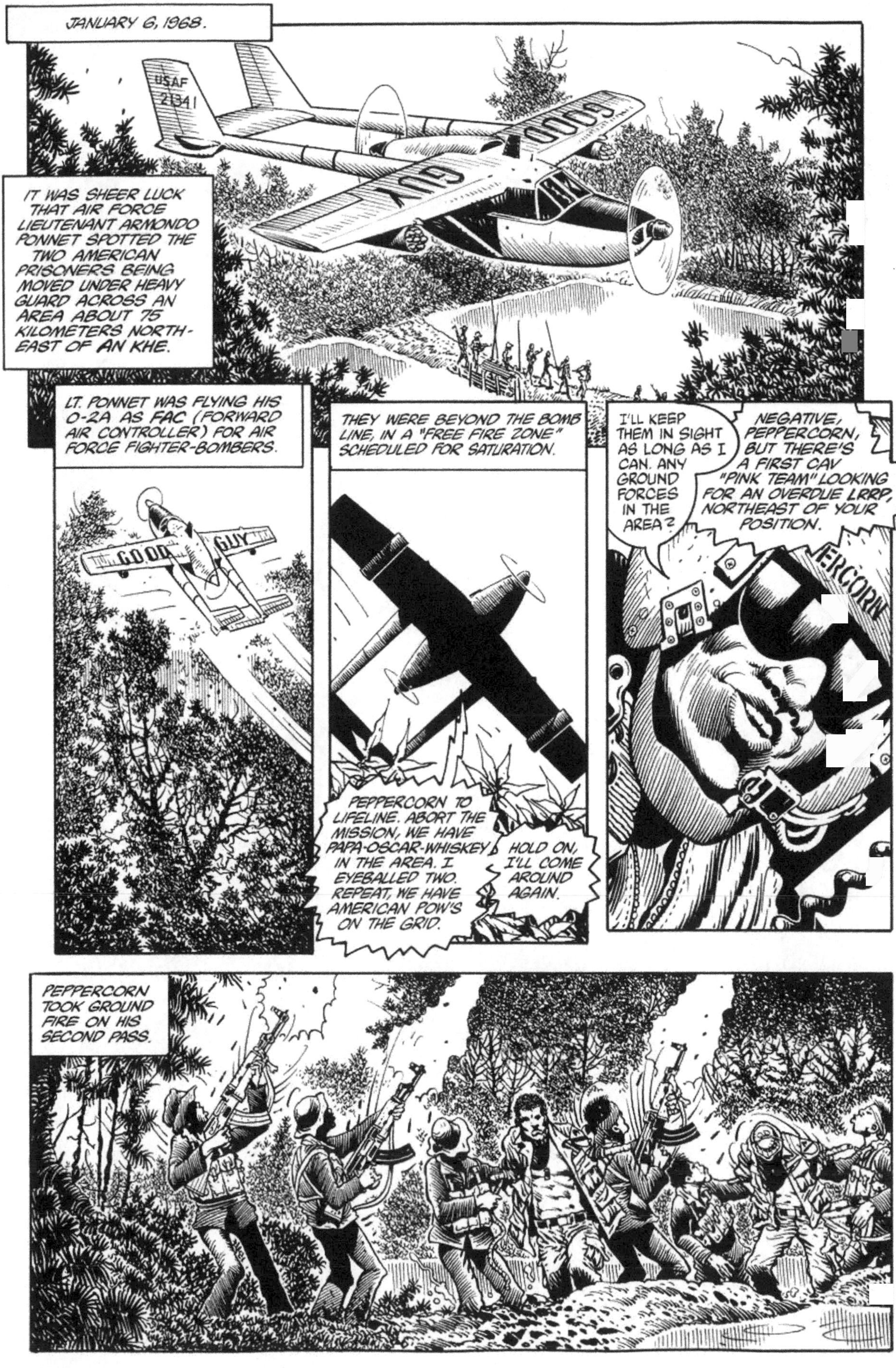
JANUARY 6, 1968.
USAF 21341
GOOD GUY
IT WAS SHEER LUCK THAT AIR FORCE LIEUTENANT ARMONDO PONNET SPOTTED THE TWO AMERICAN PRISONERS BEING MOVED UNDER HEAVY GUARD ACROSS AN AREA ABOUT 75 KILOMETERS NORTH-EAST OF AN KHE.
LT. PONNET WAS FLYING HIS O-2A AS FAC (FORWARD AIR CONTROLLER) FOR AIR FORCE FIGHTER-BOMBERS.
GOOD GUY
THEY WERE BEYOND THE BOMB LINE, IN A "FREE FIRE ZONE" SCHEDULED FOR SATURATION.
PEPPERCORN TO LIFELINE. ABORT THE MISSION, WE HAVE PAPA-OSCAR-WHISKEY IN THE AREA. I EYEBALLED TWO. REPEAT, WE HAVE AMERICAN POW'S ON THE GRID.
HOLD ON, I'LL COME AROUND AGAIN.
I'LL KEEP THEM IN SIGHT AS LONG AS I CAN. ANY GROUND FORCES IN THE AREA?
NEGATIVE, PEPPERCORN, BUT THERE'S A FIRST CAV "PINK TEAM" LOOKING FOR AN OVERDUE LRRP, NORTHEAST OF YOUR POSITION.
ERCORN
PEPPERCORN TOOK GROUND FIRE ON HIS SECOND PASS.

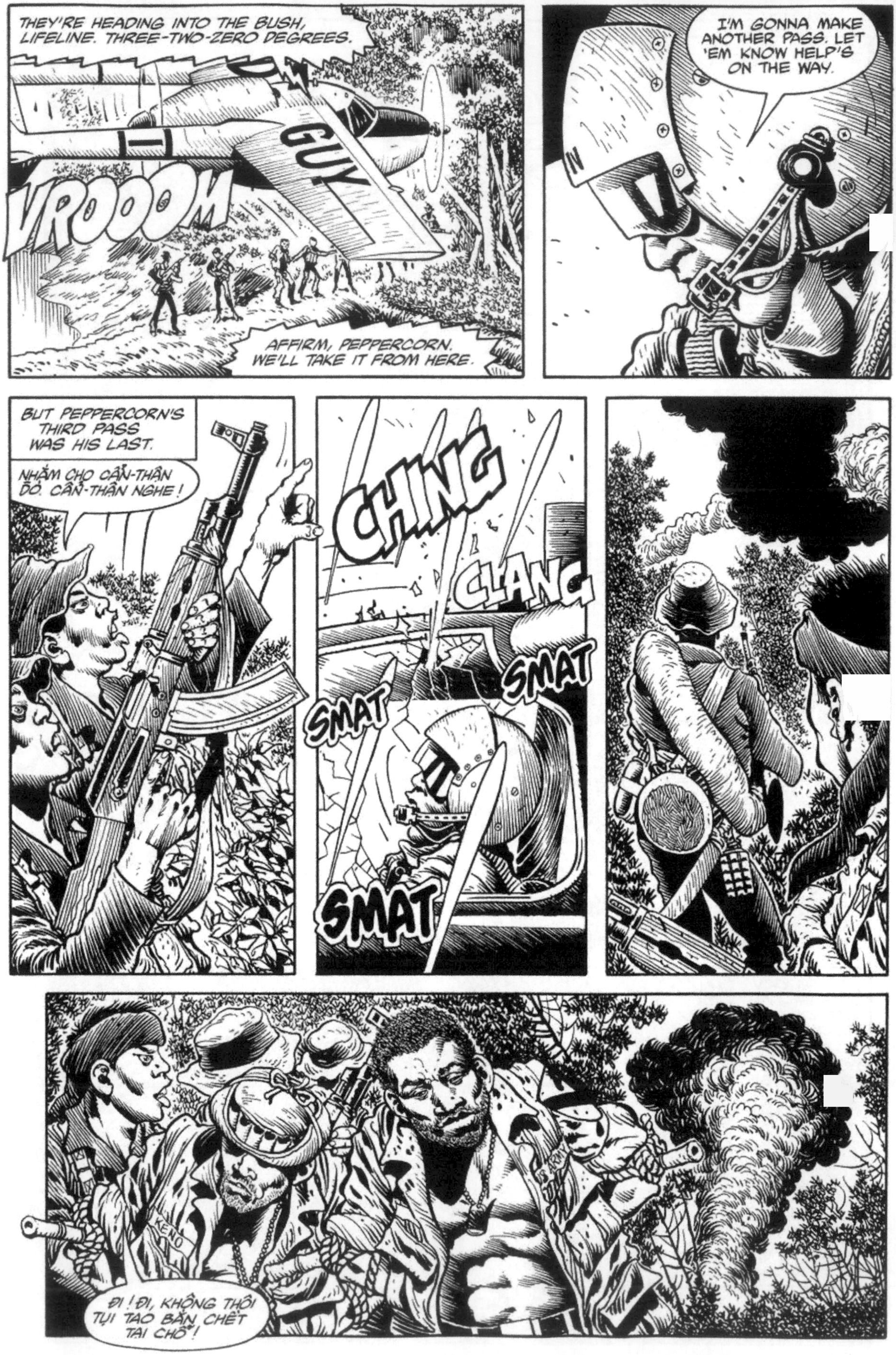

THEY'RE HEADING INTO THE BUSH, LIFELINE. THREE-TWO-ZERO DEGREES.
VROOOM
GUY
AFFIRM, PEPPERCORN. WE'LL TAKE IT FROM HERE.
I'M GONNA MAKE ANOTHER PASS. LET 'EM KNOW HELP'S ON THE WAY.
BUT PEPPERCORN'S THIRD PASS WAS HIS LAST.
NHẮM CHO CẨN-THẬN ĐỎ. CẨN-THẬN NGHE!
CHING
CLANG
SMAT
SMAT
SMAT
KENO
ĐI! ĐI, KHỘNG THÔI TỤI TAO BẮN CHẾT TẠI CHỖ!

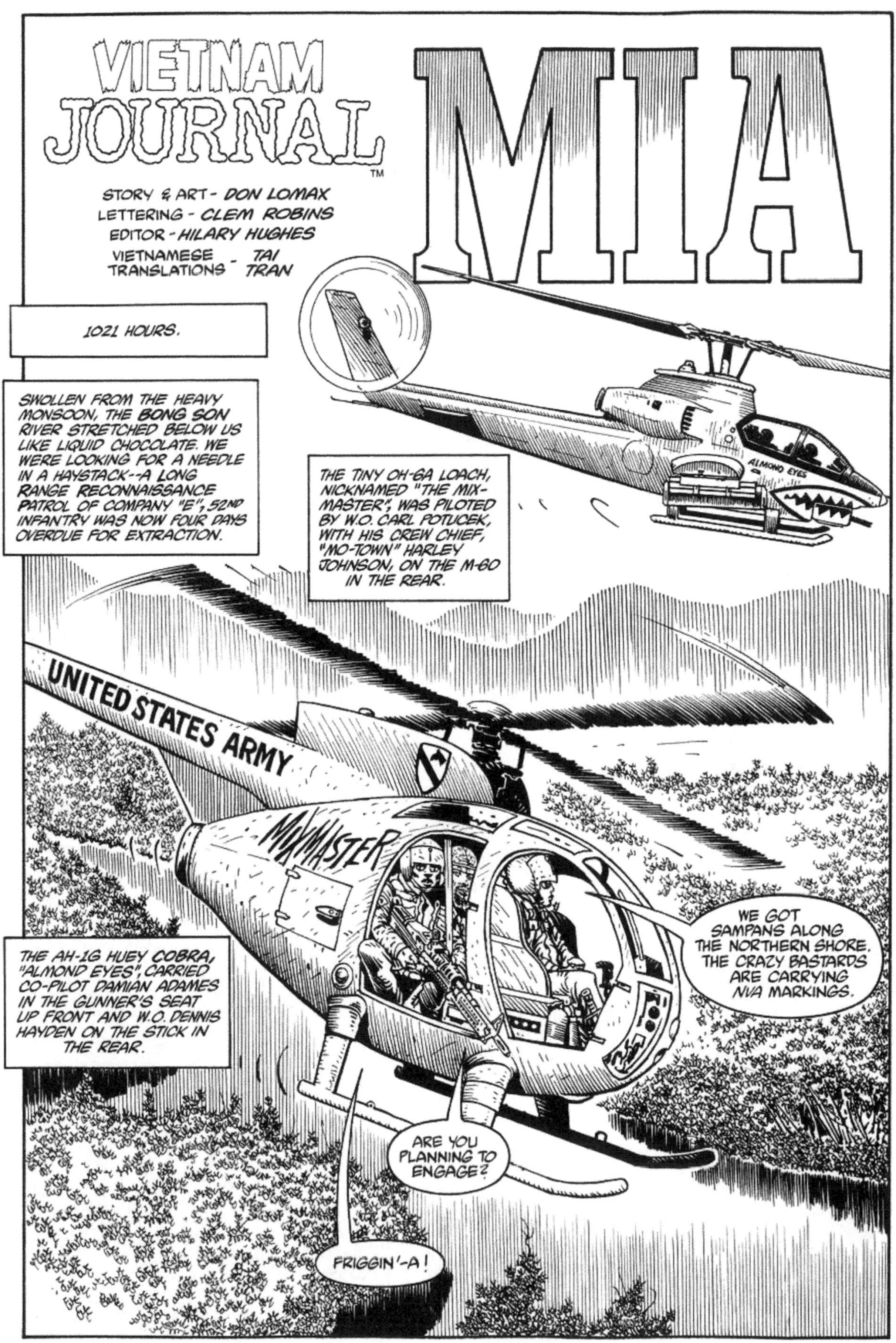
VIETNAM JOURNAL™
MIA
STORY & ART - DON LOMAX
LETTERING - CLEM ROBINS
EDITOR - HILARY HUGHES
VIETNAMESE TRANSLATIONS - TAI TRAN
1021 HOURS.
SWOLLEN FROM THE HEAVY MONSOON, THE BONG SON RIVER STRETCHED BELOW US LIKE LIQUID CHOCOLATE. WE WERE LOOKING FOR A NEEDLE IN A HAYSTACK--A LONG RANGE RECONNAISSANCE PATROL OF COMPANY "E", 52ND INFANTRY WAS NOW FOUR DAYS OVERDUE FOR EXTRACTION.
ALMOND EYES
THE TINY OH-6A LOACH, NICKNAMED "THE MIX-MASTER", WAS PILOTED BY W.O. CARL POTUCEK, WITH HIS CREW CHIEF, "MO-TOWN" HARLEY JOHNSON, ON THE M-60 IN THE REAR.
UNITED STATES ARMY
MIXMASTER
THE AH-1G HUEY COBRA, "ALMOND EYES", CARRIED CO-PILOT DAMIAN ADAMES IN THE GUNNER'S SEAT UP FRONT AND W.O. DENNIS HAYDEN ON THE STICK IN THE REAR.
WE GOT SAMPANS ALONG THE NORTHERN SHORE. THE CRAZY BASTARDS ARE CARRYING NVA MARKINGS.
ARE YOU PLANNING TO ENGAGE?
FRIGGIN'-A!

THE DOLDRUMS OF A FRUIT-LESS SEARCH CHANGED INSTANTLY TO THE ADRENALIN RUSH OF COMBAT.

HOLY--!!

HANG ON, JOURNAL! WHEN POTUCEK GOES INTO HIS SHUCK'N'JIVE--

POTUCEK ROLLED THE LOACH ON ITS RIGHT SIDE AND INITIATED A TIGHT SPIRAL DOWN TOWARD THE TREES.

THE MOST DANGEROUS TIME IS WHEN YOU'RE COMING DOWN FROM ALTITUDE. THAT'S WHEN THEY KNOW YOU'RE COMMITTING, AND IT'S THE BEST TIME FOR THEM TO CAP YOUR ASS.

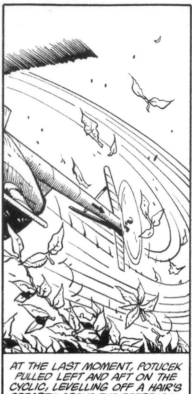

AT THE LAST MOMENT, POTUCEK PULLED LEFT AND AFT ON THE CYCLIC, LEVELLING OFF A HAIR'S BREADTH ABOVE THE TREETOPS.

THE "MIXMASTER'S" FIRST PASS WAS AT ABOUT 100 FEET OFF THE DECK, AT ABOUT 65 KNOTS.

THERE WAS AN OPENING, A TURMOIL OF FIRE, AND WE WERE BACK OVER THE TREES.

I GLIMPSED A BOAT, MAYBE, AND I HEARD THE BULLETS WHIZ PAST.

MIXMASTER TO ALMOND EYES, WE HAVE THREE SAMPANS UNLOADING IN THE TREES ALONG THE NORTH SHORE. I COUNTED 15 TO 20 REGULARS, WITH MORE IN THE TREES. THEY OPENED UP ON US WITH SOMETHING HEAVY, MAYBE A K-50.

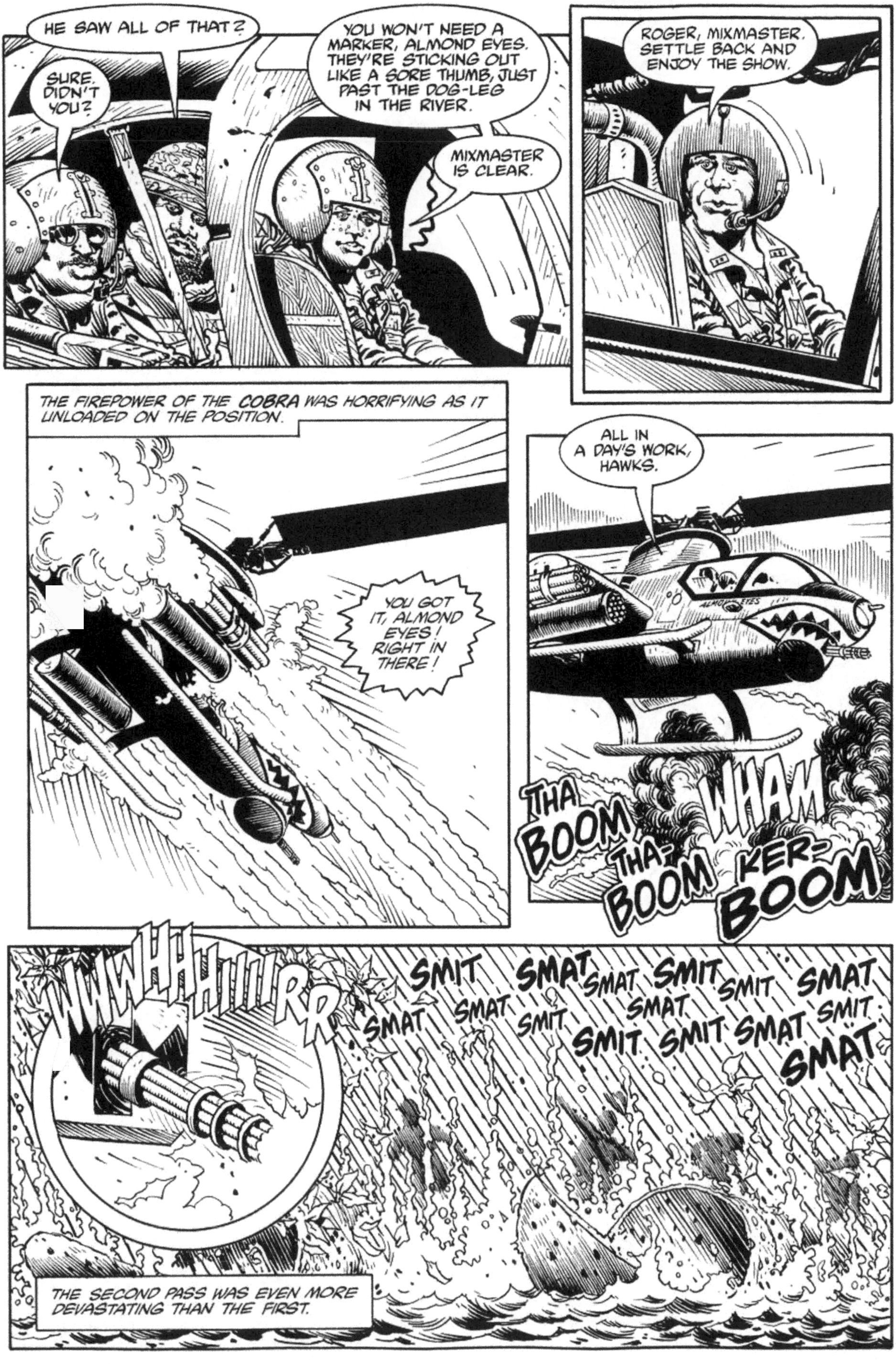
HE SAW ALL OF THAT?
SURE. DIDN'T YOU?
YOU WON'T NEED A MARKER, ALMOND EYES. THEY'RE STICKING OUT LIKE A SORE THUMB, JUST PAST THE DOG-LEG IN THE RIVER.
MIXMASTER IS CLEAR.
ROGER, MIXMASTER. SETTLE BACK AND ENJOY THE SHOW.
THE FIREPOWER OF THE COBRA WAS HORRIFYING AS IT UNLOADED ON THE POSITION.
YOU GOT IT, ALMOND EYES! RIGHT IN THERE!
ALL IN A DAY'S WORK, HAWKS.
THA BOOM THA-BOOM WHAM KER-BOOM
WWWHHHIIIRR
SMIT SMAT SMAT SMIT SMIT SMAT SMAT SMAT SMIT SMAT SMIT SMIT SMIT SMAT SMIT SMAT
THE SECOND PASS WAS EVEN MORE DEVASTATING THAN THE FIRST.

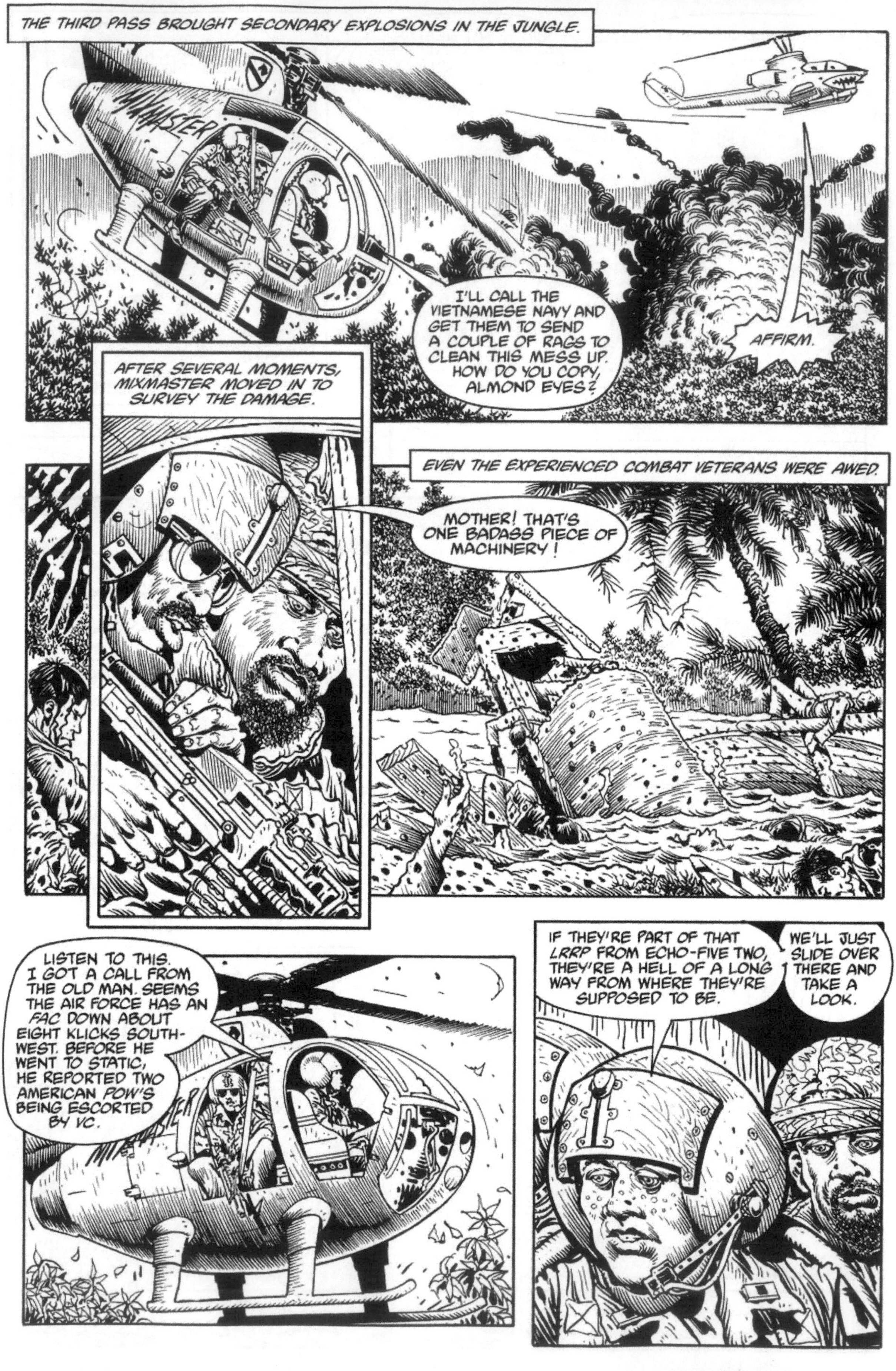

THE THIRD PASS BROUGHT SECONDARY EXPLOSIONS IN THE JUNGLE.
MIXMASTER
I'LL CALL THE VIETNAMESE NAVY AND GET THEM TO SEND A COUPLE OF RAGS TO CLEAN THIS MESS UP. HOW DO YOU COPY, ALMOND EYES?
AFFIRM.
AFTER SEVERAL MOMENTS, MIXMASTER MOVED IN TO SURVEY THE DAMAGE.
EVEN THE EXPERIENCED COMBAT VETERANS WERE AWED.
MOTHER! THAT'S ONE BADASS PIECE OF MACHINERY!
LISTEN TO THIS. I GOT A CALL FROM THE OLD MAN. SEEMS THE AIR FORCE HAS AN FAC DOWN ABOUT EIGHT KLICKS SOUTH-WEST. BEFORE HE WENT TO STATIC, HE REPORTED TWO AMERICAN POW'S BEING ESCORTED BY VC.
IF THEY'RE PART OF THAT LRRP FROM ECHO-FIVE TWO, THEY'RE A HELL OF A LONG WAY FROM WHERE THEY'RE SUPPOSED TO BE.
WE'LL JUST SLIDE OVER THERE AND TAKE A LOOK.

THE *FAC* PILOT, WITH SECOND-DEGREE BURNS AND TWO BROKEN LEGS, HAD ALREADY BEEN EVACUATED WHEN WE ARRIVED ON THE SCENE.

HARD TO BELIEVE ANYBODY COULD LIVE THROUGH THAT.

POTUCEK STARTED A CIRCULAR PATTERN IN THE DIRECTION THE POWs' CAPTORS HAD TAKEN.

THEY DIDN'T DO MUCH TO COVER THEIR TRAIL.

THEY MUST HAVE THOUGHT THE *FAC* DIDN'T HAVE A CHANCE TO REPORT IN.

WE FOLLOWED THE TRAIL FOR ABOUT A KILOMETER AND A HALF WHILE THE *COBRA* ORBITED SILENTLY ABOVE.

WHAT HAPPENS NOW?

THE TRAIL'S PETERED OUT, SO WE HEAD BACK TO REFUEL AND REARM.

IN THE MEANTIME, WE SCRAMBLE AN *ARP.* THAT'S AN *AERO RIFLE PLATOON,* TEAM BLUE. THEN WE COME BACK AND FIND OUR PEOPLE.

AND WE MAKE CHARLIE PAY.

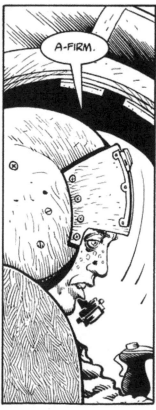

A-FIRM.

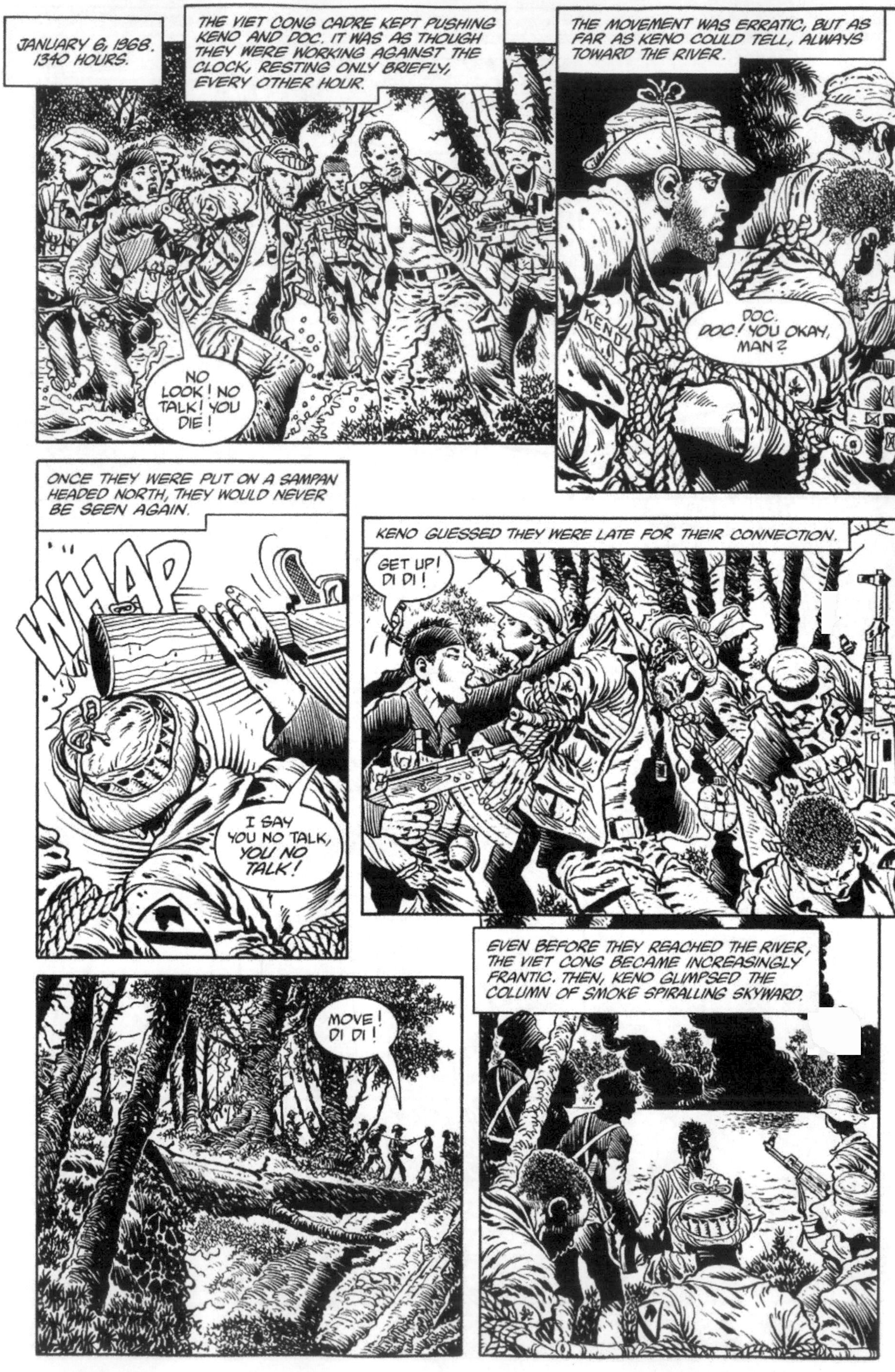

JANUARY 6, 1968. 1340 HOURS.
THE VIET CONG CADRE KEPT PUSHING KENO AND DOC. IT WAS AS THOUGH THEY WERE WORKING AGAINST THE CLOCK, RESTING ONLY BRIEFLY, EVERY OTHER HOUR.
NO LOOK! NO TALK! NO YOU DIE!
THE MOVEMENT WAS ERRATIC, BUT AS FAR AS KENO COULD TELL, ALWAYS TOWARD THE RIVER.
KENO
DOC. DOC! YOU OKAY, MAN?
ONCE THEY WERE PUT ON A SAMPAN HEADED NORTH, THEY WOULD NEVER BE SEEN AGAIN.
WHAP
I SAY YOU NO TALK, YOU NO TALK!
KENO GUESSED THEY WERE LATE FOR THEIR CONNECTION.
GET UP! DI DI!
MOVE! DI DI!
EVEN BEFORE THEY REACHED THE RIVER, THE VIET CONG BECAME INCREASINGLY FRANTIC. THEN, KENO GLIMPSED THE COLUMN OF SMOKE SPIRALLING SKYWARD.

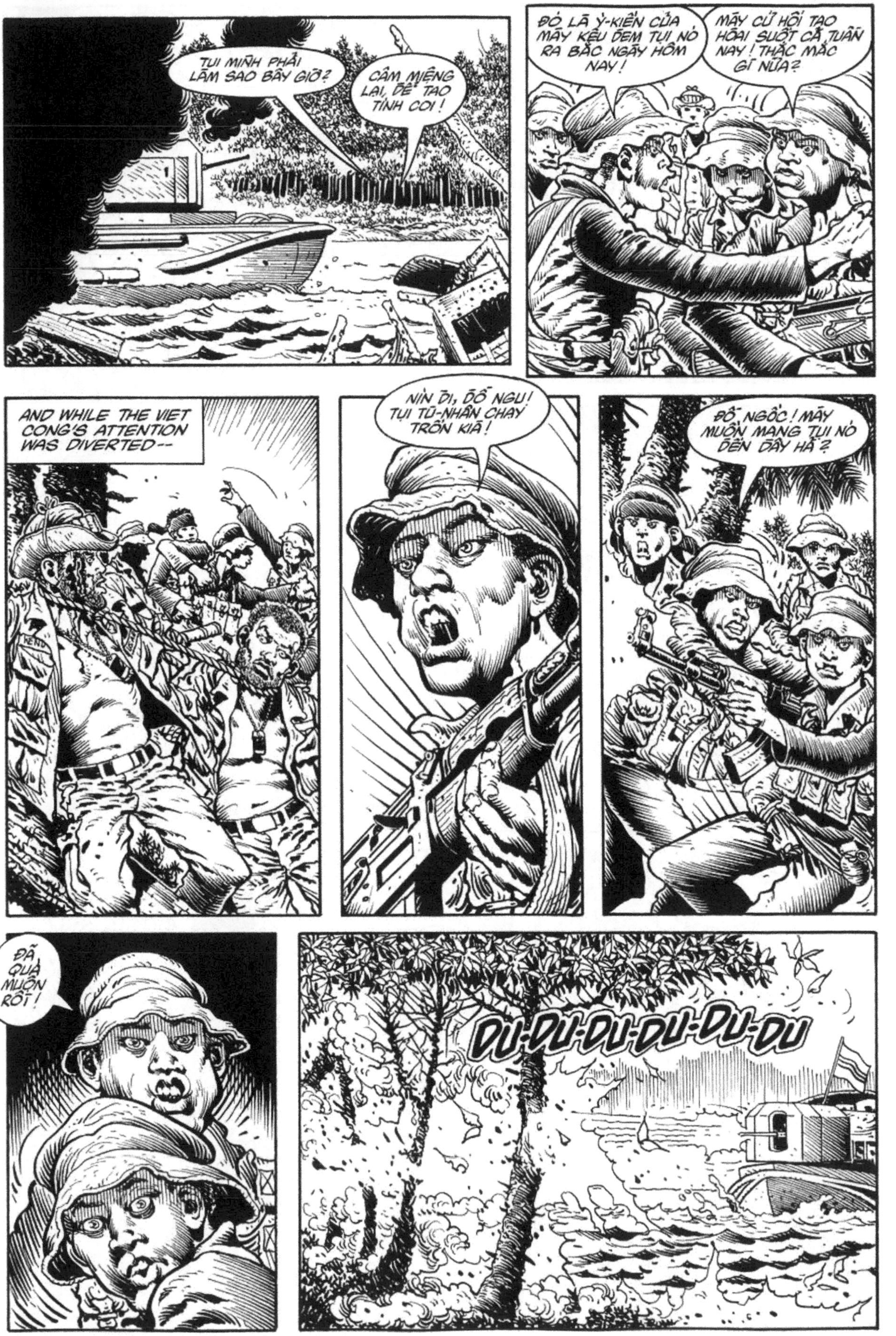
TUI MÌNH PHẢI LÀM SAO BÂY GIỜ?
CÂM MIỆNG LẠI, ĐỂ TAO TÍNH COI!
ĐÓ LÀ Ý-KIẾN CỦA MÀY KÊU ĐEM TỤI NÓ RA BẮC NGÀY HÔM NAY!
MÀY CỨ HỎI TAO HOÀI SUỐT CẢ TUẦN NAY! THẮC MẮC GÌ NỮA?
AND WHILE THE VIET CONG'S ATTENTION WAS DIVERTED--
NÌN ĐI, ĐỒ NGU! TỤI TÙ-NHÂN CHẠY TRỐN KÌA!
ĐỒ NGỐC! MÀY MUỐN MANG TỤI NÓ ĐẾN ĐÂY HẢ?
ĐÃ QUÁ MUỘN RỒI!
DU-DU-DU-DU-DU-DU-DU

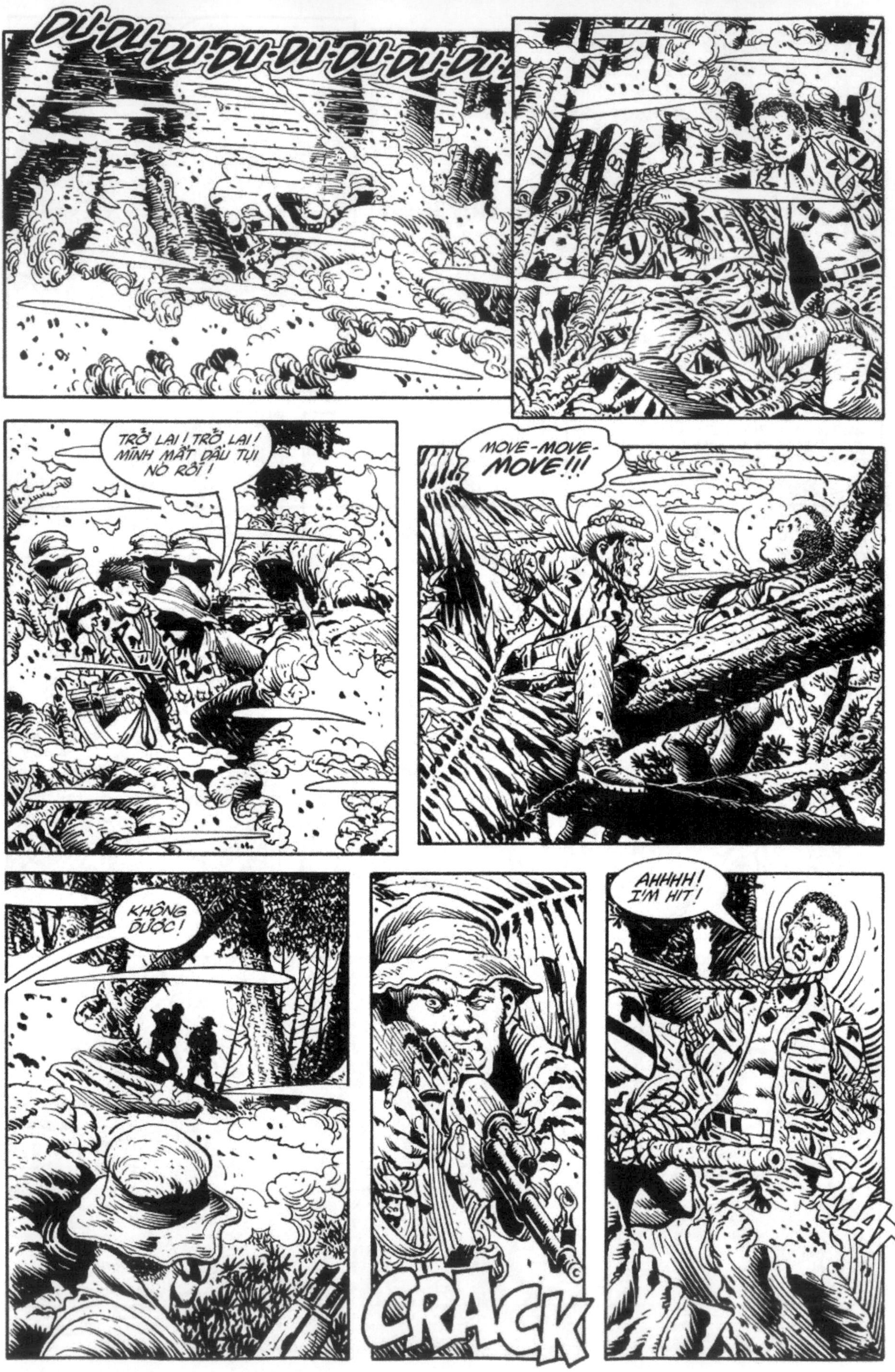
DU-DU-DU-DU-DU-DU-DU-DU-
TRỞ LẠI! TRỞ LẠI! MÌNH MẤT DẤU TỤI NÓ RỒI!
MOVE-MOVE-MOVE!!!
KHÔNG ĐƯỢC!
CRACK
AHHHH! I'M HIT!
SMAT

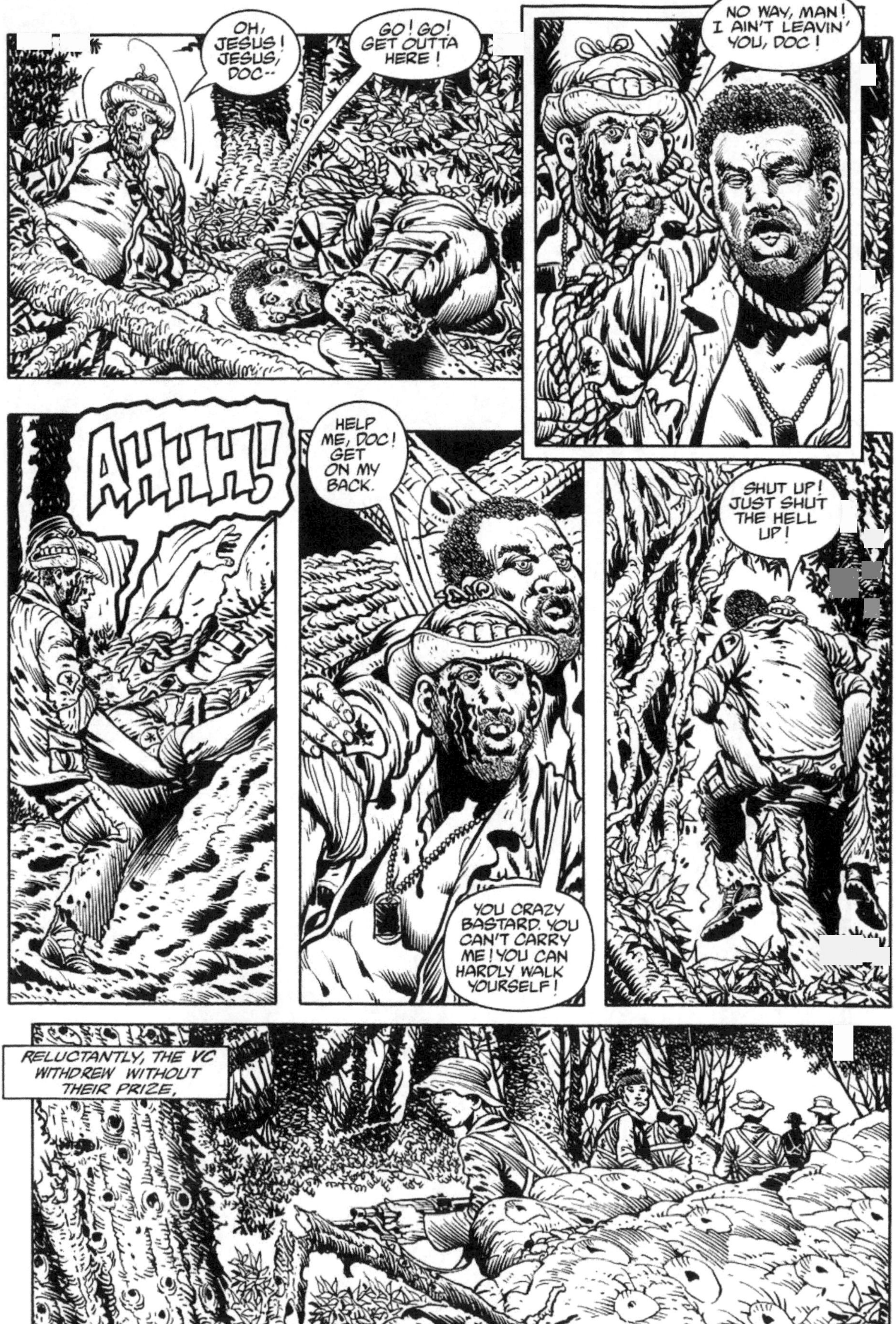
OH, JESUS! JESUS, DOC--
GO! GO! GET OUTTA HERE!
NO WAY, MAN! I AIN'T LEAVIN' YOU, DOC!
AHHH!
HELP ME, DOC! GET ON MY BACK.
YOU CRAZY BASTARD. YOU CAN'T CARRY ME! YOU CAN HARDLY WALK YOURSELF!
SHUT UP! JUST SHUT THE HELL UP!
RELUCTANTLY, THE VC WITHDREW WITHOUT THEIR PRIZE,

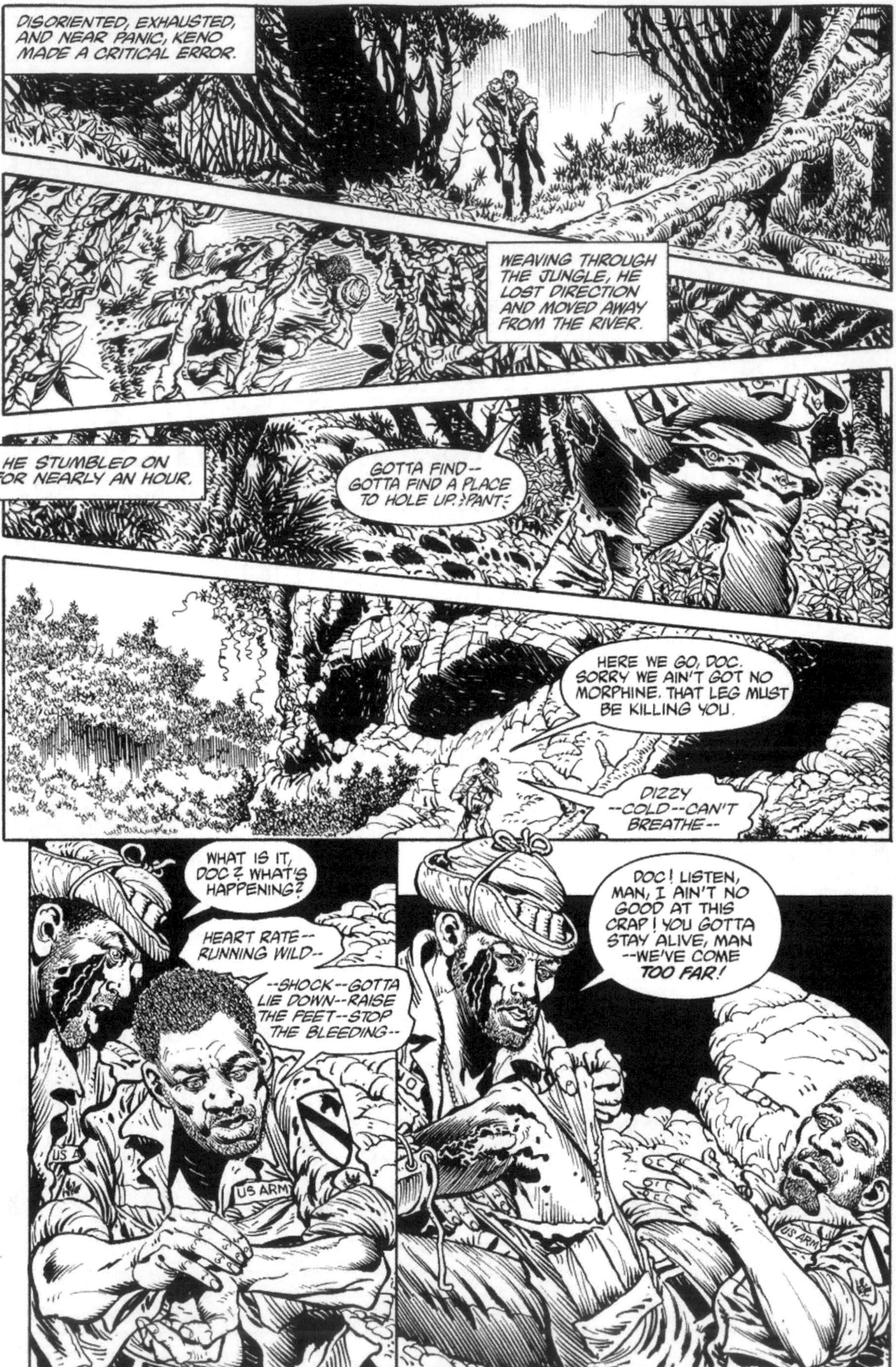
DISORIENTED, EXHAUSTED, AND NEAR PANIC, KENO MADE A CRITICAL ERROR.
WEAVING THROUGH THE JUNGLE, HE LOST DIRECTION AND MOVED AWAY FROM THE RIVER.
HE STUMBLED ON FOR NEARLY AN HOUR.
GOTTA FIND-- GOTTA FIND A PLACE TO HOLE UP. ≷PANT≷
HERE WE GO, DOC. SORRY WE AIN'T GOT NO MORPHINE. THAT LEG MUST BE KILLING YOU.
DIZZY --COLD--CAN'T BREATHE--
WHAT IS IT, DOC? WHAT'S HAPPENING?
HEART RATE-- RUNNING WILD--
--SHOCK--GOTTA LIE DOWN--RAISE THE FEET--STOP THE BLEEDING--
DOC! LISTEN, MAN, I AIN'T NO GOOD AT THIS CRAP! YOU GOTTA STAY ALIVE, MAN --WE'VE COME TOO FAR!

THE BLEEDING HAS ALMOST STOPPED ON ITS OWN, DOC --BUT YOU'VE LOST A LOT OF BLOOD, MAN!

GOTTA SPLINT IT >GASP< AND WRAP IT UP. FIND A COUPLE OF STICKS --TEAR MY PANTS LEG INTO STRIPS. BE CAREFUL YOU DON'T START IT BLEEDING AGAIN.

SHORTLY.

THAT'S THE BEST I CAN DO. I GOTTA GET SOME WATER, BUT I GOT NOTHIN' TO CARRY IT IN.

SURE YOU DO.

WHAT?

YOUR BOOT.

KENO TRIED SEVERAL TIMES TO CARRY WATER THE 50 YARDS FROM THE STREAM IN HIS HANDS, BUT IT ALWAYS LEAKED OUT.

HE FINALLY GAVE UP AND TOOK DOC'S SUGGESTION.

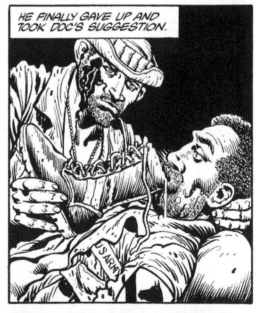

BY LATE AFTERNOON, DOC'S THIRST WAS QUENCHED FOR THE TIME BEING, AND THEY BOTH RESTED.

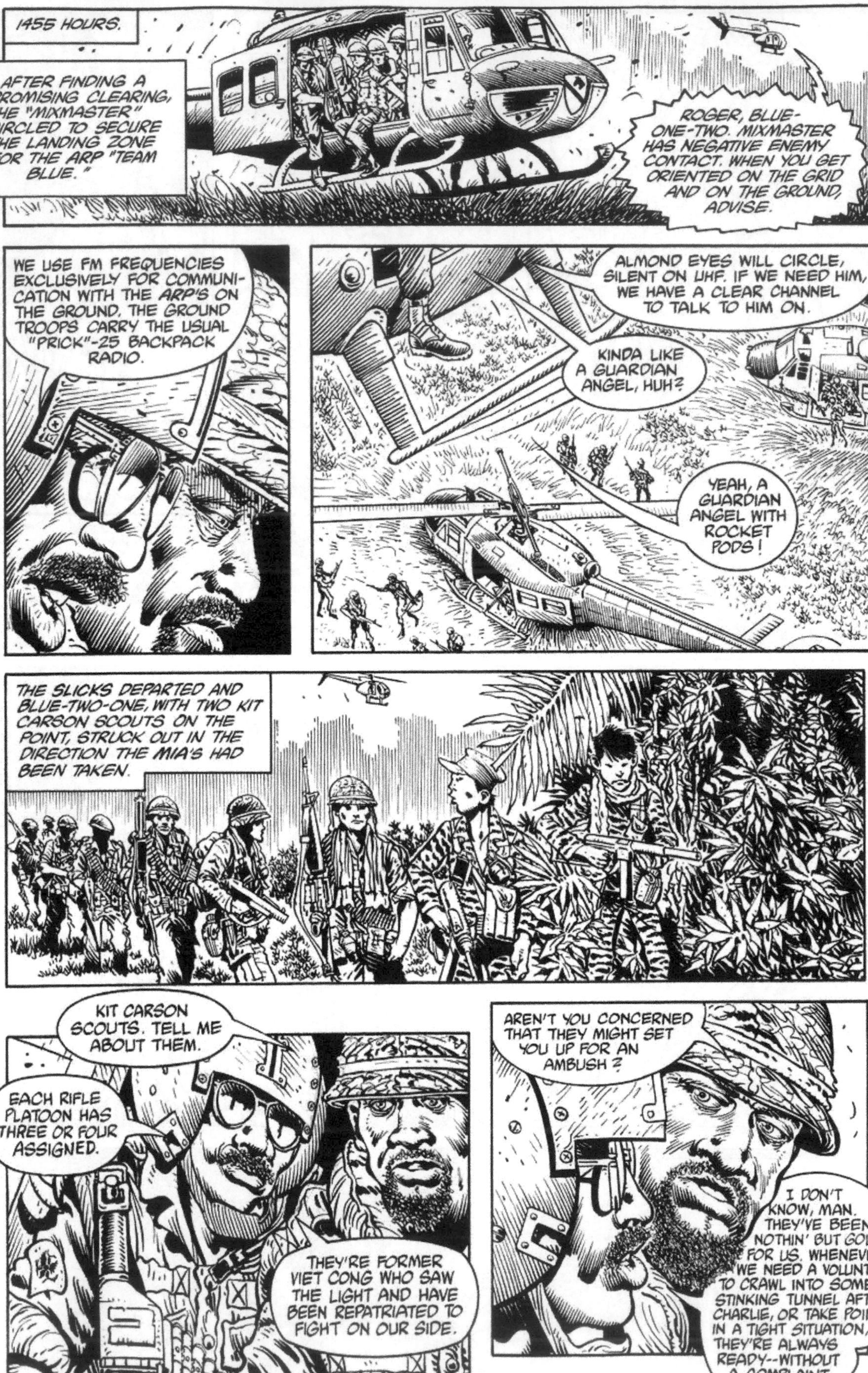
1455 HOURS.
AFTER FINDING A PROMISING CLEARING, THE "MIXMASTER" CIRCLED TO SECURE THE LANDING ZONE FOR THE ARP "TEAM BLUE."
ROGER, BLUE-ONE-TWO. MIXMASTER HAS NEGATIVE ENEMY CONTACT. WHEN YOU GET ORIENTED ON THE GRID AND ON THE GROUND, ADVISE.
WE USE FM FREQUENCIES EXCLUSIVELY FOR COMMUNICATION WITH THE ARP'S ON THE GROUND. THE GROUND TROOPS CARRY THE USUAL "PRICK"-25 BACKPACK RADIO.
ALMOND EYES WILL CIRCLE, SILENT ON UHF. IF WE NEED HIM, WE HAVE A CLEAR CHANNEL TO TALK TO HIM ON.
KINDA LIKE A GUARDIAN ANGEL, HUH?
YEAH, A GUARDIAN ANGEL WITH ROCKET PODS!
THE SLICKS DEPARTED AND BLUE-TWO-ONE, WITH TWO KIT CARSON SCOUTS ON THE POINT, STRUCK OUT IN THE DIRECTION THE MIA'S HAD BEEN TAKEN.
KIT CARSON SCOUTS. TELL ME ABOUT THEM.
EACH RIFLE PLATOON HAS THREE OR FOUR ASSIGNED.
THEY'RE FORMER VIET CONG WHO SAW THE LIGHT AND HAVE BEEN REPATRIATED TO FIGHT ON OUR SIDE.
AREN'T YOU CONCERNED THAT THEY MIGHT SET YOU UP FOR AN AMBUSH?
I DON'T KNOW, MAN. THEY'VE BEEN NOTHIN' BUT GOLD FOR US. WHENEVER WE NEED A VOLUNTEER TO CRAWL INTO SOME STINKING TUNNEL AFTER CHARLIE, OR TAKE POINT IN A TIGHT SITUATION, THEY'RE ALWAYS READY--WITHOUT A COMPLAINT.

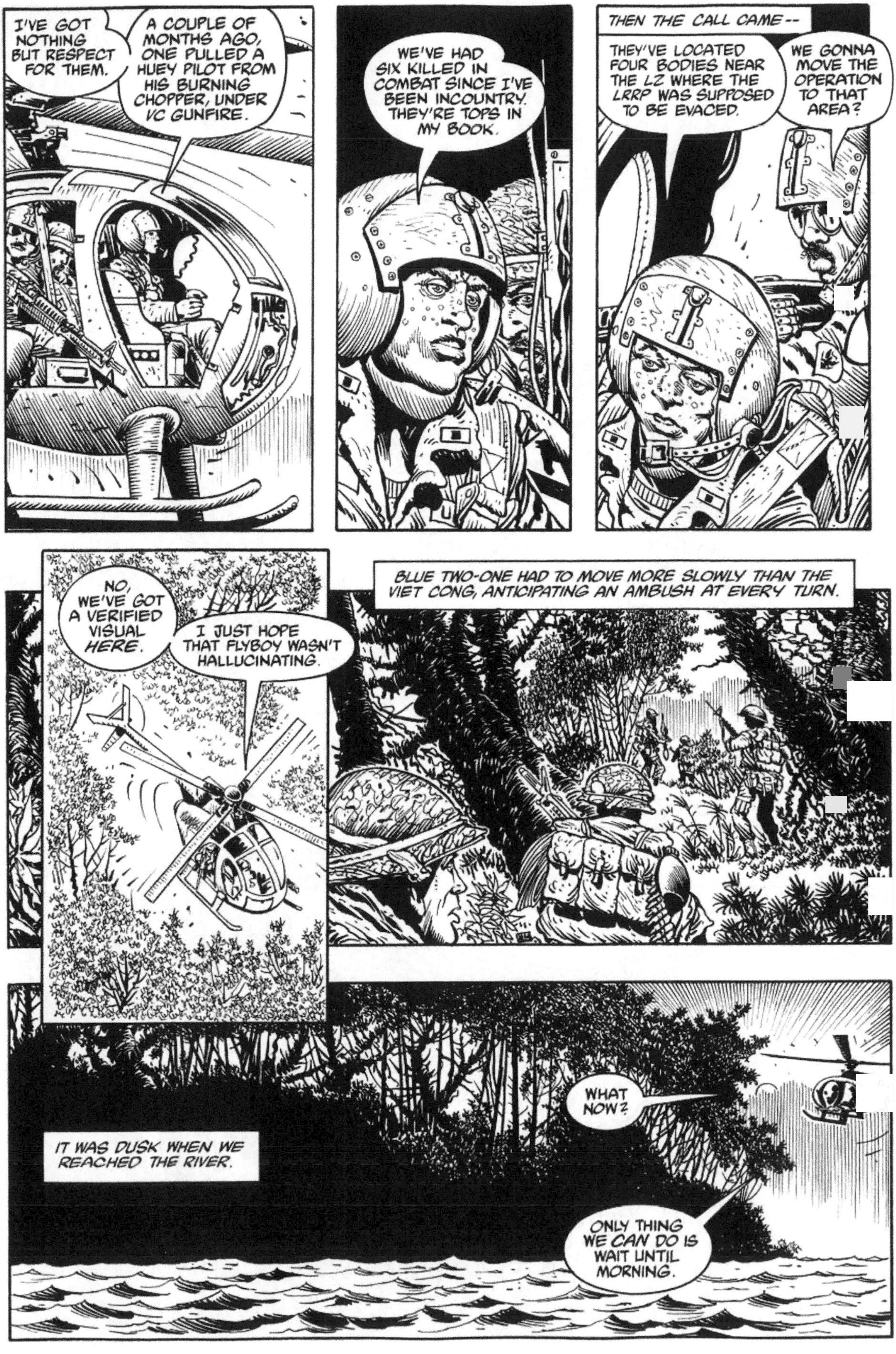
I'VE GOT NOTHING BUT RESPECT FOR THEM.
A COUPLE OF MONTHS AGO, ONE PULLED A HUEY PILOT FROM HIS BURNING CHOPPER, UNDER VC GUNFIRE.
WE'VE HAD SIX KILLED IN COMBAT SINCE I'VE BEEN INCOUNTRY. THEY'RE TOPS IN MY BOOK.
THEN THE CALL CAME--
THEY'VE LOCATED FOUR BODIES NEAR THE LZ WHERE THE LRRP WAS SUPPOSED TO BE EVACED.
WE GONNA MOVE THE OPERATION TO THAT AREA?
NO, WE'VE GOT A VERIFIED VISUAL HERE.
I JUST HOPE THAT FLYBOY WASN'T HALLUCINATING.
BLUE TWO-ONE HAD TO MOVE MORE SLOWLY THAN THE VIET CONG, ANTICIPATING AN AMBUSH AT EVERY TURN.
IT WAS DUSK WHEN WE REACHED THE RIVER.
WHAT NOW?
ONLY THING WE CAN DO IS WAIT UNTIL MORNING.

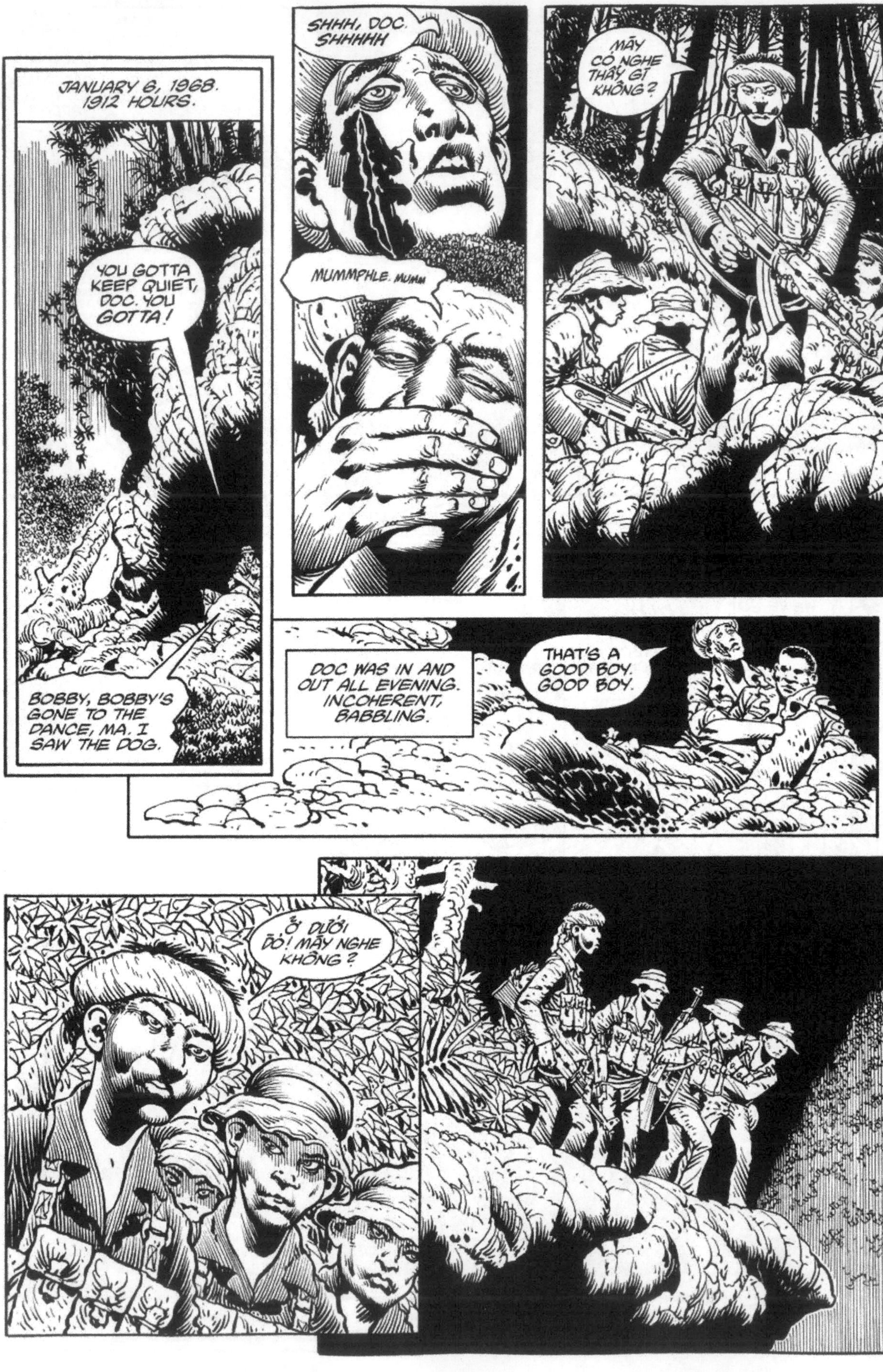
JANUARY 6, 1968.
1912 HOURS.
YOU GOTTA KEEP QUIET, DOC. YOU GOTTA!
BOBBY, BOBBY'S GONE TO THE DANCE, MA. I SAW THE DOG.
SHHH, DOC. SHHHHH
MUMMPHLE. MUMM
MÃY CÓ NGHE THẤY GÌ KHÔNG?
DOC WAS IN AND OUT ALL EVENING. INCOHERENT, BABBLING.
THAT'S A GOOD BOY. GOOD BOY.
Ở DƯỚI ĐÓ! MÃY NGHE KHÔNG?

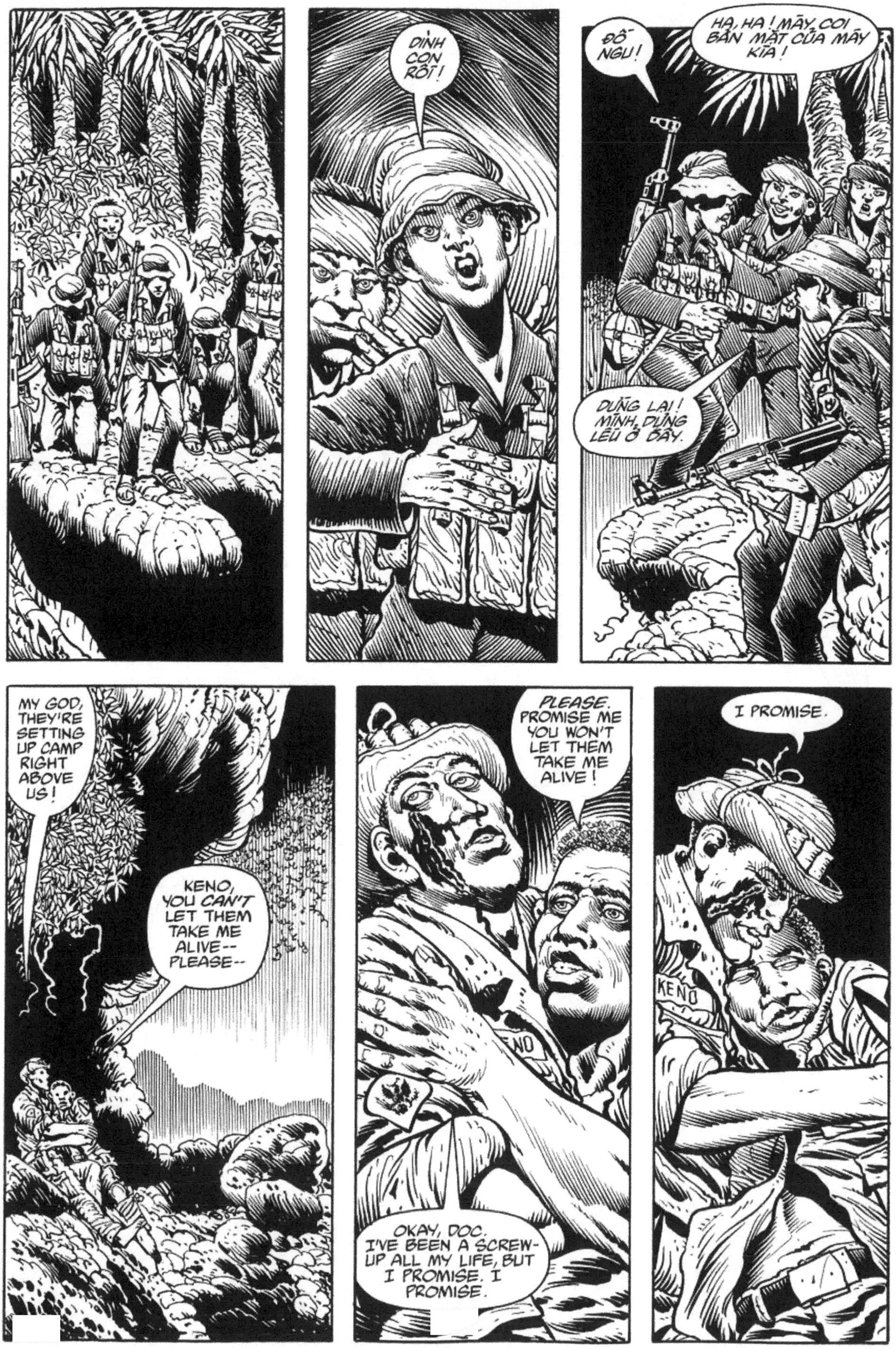
DÍNH CON RỒI!
ĐỒ NGU!
HA, HA! MÀY, COI BẢN MẶT CỦA MÀY KÌA!
DỪNG LẠI! MÌNH, DỰNG LỀU Ở ĐÂY.
MY GOD, THEY'RE SETTING UP CAMP RIGHT ABOVE US!
KENO, YOU *CAN'T* LET THEM TAKE ME ALIVE-- PLEASE--
PLEASE. PROMISE ME YOU WON'T LET THEM TAKE ME ALIVE!
OKAY, DOC. I'VE BEEN A SCREW-UP ALL MY LIFE, BUT I PROMISE. I PROMISE.
I PROMISE.
KENO
KENO

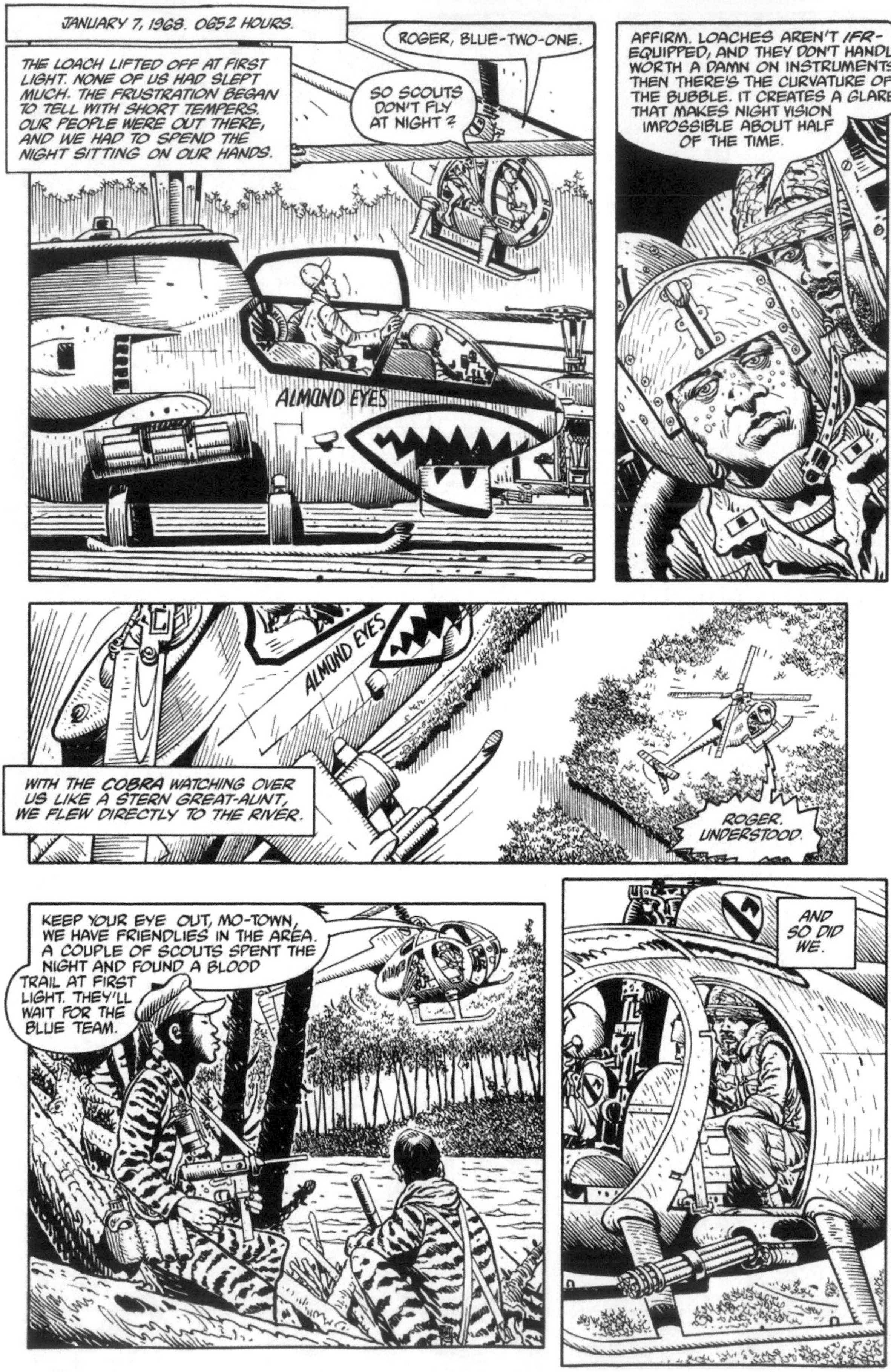

JANUARY 7, 1968. 0652 HOURS.
THE LOACH LIFTED OFF AT FIRST LIGHT. NONE OF US HAD SLEPT MUCH. THE FRUSTRATION BEGAN TO TELL WITH SHORT TEMPERS. OUR PEOPLE WERE OUT THERE, AND WE HAD TO SPEND THE NIGHT SITTING ON OUR HANDS.
ROGER, BLUE-TWO-ONE.
SO SCOUTS DON'T FLY AT NIGHT?
ALMOND EYES
AFFIRM. LOACHES AREN'T IFR-EQUIPPED, AND THEY DON'T HANDLE WORTH A DAMN ON INSTRUMENTS. THEN THERE'S THE CURVATURE OF THE BUBBLE. IT CREATES A GLARE THAT MAKES NIGHT VISION IMPOSSIBLE ABOUT HALF OF THE TIME.
ALMOND EYES
WITH THE COBRA WATCHING OVER US LIKE A STERN GREAT-AUNT, WE FLEW DIRECTLY TO THE RIVER.
ROGER. UNDERSTOOD.
KEEP YOUR EYE OUT, MO-TOWN, WE HAVE FRIENDLIES IN THE AREA. A COUPLE OF SCOUTS SPENT THE NIGHT AND FOUND A BLOOD TRAIL AT FIRST LIGHT. THEY'LL WAIT FOR THE BLUE TEAM.
AND SO DID WE.

KENO'S FIRST MOVE ON AWAKENING WAS TO CHECK ON DOC.

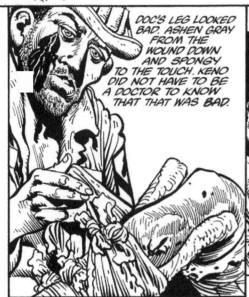

DOC'S LEG LOOKED BAD. ASHEN GRAY FROM THE WOUND DOWN AND SPONGY TO THE TOUCH. KENO DID NOT HAVE TO BE A DOCTOR TO KNOW THAT THAT WAS BAD.

HE KNEW DOC NEEDED WATER, BUT THOUGH HE HAD NOT HEARD ANY MOVEMENT FROM ABOVE, THE VIET CONG PATROL COULD BE SLEEPING JUST ABOVE THEIR POSITION.

=MOAN=

EASY, DOC.

HE KNEW THAT DOC'S ONLY CHANCE WAS FOR HIM TO WALK OUT AND BRING BACK HELP.

THEN--

TOÀN BIÊN-PHÒNG VIỆT-CỘNG ĐÃ NGHĨ ĐÊM NƠI ĐÂY.

ĐƯỜNG MÒN MÁU CHẬM-DỨT VẢI "MÉT" Ở PHÍA SAU.

KENO, KNOWING ONLY THAT THE VOICES WERE VIETNAMESE, ASSUMED THAT THE KIT CARSON SCOUTS WERE THE VIET CONG PATROL, RETURNING.

THỬ XUỐNG PHÍA DƯỚI COI. TUI NÓ QUANH-QUẨN ĐẦU ĐÂY THÔI.

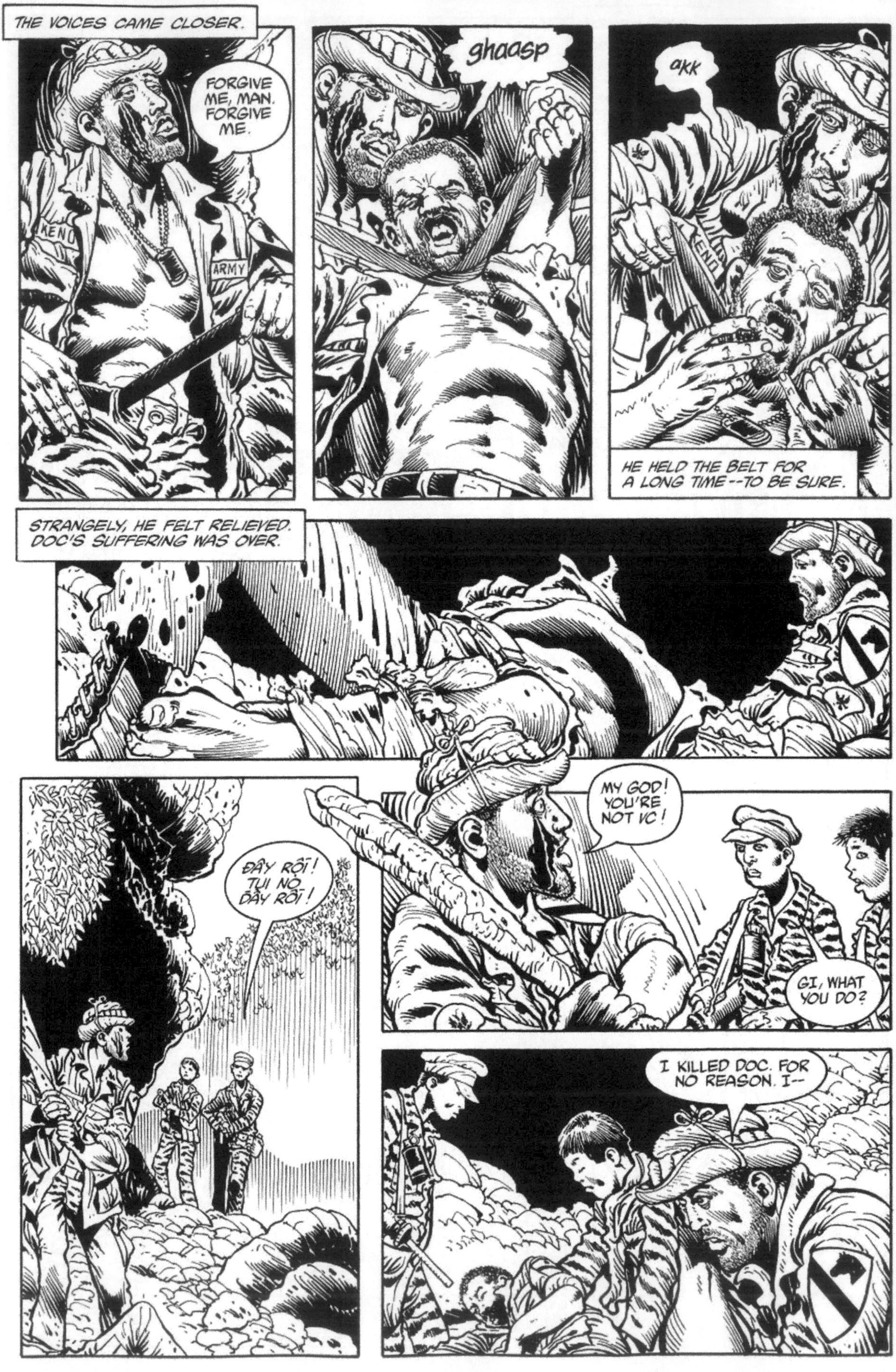
THE VOICES CAME CLOSER.
FORGIVE ME, MAN. FORGIVE ME.
KENO
ARMY
ghaasp
akk
HE HELD THE BELT FOR A LONG TIME--TO BE SURE.
STRANGELY, HE FELT RELIEVED. DOC'S SUFFERING WAS OVER.
ĐÂY RỒI! TUI NÓ ĐÂY RỒI!
MY GOD! YOU'RE NOT VC!
GI, WHAT YOU DO?
I KILLED DOC. FOR NO REASON. I--

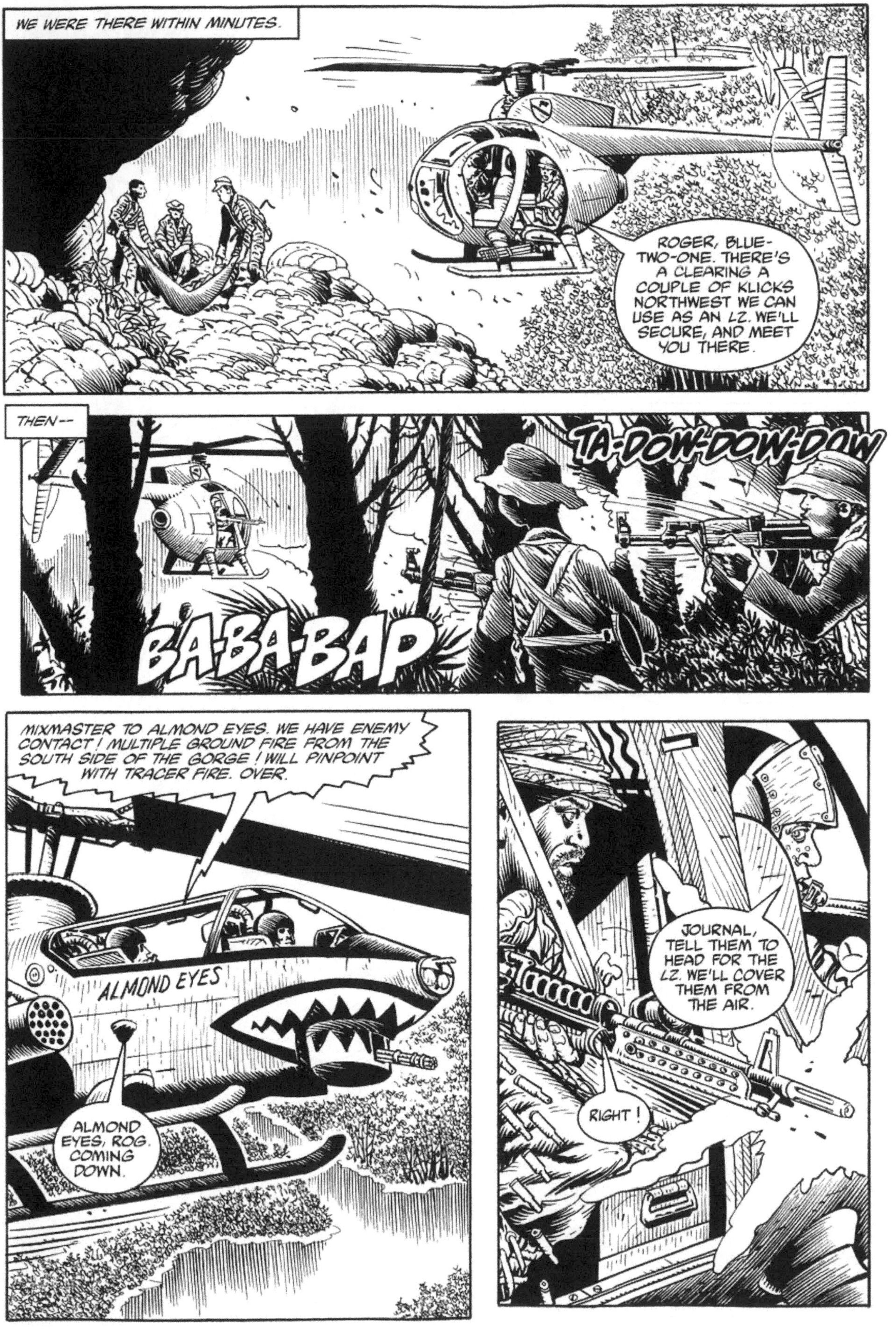
WE WERE THERE WITHIN MINUTES.
ROGER, BLUE-TWO-ONE. THERE'S A CLEARING A COUPLE OF KLICKS NORTHWEST WE CAN USE AS AN LZ. WE'LL SECURE, AND MEET YOU THERE.
THEN--
TA-DOW-DOW-DOW
BA-BA-BAP
MIXMASTER TO ALMOND EYES. WE HAVE ENEMY CONTACT! MULTIPLE GROUND FIRE FROM THE SOUTH SIDE OF THE GORGE! WILL PINPOINT WITH TRACER FIRE. OVER.
ALMOND EYES
ALMOND EYES, ROG. COMING DOWN.
JOURNAL, TELL THEM TO HEAD FOR THE LZ. WE'LL COVER THEM FROM THE AIR.
RIGHT!

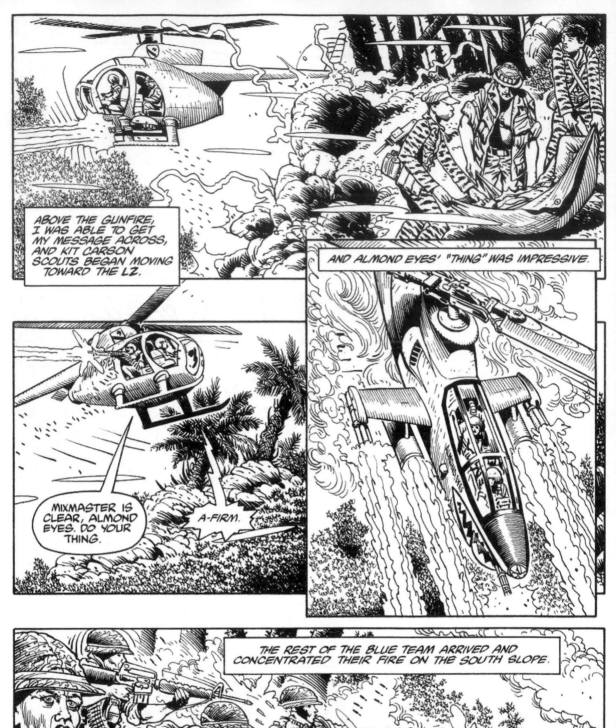

ABOVE THE GUNFIRE, I WAS ABLE TO GET MY MESSAGE ACROSS, AND KIT CARSON SCOUTS BEGAN MOVING TOWARD THE *LZ*.

AND ALMOND EYES' "THING" WAS IMPRESSIVE.

MIXMASTER IS CLEAR, ALMOND EYES. DO YOUR THING.

A-FIRM.

THE REST OF THE BLUE TEAM ARRIVED AND CONCENTRATED THEIR FIRE ON THE SOUTH SLOPE.

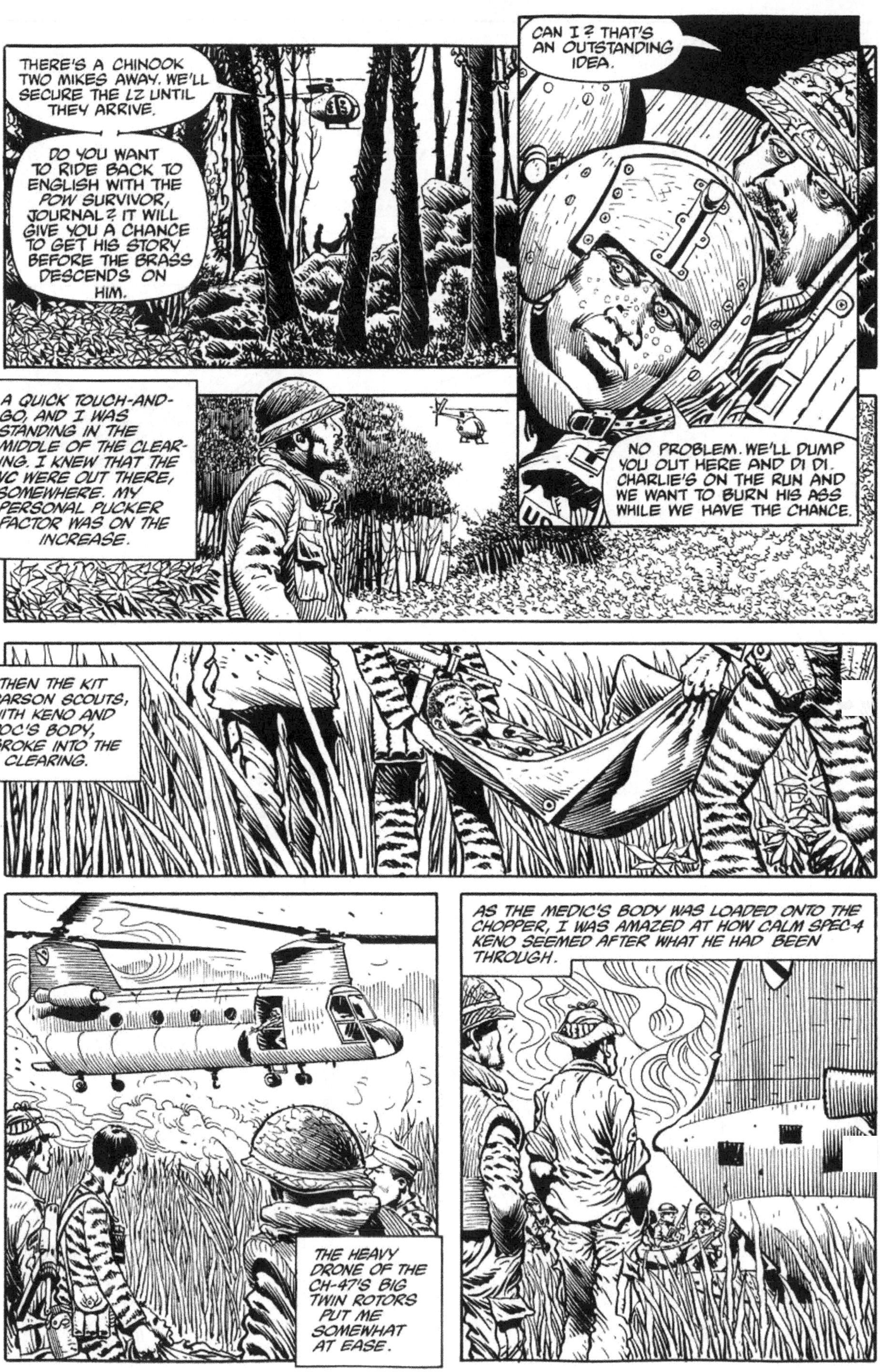
THERE'S A CHINOOK TWO MIKES AWAY. WE'LL SECURE THE LZ UNTIL THEY ARRIVE.
DO YOU WANT TO RIDE BACK TO ENGLISH WITH THE POW SURVIVOR, JOURNAL? IT WILL GIVE YOU A CHANCE TO GET HIS STORY BEFORE THE BRASS DESCENDS ON HIM.
CAN I? THAT'S AN OUTSTANDING IDEA.
NO PROBLEM. WE'LL DUMP YOU OUT HERE AND DI DI. CHARLIE'S ON THE RUN AND WE WANT TO BURN HIS ASS WHILE WE HAVE THE CHANCE.
A QUICK TOUCH-AND-GO, AND I WAS STANDING IN THE MIDDLE OF THE CLEARING. I KNEW THAT THE VC WERE OUT THERE, SOMEWHERE. MY PERSONAL PUCKER FACTOR WAS ON THE INCREASE.
THEN THE KIT CARSON SCOUTS, WITH KENO AND DOC'S BODY, BROKE INTO THE CLEARING.
THE HEAVY DRONE OF THE CH-47'S BIG TWIN ROTORS PUT ME SOMEWHAT AT EASE.
AS THE MEDIC'S BODY WAS LOADED ONTO THE CHOPPER, I WAS AMAZED AT HOW CALM SPEC-4 KENO SEEMED AFTER WHAT HE HAD BEEN THROUGH.

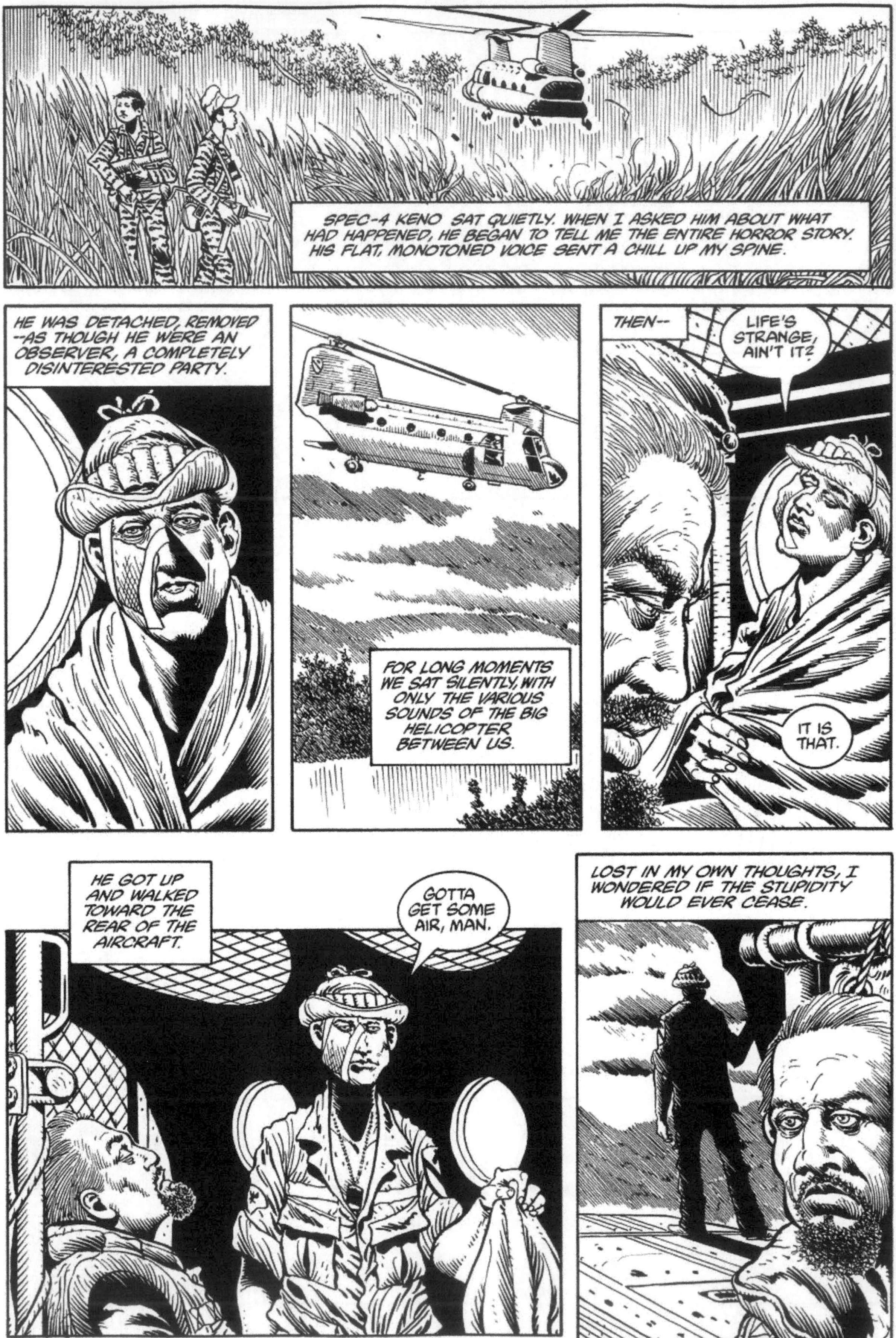
SPEC-4 KENO SAT QUIETLY. WHEN I ASKED HIM ABOUT WHAT HAD HAPPENED, HE BEGAN TO TELL ME THE ENTIRE HORROR STORY. HIS FLAT, MONOTONED VOICE SENT A CHILL UP MY SPINE.
HE WAS DETACHED, REMOVED --AS THOUGH HE WERE AN OBSERVER, A COMPLETELY DISINTERESTED PARTY.
FOR LONG MOMENTS WE SAT SILENTLY, WITH ONLY THE VARIOUS SOUNDS OF THE BIG HELICOPTER BETWEEN US.
THEN--
LIFE'S STRANGE, AIN'T IT?
IT IS THAT.
HE GOT UP AND WALKED TOWARD THE REAR OF THE AIRCRAFT.
GOTTA GET SOME AIR, MAN.
LOST IN MY OWN THOUGHTS, I WONDERED IF THE STUPIDITY WOULD EVER CEASE.

ONE MOMENT HE WAS STANDING THERE. THE NEXT HE WAS GONE.

WHAT--?

I RUSHED TO THE REAR, NEARLY GOING OUT THE DOOR MYSELF IN MY ALARM.

OH, NO--

OH GOD, KID. I SHOULD HAVE SEEN IT COMING.

I SHOULD HAVE SEEN IT.

GOLDEN GOOSE
RESTAURANT

YOU'RE A HARD MAN TO FIND, JOURNAL.

YOU BEEN LOOKING FOR ME? AW, AIN'T THAT SWEET?

HAVE YOU MET MY LITTLE BUDDY? WHAT'S YOUR NAME AGAIN?

POTUCEK AND MO-TOWN FOUND ME TWO DAYS LATER IN THE GOLDEN GOOSE BAR, ON ONE OF BONG SON'S FILTHY BACK STREETS.

HO.

KEITHAMMER

POTUCEK   US

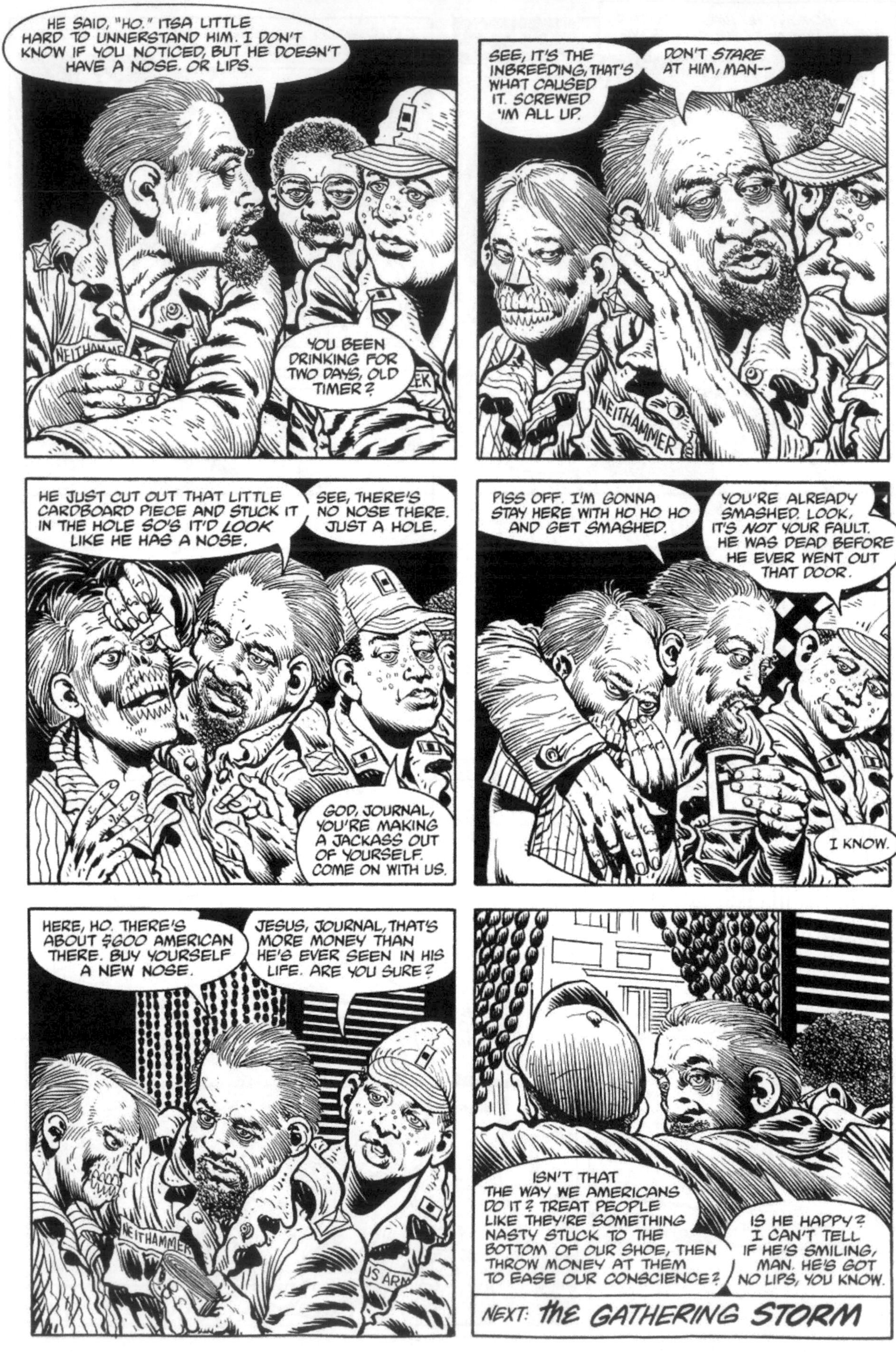
HE SAID, "HO." ITSA LITTLE HARD TO UNNERSTAND HIM. I DON'T KNOW IF YOU NOTICED, BUT HE DOESN'T HAVE A NOSE. OR LIPS.
NEITHAMMER
YOU BEEN DRINKING FOR TWO DAYS, OLD TIMER?
SEE, IT'S THE INBREEDING, THAT'S WHAT CAUSED IT. SCREWED 'IM ALL UP.
DON'T STARE AT HIM, MAN--
NEITHAMMER
HE JUST CUT OUT THAT LITTLE CARDBOARD PIECE AND STUCK IT IN THE HOLE SO'S IT'D LOOK LIKE HE HAS A NOSE.
SEE, THERE'S NO NOSE THERE. JUST A HOLE.
GOD, JOURNAL, YOU'RE MAKING A JACKASS OUT OF YOURSELF. COME ON WITH US.
PISS OFF. I'M GONNA STAY HERE WITH HO HO HO AND GET SMASHED.
YOU'RE ALREADY SMASHED. LOOK, IT'S NOT YOUR FAULT. HE WAS DEAD BEFORE HE EVER WENT OUT THAT DOOR.
I KNOW.
HERE, HO. THERE'S ABOUT $600 AMERICAN THERE. BUY YOURSELF A NEW NOSE.
JESUS, JOURNAL, THAT'S MORE MONEY THAN HE'S EVER SEEN IN HIS LIFE. ARE YOU SURE?
NEITHAMMER
ISN'T THAT THE WAY WE AMERICANS DO IT? TREAT PEOPLE LIKE THEY'RE SOMETHING NASTY STUCK TO THE BOTTOM OF OUR SHOE, THEN THROW MONEY AT THEM TO EASE OUR CONSCIENCE?
IS HE HAPPY? I CAN'T TELL IF HE'S SMILING, MAN. HE'S GOT NO LIPS, YOU KNOW.
NEXT: THE GATHERING STORM

Missing Americans™

POW Forum: Summing up the evidence that live POWs are still being held in Vietnam

On February 1, 1988, The Connecticut chapter of the National Forget-Me-Not Association sponsored a Prisoner-of-War Forum at Western Connecticut State University in Danbury, Connecticut.

Participants included Bill Paul, a reporter for The Wall Street Journal, and then-U.S. Rep. John Rowland (R-Conn.), a leader in Congress on the issue of POWs abandoned in Vietnam.

In this, the sixth and final part of our edited transcript of those proceedings, Mr. Paul concludes his historical overview of the issue...

About a year and a half ago, a Vietnamese foreign ministry official announced that there might be men in the countryside — beyond the government's control. Remember, for years they've been saying, "Nobody here." Suddenly, in front of an American camera crew he says, "They might be here."

Then you have Robert McFarlane, formerly President Reagan's National Security Advisor. Two years ago, Robert McFarlane, at an off-the-record press session — which by the way was sponsored by *newsmen*, that's the crime of it all — announced, "Yes, I believe there are still Americans in Southeast Asia." For this then to go unreported is *too much.* How do you deal with this?

Well, [the administration] quickly backtracked and said that's only his *personal* opinion. I defy you to tell me how you separate the professional and personal opinions of President Reagan's top national security man.

So what have you got? You have the Vietnamese saying they're there. You've got [a high-ranking] official in the Reagan administration saying, in his *personal* belief, they are there. You have a bugged conversation that the CIA doesn't want to come forward with. You have Bob Garwood who came back out to tell us they were there. You have the former head of the Defense Intelligence Agency saying he was expecting *hundreds* more in 1973. You have a former intelligence operative, Jerry Mooney, who said, "I was checking my list and only 5% came back and the ones who didn't come back were the ones who would've been of use to the Vietnamese."

There's more. Those are the highlights. I haven't gone into the evidence on Korea and World War II.

Can things change? Can we get the men back? Yes, yes. We will get them back, but I can't tell you when. Sorry if that's a cop-out.

But I do know this — for 45 years or so, the Soviets said Raoul Wallenberg was dead. They further said he was a traitor to mankind. [In January,] the Soviet prime minister, Nicholai Ryzhkov, in Stockholm no less — did not say he's alive — but did suddenly decide that Raoul Wallenberg was a great humanitarian. The reporter for Reuters was totally dumbfounded by this.

"How many men really were left behind?" — Bill Paul
Photo by Carol Kaliff. Copyright ©1991 The Danbury (Ct.) News-Times

What I'm saying is, things turn on a dime. If it suits somebody's purpose, and it may now suit the Russians' purpose, they'll move. I don't think Washington wants to move. I think 1) they're trapped by the embarrassment of so many years having gone by, 2) they have been convinced that there is another agenda here that takes precedence — that's worth more than a handful of soldiers. Or so they think.

One last thought.

The official MIA list has 2,414 names on it. And everybody assumes that's the starting point. The U.S. says, "Yes they're missing, but most of them got killed — airplane crashes, they exploded in mid-air." And they're right — a lot of those men are not alive. But in light of what I've said, ask yourself how many men did the communists take that we simply wrote off as "killed in action, body not recovered"? How many had skills that the Vietnamese wanted, that the Russians wanted before them, and the Koreans wanted as well? How many men *really* were left behind?

I submit that for every one we got back, we left ten there. That the real, honest-to-God number of men who were left behind is 5,000-plus. And let's assume they brutalized 80% of them — we still then have more than 1,000 men there. The 1,000 men we're saving if, you folks I guess, will convince the governments that it's in everybody's best [interests].

Thank you.

ABOUT DON LOMAX

DON LOMAX was drafted into the Army in 1965 and, along with most draftees went to Vietnam in the fall of 1966 during President Johnson's targeted build-up to reach his goal of half a million troops in-country by the summer of 1967. Being an orphan company without a particular mission at the time, upon arriving in the Cha Rang Valley on Highway 19 in the near geological center of the country, his unit (the 98th Light Equipment Maintenance Company) was assigned a plethora of duties from convoying supplies, to airport guard duty at Qui Nhon Airport, to repairing Fuel bladders, with a little shit burning thrown in for fun. All the while he took mental notes and sketched the people, the gear, and the countryside thinking, "This would make a great comic." And it did.

VIETNAM JOURNAL, the comic book was first published by Apple Publishing in 1987 and was eventually nominated for a Harvey Award. He has had a long career now approaching 50 years in magazine and comic books including a stint at writing The 'Nam and The Punisher for Marvel in the '90s. Other spin-offs, High Shining Brass, Valley of Death, and Tet '68 are still available in print and download on-line, as well as the Vietnam Journal series from Caliber Comics.

But Don Lomax is by no means a one trick pony. For nearly 50 years he has had comics and cartoons appearing in a score of national magazines on a regular basis including Easyrider, CARtoons, Heavy Metal, Overdrive (Knights of the Road), Police and Security News (Above and Beyond), American Towman, and many others. But he also worked for most of the major comic book imprints including Pacific, Marvel, First, Americomics, Fantagraphics,Transfuzion, Eros and of course Caliber.

Lomax has four great children, two girls and two boys with ten grandchildren, and twelve great grandchildren (at last count). His sons are both veterans, his oldest Bryan served in Panama during operation Just Cause and Torrin with the Special Forces during several tours in Iraq and Afghanistan. Both are retired now. Lomax now lives in Illinois with the light of his life, his wife, Zenaida and is hard at work on Series Two of Vietnam Journal. (well, not THAT hard at work. When you love what you do it can't really be called work, can it?)

COMING NEXT:

TET '68

VIETNAM
JOURNAL
BOOK FIVE - TET '68
DON LOMAX

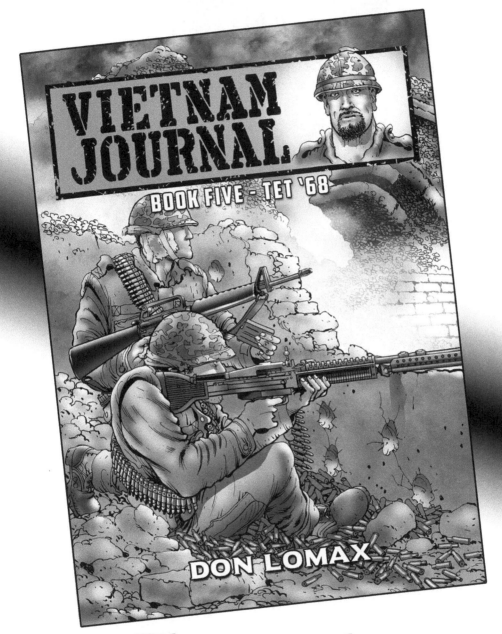

The complete 6 issue series!

Check out the Preview...

SPECIAL PREVIEW

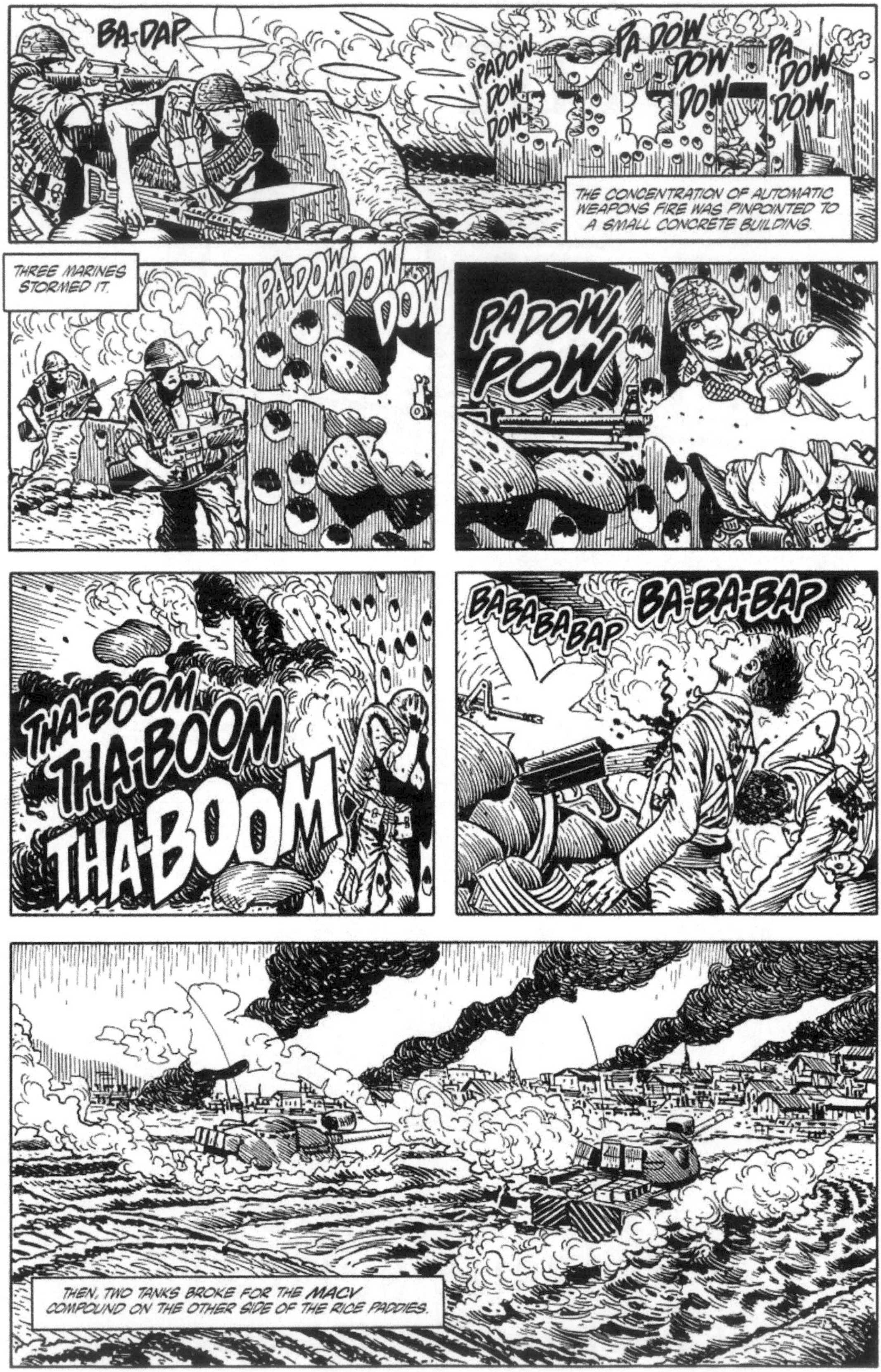
BA-DAP
PADOW DOW DOW
PA DOW DOW DOW
PA DOW DOW
THE CONCENTRATION OF AUTOMATIC WEAPONS FIRE WAS PINPOINTED TO A SMALL CONCRETE BUILDING.
THREE MARINES STORMED IT.
PA-DOW DOW DOW
PADOW POW
THA-BOOM THA-BOOM THA-BOOM
BABABABAP
BA-BA-BAP
THEN, TWO TANKS BROKE FOR THE MACV COMPOUND ON THE OTHER SIDE OF THE RICE PADDIES.

Book Five: TET '68

SPECIAL PREVIEW

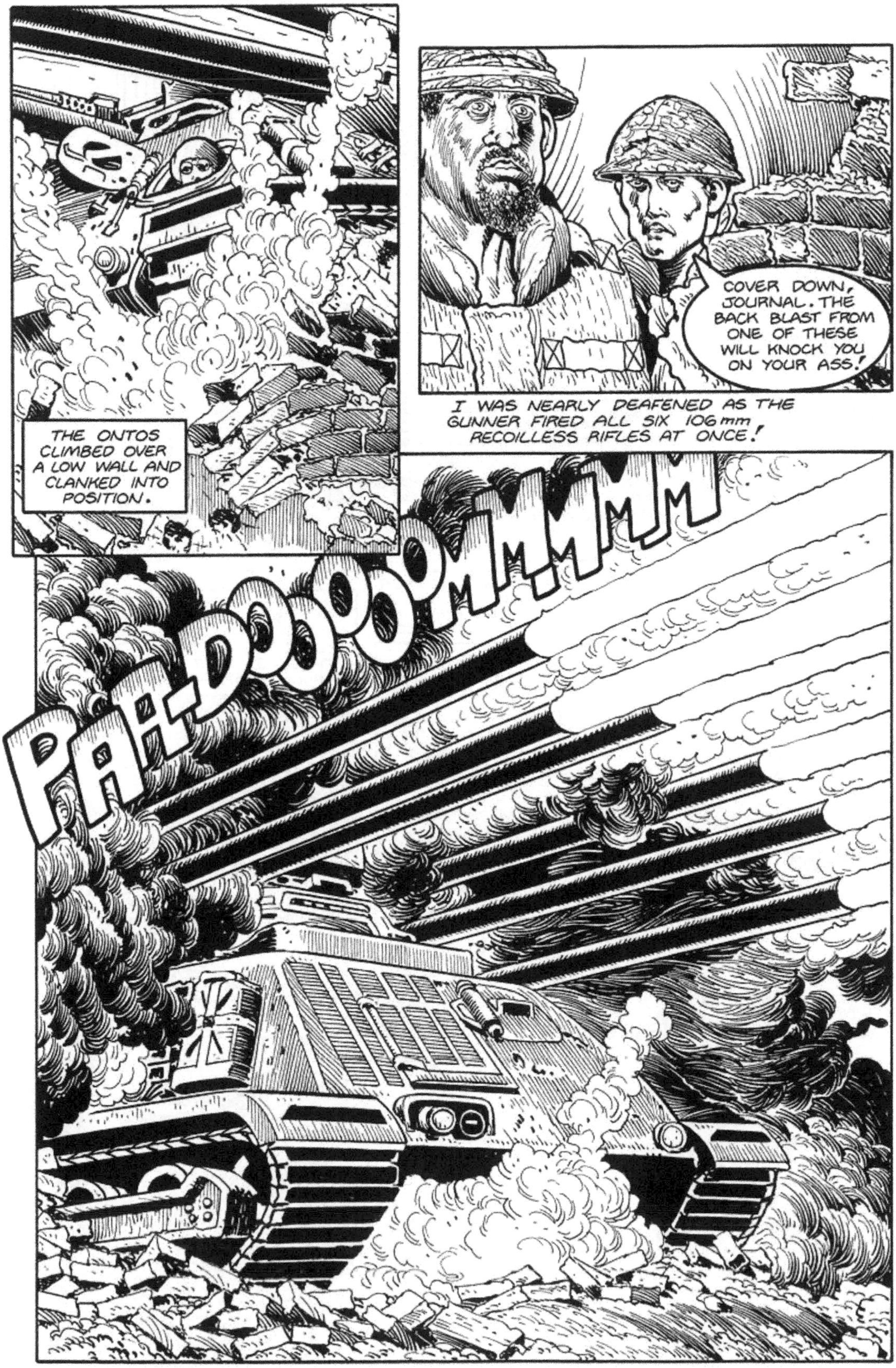

THE ONTOS CLIMBED OVER A LOW WALL AND CLANKED INTO POSITION.
COVER DOWN, JOURNAL. THE BACK BLAST FROM ONE OF THESE WILL KNOCK YOU ON YOUR ASS!
I WAS NEARLY DEAFENED AS THE GUNNER FIRED ALL SIX 106mm RECOILLESS RIFLES AT ONCE!
PAA-DOOOOOMMMMMMM

Book Five: TET '68

SPECIAL PREVIEW

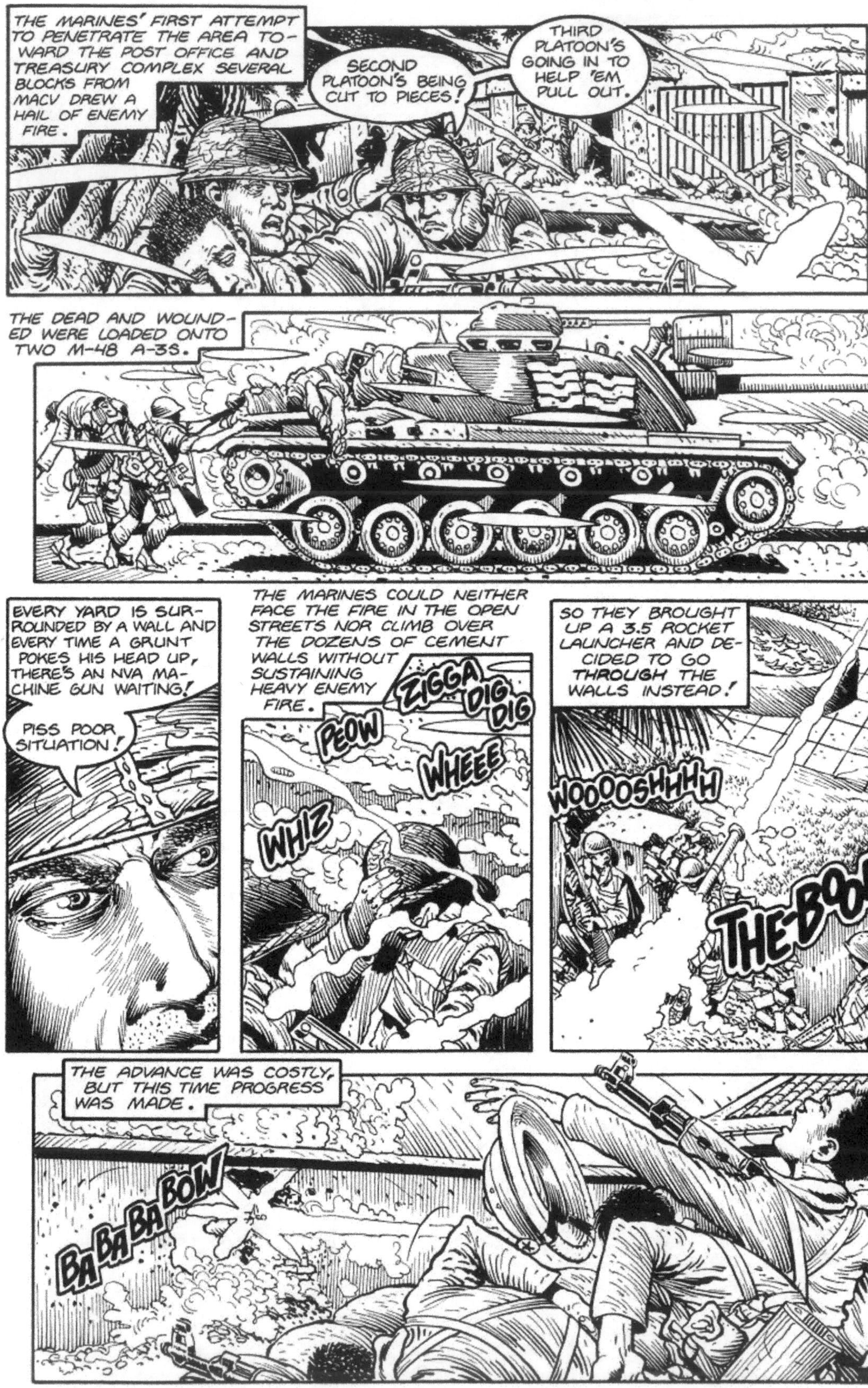
THE MARINES' FIRST ATTEMPT TO PENETRATE THE AREA TO-WARD THE POST OFFICE AND TREASURY COMPLEX SEVERAL BLOCKS FROM MACV DREW A HAIL OF ENEMY FIRE.
SECOND PLATOON'S BEING CUT TO PIECES!
THIRD PLATOON'S GOING IN TO HELP 'EM PULL OUT.
THE DEAD AND WOUND-ED WERE LOADED ONTO TWO M-48 A-3S.
EVERY YARD IS SUR-ROUNDED BY A WALL AND EVERY TIME A GRUNT POKES HIS HEAD UP, THERE'S AN NVA MA-CHINE GUN WAITING!
PISS POOR SITUATION!
THE MARINES COULD NEITHER FACE THE FIRE IN THE OPEN STREETS NOR CLIMB OVER THE DOZENS OF CEMENT WALLS WITHOUT SUSTAINING HEAVY ENEMY FIRE.
ZIGGA DIG DIG
PEOW
WHEEE
WHIZ
SO THEY BROUGHT UP A 3.5 ROCKET LAUNCHER AND DE-CIDED TO GO THROUGH THE WALLS INSTEAD!
WOOOOSHHHH
THE-BOOM
THE ADVANCE WAS COSTLY, BUT THIS TIME PROGRESS WAS MADE.
BABABABOW

Book Five: TET '68

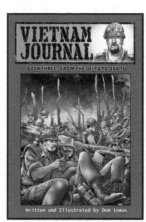

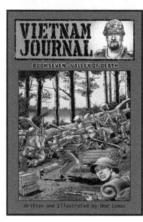

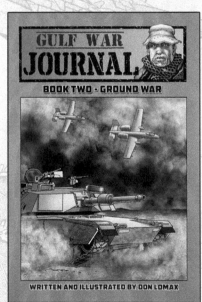

ALSO AVAILABLE FROM CALIBER COMICS

QUALITY GRAPHIC NOVELS TO ENTERTAIN

THE SEARCHERS: VOLUME 1
The Shape of Things to Come

Before *League of Extraordinary Gentlemen* there was *The Searchers*. At the dawn of the 20th Century the greatest literary adventurers from the minds of Wells, Doyle, Burroughs, and Haggard were created. All thought to be the work of pure fiction. However, a century later, the real-life descendents of those famous characters are recuited by the legendary Professor Challenger in order to save mankind's future. Series collected for the first time.

"Searchers is the comic book I have on the wall with a sign reading - 'Love books? Never read a comic? Try this one! ....money back guarantee..." - Dark Star Books.

WAR OF THE WORLDS: INFESTATION

Based on the H.G. Wells classic! The "Martian Invasion" has begun again and now mankind must fight for its very humanity. It happened slowly at first but by the third year, it seemed that the war was almost over... the war was almost lost.

"Writer Randy Zimmerman has a fine grasp of drama, and spins the various strands of the story into a coherent whole... imaginative and very gritty."
- war-of-the-worlds.co.uk

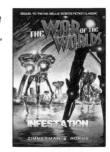

HELSING: LEGACY BORN

From writer Gary Reed (Deadworld) and artists John Lowe (Captain America), Bruce McCorkindale (Godzilla). She was born into a legacy she wanted no part of and pushed into a battle recessed deep in the shadows of the night. Samantha Helsing is torn between two worlds...two allegiances...two families. The legacy of the Van Helsing family and their crusade against the "night creatures" comes to modern day with the most unlikely of all warriors.

"Congratulations on this masterpiece..."
- Paul Dale Roberts, Compuserve Reviews

DEADWORLD

Before there was The Walking Dead there was Deadworld. Here is an introduction of the long running classic horror series, Deadworld, to a new audience! Considered by many to be the godfather of the original zombie comic with over 100 issues and graphic novels in print and over 1,000,000 copies sold, Deadworld ripped into the undead with intelligent zombies on a mission and a group of poor teens riding in a school bus desperately try to stay one step ahead of the sadistic, Harley-riding King Zombie. Death, mayhem, and a touch of supernatural evil made Deadworld a classic and now here's your chance to get into the story!

DAYS OF WRATH

Award winning comic writer & artist Wayne Vansant brings his gripping World War II saga of war in the Pacific to Guadalcanal and the Battle of Bloody Ridge. This is the powerful story of the long, vicious battle for Guadalcanal that occurred in 1942-43. When the U.S. Navy orders its outnumbered and out-gunned ships to run from the Japanese fleet, they abandon American troops on a bloody, battered island in the South Pacific.

"Heavy on authenticity, compellingly written and beautifully drawn."
- Comics Buyers Guide

THE BOBCAT

Described as the Native American *Black Panther*.
1898. Indian Territory. Will Firemaker is a Cherokee Blacksmith who is finding out that the world of ancient lore and myth of his Tribe, that Will had always thought of as tribal fairytales, are actually true, and they're telling him he must replace his best friend from the animal kingdom, The Great Cat, as the guardian of his people. This sends him down a path of shock and disbelief as beings from the ancient past begin to manifest themselves in the world of reality. And as malevolent forces rise up in the wake of the fledgling Industrial Age, the future rushes head on into the Old West. Tahlequah will never be the same...

CALIBER PRESENTS

The original Caliber Presents anthology title was one of Caliber's inaugural releases and featured predominantly new creators, many of which went onto successful careers in the comics' industry. In this new version, Caliber Presents has expanded to graphic novel size and while still featuring new creators it also includes many established professional creators with new visions. Creators featured in this first issue include nominees and winners of some of the industry's major awards including the Eisner, Harvey, Xeric, Ghastly, Shel Dorf, Comic Monsters, and more.

LEGENDLORE

From Caliber Comics now comes the entire Realm and Legendlore saga as a set of volumes that collects the long running critically acclaimed series. In the vein of The Lord of The Rings and The Hobbit with elements of Game of Thrones and Dungeon and Dragons.

Four normal modern day teenagers are plunged into a world they thought only existed in novels and film. They are whisked away to a magical land where dragons roam the skies, orcs and hobgoblins terrorize travelers, where unicorns prance through the forest, and kingdoms wage war for dominance. It is a world where man is just one race, joining other races such as elves, trolls, dwarves, changelings, and the dreaded night creatures who steal the night.

TIME GRUNTS

What if Hitler's last great Super Weapon was – Time itself! A WWII/time travel adventure that can best be described as *Band of Brothers* meets *Time Bandits*.

October, 1944. Nazi fortunes appear bleaker by the day. But in the bowels of the Wenceslas Mines, a terrible threat has emerged . . . the Nazis have discovered the ability to conquer time itself with the help of a new ominous device!

Now a rag tag group of American GIs must stop this threat to the past, present, and future . . . While dealing with their own past, prejudices, and fears in the process.

CALIBER
COMICS

www.calibercomics.com

CPSIA information can be obtained
at www.ICGtesting.com
Printed in the USA
LVHW111516110122
708310LV00008B/763

9 781942 351467